Pouring Six Beers at a Time

And Other Stories from a Lifetime in Baseball

Bill Giles

with Doug Myers

TRIUMPH
BOOKS

Library of Congress Cataloging-in-Publication Data

Giles, Bill, 1934–
    Pouring six beers at a time : and other stories from a lifetime in baseball / Bill Giles.
      p.cm.
    Includes bibliographical references and index.
    ISBN-13: 978-1-57243-931-3
    ISBN-10: 1-57243-931-9
        1. Giles, Bill, 1934– 2. Baseball team owners—Pennsylvania—Philadelphia—Biography. 3. Baseball—Pennsylvania—Philadelphia—History. 4. Philadelphia Phillies (Baseball team)—History. I. Title.
    GV865.G56A3 2006
    796.357092—dc22
    [B]
                                                    2006028163

This book is available in quantity at special discounts for your group or organization. For further information, contact:

Triumph Books
542 South Dearborn Street
Suite 750
Chicago, Illinois 60605
(312) 939-3330
Fax (312) 663-3557

Printed in U.S.A.
ISBN: 978-1-57243-931-3
Design by Amy Carter
All photos courtesy of Bill Giles unless otherwise noted.

To my lovely, gentle, sweet, caring wife of over 50 years—Nancy—for putting up with me

Contents

Foreword

Baseball is a game of dreams. Bill Giles is a man of dreams. So they had no choice but to find each other. How would either have survived without the other?

Baseball was just baseball before Bill Giles got mixed up in it. The men who ran it thought all they were supposed to do was open the gates, get their 27 outs a night, and hope somebody might watch if the planets all lined up. But Bill Giles dreamed different dreams. He had this goofy idea that you might be able to get people to show up at a baseball game for reasons other than the fact that somebody happened to be playing one. Turns out, this made him a man ahead of his time. Back then, however, *visionary* wasn't exactly the most popular word his buddies in baseball used to describe him.

Scoreboards exploded in Bill Giles's dreams. Kitemen whooshed through the sky (in theory, at least) to deliver the first baseball of the season in Bill Giles's dreams. Flying Wallendas tightroped above the stadium in Bill Giles's dreams. A guy got all dressed up in a giant bird suit and made people laugh in Bill Giles's dreams.

In Bill Giles's dreams, baseball was always more than just a game. It was a show. It was a show you could sell to women and to kids and to folks who barely knew a baseball from a beach ball. It could be part sport and part Disney World. It was a spectacle to be hyped up and promoted, kind of like the circus coming to town 81 days a year. What Bill Veeck was to baseball in Cleveland, St. Louis, and Chicago, that's what Bill Giles was to baseball in Houston and Philadelphia.

His dreams weren't always as brilliant as they seemed in his turbo-driven imagination. His wacky brainstorms didn't always work the way the master brainstormer drew them. Kiteman kept crashing instead of whooshing. His World's Highest-Jumping Easter Bunny literally went up in flames. His ostrich and duck races never did threaten to supplant the Kentucky Derby as America's most beloved racing extravaganza. But Bill Giles just laughed and moved on to the next can't-miss dream that popped into his head. One man's promotional catastrophe was this man's hilarious Book Chapter Waiting to Happen. So in retrospect, wasn't all that dreaming worth it?

But Bill Giles dreamed other dreams, too. He was, after all, the son of a baseball man. So he dreamed the same kind of baseball dreams we all dream. He dreamed about trades and signings and lineup cards that would make the customers in his world happier than they had ever been in their entire lives. Not that the baseball guys around him would actually make those deals. But that didn't mean those dreams weren't worth dreaming.

The first time I ever met Bill Giles, he was leaning back in a chair in the old Veterans Stadium press room, showing off the latest list of ingenious ideas he had scribbled on the nearest napkin. All he ever needed was an audience and some general manager who would just see the wisdom of trading him Dave Winfield for, say, Rudy Meoli, and it was only going to be a matter of time before Philadelphia understood what a heroic figure he aspired to become.

But in reality, it would have been a matter of a really, really, really long time—centuries, possibly—had Bill Giles not had yet one more dream. He dreamed of running his own baseball team. And then, whaddayaknow, he looked up one day in 1981 and discovered that the Phillies team he worked for happened to have a For Sale sign pasted on its front door. I can still recall running into him, very early on a spring-training morning, two days after owner Ruly Carpenter had announced he had to get out of this crazy business.

Luckily, I was awake enough to ask Bill if he had any interest in buying the Phillies. More luckily for me, he was a man who was never afraid to blurt out an answer like this to a reporter: "Yeah...In fact, I've been working on it already." Eight months later, he was president of the Phillies. And you could practically see all those dreams he'd scrawled on all those napkins and legal pads springing to life.

The day he took over as *el presidente,* Bill Giles, in that sunny way of his, predicted the Phillies were going to be the Team of the Decade in the 1980s. Okay, so it didn't quite work out that way (although it's possible his Team of the Decade trophy was just lost in the mail). But in Philadelphia, where the beer mugs are always half empty, this guy doesn't get nearly enough credit for the good things that have happened since he showed up in town. He didn't just make baseball more fun. He didn't just put his stamp on one of America's most beautiful ballparks. He left his imprint on the product itself, too. Remember, the Phillies had made it to the postseason twice in the pre–Bill Giles history of the franchise. They've made it seven times since. And nobody wishes that number was higher more than Bill Giles does, even if some people in his town never figured that out.

Dreamers don't dream about losing. They dream about riding around on parade floats. Dreamers don't dream about all the empty seats and disgruntled talk-show callers they can inspire. They dream about how to make people so happy that the only cause for debate is whether to name that street next to the ballpark Bill Giles Boulevard or Bill Giles Way. Well, maybe Bill Giles's way of owning a baseball team didn't work out quite so well in real life as it looked in Dreamland. But in great part, that was because his heart was too big, not too small. If I had a choice between Bill Giles running my baseball team and some lifelong bigwig from International Conglomerate Megacorporate Holdings Co. Inc., give me Bill Giles a hundred times out of a hundred.

Give me a guy who has spent his entire life hanging around baseball parks and baseball people. Give me a guy who, at any given second, can tell you a funny tale, from his very own lifetime, about anyone from Ernie "the Schnozz" Lombardi to John Kruk to Benny the Bomb. Bill Giles is a man with so many of those tales, he just had to write this book. And when you're finished reading it, you'll understand that his dreams sure had a lot in common with all of our dreams, except with one big difference: Bill Giles's dreams came true.

—Jayson Stark

Acknowledgments

This book would not have been written without the encouragement of my great friend John Mashek. John is a former political writer with *U.S. News & World Report*, *The Boston Globe*, and *The Atlanta Journal-Constitution* and is a Phillies Phanatic. The first time I ever met John, he told me that he wanted to be buried at home plate in Crosley Field in Cincinnati, Ohio. It is no wonder we became lifetime friends.

Special thanks to Dr. John B. Lord, a professor at Saint Joseph's University in Philadelphia, who did a lot of research on the labor and business aspects of baseball and helped rewrite some of the chapters. And to Doug Myers, for making the book flow so well and adding a number of interesting sidebars. We bonded well, and he is a great wordsmith.

Thanks and a beer or two go to past and current Phillies employees —Dan and Cathy Baker, Ronnie and Mike Carroll, Larry Shenk, Dave Montgomery, Bill Webb, Dallas Green, Larry Andersen, Harry Kalas, Pat Gillick, Mike Dimuzio, Rosie Rahn, Paul Callahan, Adele Macdonald, Nancy Nolan, Chris Leagult—all of whom helped with my recall of many of the stories you will read. If I left anyone out, my deepest apologies.

Thanks to Tal Smith, president of the Houston Astros, for his editing of the chapters about my Astrodome experiences and to Tal, Gene Elston, and Mike Acosta of Houston for some of the pictures.

Thanks to my assistant, Lynn Samuels, for typing all of the original drafts of the book. Thanks to my wife, Nancy, and sons Mike, Joe, and Chris for their constructive criticism.

Thanks to author David Halberstam for pushing me to write the book.

And, finally, thanks to all the players, baseball personnel, and fans who have made my baseball life so fulfilling.

Introduction

"The period of time from the last World Series game to the next spring-training game."

—*Roger Angell on the definition of* eternity

In my case, Roger Angell's statement rings very true. I was practically raised in a ballpark—Crosley Field in Cincinnati, Ohio—and have spent most of my time in or around one ever since. My mother died when I was seven years old; an only child, I hung out with my dad, who was a sports celebrity.

My godfather is Hall of Famer Branch Rickey, truly one of the sport's great names and a key architect of modern baseball. My father is also in the National Baseball Hall of Fame, having been recognized for his contributions to the game in the front office of the Cincinnati Reds and the league office of the National League. The lives of Warren Giles and me—his son, Bill—have spanned more than three generations of players, owners, and, of course, the fans who have made the game our national pastime.

My father was president and general manager of the Cincinnati Reds from 1937 until 1951, when he became president of the National League before retiring in 1970. As for me...well, the baseball didn't roll too far from the dugout. I went on to be a minor league operator, traveling secretary, publicity director, promotions director, marketing director, vice president of business operations, CEO, owner of a major league team, and honorary president of the National League. Not bad for a guy who first made the front pages at the age of five for making unauthorized improvements to the family homestead…but more on that later.

I grew up with the Reds in the 1930s, '40s, and '50s; did my part to help bring baseball to Houston (and eventually inside a dome) in the 1960s; had a front-row seat for some of the greatest moments in Phillies history in the 1970s, '80s, and '90s; and realized my dream of bringing an old-style ballpark back to Philadelphia in the new century.

I had the honor of negotiating contracts with Mike Schmidt, Steve Carlton, Pete Rose, and Joe Morgan—four of the greatest players of the 20th century—and the pleasure of watching them play for many years. I saw the Philadelphia Phillies, the team I worked for and eventually owned, participate in three World Series in 14 years—after having been in two over the previous 77. I experienced the joy of Tug McGraw's final strike of the 1980 season and the pain of Joe Carter ending the 1993 season a game too early.

I've had 70 wonderful years of living and loving the game of baseball, riding the highs and suffering the lows. And, yes, I cried watching every baseball movie except *Bull Durham*. As Bart Giamatti once said about the game, "Baseball will break our hearts." My own may have been broken a few times, but it always healed.

I am a baseball "lifer," and this book is about my baseball life, my memories and experiences. Some are happy, some are sad, a lot are funny, and a few are downright strange. It features characters and events that prove the old adage that truth is stranger than fiction. I'll tell you about baseball stars, owners, and every commissioner who ever served. About prizefights, bullfights, and the purchase of the Ringling Bros. and Barnum & Bailey circus. About the thrill of victory, the agony of defeat, and the aerodynamic misadventures of the magnificent Kiteman.

Perhaps the toughest part of writing this book was to come up with a title that captured the great fun and significant challenges that come with a life spent in the baseball front office. Straddling the worlds of baseball the game and baseball the business, loving the game as much as any fan while being forced to make cold and calculated business decisions, coming up with wacky ideas like tightrope walkers and ostrich races to bring smiles to the faces of fans while always recognizing that the game comes first—it's a balancing act that requires an array of skills that no business school will teach you. You've got to do your best to do it all and do it all at once, and it still may not be enough. Kind of like pouring six beers at a time...but more on that later.

Just as I've always done, I've tried my best to be truthful and have some fun without hurting anybody—whether I'm telling you what I like about the game, what I'm not so fond of, what I tried that worked, the many mistakes I made along the way, and what I'd do if I were king for a day.

So relax, have a seat, and enjoy a day at the ballpark. Or, in my case, 70-plus years and counting.

Raised in a Ballpark

Opening Day and the Immortal Kiteman

For me, the opening day of a baseball season was the third most important day of the year, falling behind only Thanksgiving and Christmas. Ever since we dropped a ball from a helicopter to our backup catcher to open Veterans Stadium in 1971, I knew we had to deliver each season's first ball in Philadelphia in some unique manner.

So how to top that in '72? I had read an article in *Sports Illustrated* about a man who jumped off cliffs with a kite on his back and sailed through the air. I envisioned him jumping off the roof of Veterans Stadium and sailing into home plate with the first ball. I contacted him and asked him to fly from his home in Seattle to Philadelphia.

Kiteman took a look at my idea and said he could only do it if we built an 80-foot ramp on top of the seats in right field. He would water ski down the ramp to get enough draft under his kite. I decided to give it a try. A month before Opening Day, I spent $5,000 to build a ramp on top of the right-field seats.

You know what they say about best-laid plans. The players ended up going on strike, which delayed the start of the season by a week. I received a call from my Kiteman friend.

"Bill, I can't come a week later."

"You can't?"

"I have to go to Mexico and teach the president of Mexico how to water ski."

I was stuck. We had advertised heavily: "Come See the Kiteman!"

I looked in the yellow pages, but there was no Kiteman to be found. A man who owned a local hardware store in Paoli read that I was stuck with no Kiteman. He called to tell me that he had a friend, Richard Johnson, who flew kites in shows in Cypress Gardens, Florida, and that he could probably be the new Kiteman.

I flew Mr. Johnson up to Philly to look at our ramp. He said he could not do the ramp, but that if I got him some roller skates and pulled him behind a car down the street in front of the Vet, he could sail up and over the roof and glide down to home plate.

That sounded pretty cool.

I called police commissioner Frank Rizzo and explained the plan. He rejected it because it would "mess up traffic."

I really needed the Kiteman show to go on, so I went back to Mr. Johnson and offered him $1,500 instead of the original $1,000.

"Okay, I'll give it a try."

"Great!" I responded. "Would you like to practice?"

"Mr. Giles," he said, "if I'm going to kill myself, I want someone other than just you watching me."

Kiteman's big moment came on a cool, windy night before 38,000 fans as the Phillies opened the 1972 home season at the Vet against St. Louis. I had asked one of my sales guys, Paul Callahan, to accompany Kiteman to the upper deck, where his ramp had been built. I went into the public announcer's booth to orchestrate the Kiteman show.

Dan Baker was our PA man. Before Baker came to the Phillies, he'd worked the "thrill circuit" up in New England, announcing Evel Knievel and others, so he knew how to sell it.

"Never before seen in a major league stadium," Baker said, his voice booming out across the Vet, "the world-renowned Kiteman will fly high above the stadium to deliver the first ball of the 1972 season." He had worked out a 30-second introduction that built to a crescendo—a peak of emotion to get the fans revved up—closing with: "Here's the Kiteman!"

The organist did a drum roll.

The fans stared anxiously at the ramp in right field.

The Kiteman did not move.

I turned to Baker and said, "He must not be able to hear us. Introduce him again."

Baker said, "Ladies and gentlemen, the Kiteman is summoning up the courage to take on this death-defying stunt." He went through yet another intro that built to yet another peak, then finally said, "Here's the Kiteman!"

The organist did yet another drum roll.

The Kiteman still did not move.

You have to understand Phillies fans. They are not the most patient people in the world. They were already booing.

I got on the walkie-talkie with Callahan and asked, "Does he hear the PA?"

"Yes, he hears it."

"Well, then what's the problem?"

"The problem? The problem is that he's scared to death. He's frozen."

In a touching display of sensitivity and sympathy, I told Callahan, "Give him a little push."

But Callahan couldn't give him a push because he was down in the front row of the upper deck in the 500 Level, having been given explicit orders by Kiteman to catch him if he wasn't airborne by then. Little did Kiteman know that Callahan had already figured out that if you grab someone skiing down a ramp right before he goes over an upper deck railing, you're going over with him. Kiteman had only 48 rows of seats to get airborne or he'd be falling into the lower level—Callahan or no Callahan.

Kiteman finally started down the ramp on his water skis. Halfway down the 600 Level, a gust of wind knocked him sideways off the ramp. He crashed through row after row of seats and into the railing of the upper deck.

I thought he was dead.

The fans were booing lustily.

Callahan, having figured that Kiteman had at least two broken legs and possibly a broken back, rushed over to him. Someone had to throw out the first ball, you understand, and it was taped to the kite.

"Give me the ball," Callahan said.

"That's my job," Kiteman replied.

Miraculously, Kiteman got to his feet and heaved the ball—as if he thought it would sail to the pitcher's mound from the 500 Level. It ended up in the Phillies bullpen behind the outfield fence.

The fans booed even louder.

As for me, I was just relieved that he was alive. Generally speaking, a dead body is not a good omen for the start of a baseball season.

Youngest Member of the Gas House Gang

You might be wondering how a 37-year-old man—an armed-forces veteran, devoted husband, and loving father—found himself in the position of finding kite-flying daredevils for a living. To answer that question, we'll have to start at the beginning.

Like most boys born in the 1930s, I wanted to be a big-league baseball player. Unlike most boys, I had the advantage of being born into a world of baseball. It was September 7, 1934, in Rochester, New York. My parents, Jane and Warren Giles, were playing bridge with a friend and baseball associate, Gabe Paul, and his wife, Mary. The game must have been a bit boring because my mother decided to add some excitement by going into labor. She was rushed to the hospital and brought me into the world that night.

At the time, my father was president of the Rochester Red Wings baseball team, which was the top affiliate of the St. Louis Cardinals. So I guess you could say I came into life as a Cardinal—or, at that time, the legendary Gas House Gang. They were seven games back in the standings when I was born, but about to go 18–5 to take the National League pennant from Carl Hubbell and the New York Giants. Too bad I was a bit young to remember much of that—though I'd have my own experiences with the modern-day equivalent of that band of crazies 59 years later.

In addition to running the Red Wings, my father was also president of the entire International League. The International League was one of three Triple A circuits, along with the American

Association and the Pacific Coast League. My father had gotten his start in baseball after returning to Illinois from military service in World War I. In 1919 he came to a town meeting to discuss the future of the Three-I League and left it as the newly elected president of the team in Moline. A few years later he joined the St. Louis Cardinals farm system as general manager of one of their minor league teams in St. Joseph, Missouri. Eventually he became president of the Rochester Red Wings. In 1937 he took on the job of president of the Cincinnati Reds and then served as president of the National League from 1951 to 1969—the longest tenure of any man who ever held the position. His name is now on the trophy that is given each year to the champions of the National League.

MEMORIES OF A BASEBALL CHILDHOOD

It is interesting which memories stand the test of time. As I think back to life with the Cincinnati Reds way back when, these are some of the memories that have stayed with me for nearly 70 years.

Crosley Field

Back when I was a kid, the Cincinnati Reds played at Crosley Field, named after Powel Crosley Jr., owner of the team. Mr. Crosley's company made radios, refrigerators, and small automobiles. Crosley Field had grass terraces in left and center fields running about 15 feet from the walls down toward the infield. The center-field terrace in Houston's Minute Maid Park was inspired by this feature of Crosley Field. There was also a big sign on top of a laundry beyond the left-field fence that said: Hit This Sign and Win a New Suit. I can remember a few guys hitting it, Eddie Miller and Frank McCormick in particular.

Eddie Miller

Eddie Miller was a power-hitting shortstop, at least by the standards of the 1940s. Nowadays, 19 home runs from a shortstop is no big deal; not so back when Eddie played. He was the only player I ever saw who didn't go to his dugout between innings. If he didn't think he was going to come up to bat in a particular inning, he would sit on the ground next to the stands by third base. This was at the time when players would leave their gloves on the field between innings. Miller would also cut the leather out of the pocket of his glove so he could feel the ball better with his bare hand. He once gave me one of his old gloves, which I used to play softball.

Frank McCormick

Frank McCormick was the Reds' best power hitter in the late '30s and early '40s. In his prime, he hit over .300 and knocked in more than 100 runs three years in a row. In addition to the occasional suit, McCormick won a fair share of cereal, too. For every home run, a player would win a case of Wheaties.

"There's another case of Wheaties for McCormick," the radio announcer would say.

Frank would frequently give me some of his Wheaties. McCormick's name is not as well known as it should be. He was a very underrated first baseman whose power ended up being sapped in the prime of his career by a freak back injury. McCormick injured his back diving off a hotel diving board in Havana when the Reds were in Cuba playing an exhibition game. That injury really shortened his career. Probably cost him 2,000 hits and a .300 lifetime batting average. A Don Mattingly of the '30s and '40s, I guess you could say.

Hank Sauer

If McCormick was a Mattingly of the '30s and '40s, power-hitting left fielder Hank Sauer was an Andre Dawson—let go by one National League franchise only to go on to win an MVP award for a lousy Chicago Cubs team. The Reds gave up on Sauer after a horrific slump in early 1949 that made his impressive 1948 season look like a fluke. But you can't see the whole story in the statistics. Because Sauer was such a dead-pull hitter, the opposing teams would put all their players on the left side of second base except the first baseman and right fielder. Manager Bucky Walters, a great pitcher in his day, insisted that Sauer hit the ball to right field. It messed up Hank's swing so bad that he couldn't hit. My father ended up dealing him to the Cubs for Peanuts Lowrey and Harry Walker.

Lowrey and Walker never did much for the Reds, while Sauer went back to pulling the ball for the Cubs and had great success. He had a number of big seasons in Chicago, even leading the league in home runs and winning the MVP in 1952.

Kenny Raffensberger

The Cubs were always one of my favorite teams, and Wrigley Field was always my favorite park. Pitcher Kenny Raffensberger could say the same thing, though for very different reasons. Wrigley Field has a reputation for being a hitter's park, but usually not when Raffy was throwing. The wind at Wrigley does not always blow out—turning routine fly balls into long home runs and putting crooked numbers up on the scoreboard. The wind would often blow in, and, when it did, it was very hard to score runs. That's when the Reds would trot out Raffensberger, even if he had only a day or two of rest. Raffy did not throw very hard, and he would throw the ball right down the middle of the plate. The Cubs would hit the heck out of the ball, but the wind kept it in the park. He pitched a lot of shutouts at Wrigley. In fact, when Raffy got a win it often was a shutout. Though he "only" won 119 games in a 15-year career, he piled up almost as many shutouts as Carl Hubbell and more than Dizzy Dean—31 in all. Just goes to show that good things can happen when you trust your defense.

The War Years

Getting to see some of the all-time greats in their prime was something I'll never forget. So was seeing some of the players who filled in for the regulars during World War II. Players like Pete Gray, who played with the St. Louis Browns in 1945. One of his arms was only a stub. He would catch a ball in the glove worn on his one good hand, toss the ball a foot in the air, put the glove under the stump of his other arm, catch the ball again with his original glove hand, and throw to a base. He was actually a fairly effective player because he could steal some bases.

Gray was a great example of what happened during the war years when a lot of the league's best players had to go into the military. Because it was hard to find good players during the war, my dad had to sign two 40-something pitchers: Hod Lisenbee, who had been retired for nine years, and Boom-Boom Beck. One story of how Beck got his nickname, Boom-Boom, says that it was because of the sound his pitches made after they clanged off the wall at Ebbets Field, where he once lost 20 games for the Dodgers. Not exactly the best nickname for a pitcher to have.

Joe Nuxhall was another interesting player from the war years. In 1944, at age 15, he became the youngest pitcher ever to appear in a major league game. I saw that game. He threw his first pitch over the backstop. He got two outs, walked five, and got tagged for five runs. Didn't pitch in the big leagues again for eight years. When he did finally get back, he stayed for 15 years with modest success. He ended up becoming a very popular broadcaster with the Cincinnati Reds.

Opening Day

When I was growing up in Cincinnati, Opening Day of the baseball season was just short of a religious holiday.

The schools would close at noon to permit kids to go to the game. There was the Liberty Street Parade with many bands and floats prior to the game, and the game was always sold out months in advance. They had to put rope barriers on the field to allow 5,000 people to stand in the outfield. If a player hit a ball into the crowd, it was ruled a ground-rule double. Historically, Cincinnati always had the first true opening game because it was the first professional team, dating all the way back to 1869. In later years, ESPN negotiated a TV deal for opening night on Sunday with one of the previous season's World Series teams as one of the participants. This did not make the Reds very happy, but it did not change the tradition of a full house in Cincinnati for the season opener.

Cincinnati was and is a great baseball town and, as you've seen, the site of some of my fondest baseball memories.

On the Front Page at Five

My formal introduction to baseball began shortly after my father's move to the Reds when, at the age of four, I started going to games with my mom and dad. I made the front page of a newspaper for the first time in 1939 at the tender age of five—and, of course, it had to do with Major League Baseball and the Cincinnati Reds. The Reds were in first place in the National League pennant race. I had been painting my wagon and had some red paint left over. So I started to paint our white colonial house red. I don't know who took the photo or how it got into the hands of the newspaper, but someone at the paper thought it was cute. The next day, alluding to the first place standing of the team, the paper carried the headline, "Warren Giles Sees Red," along with a picture of me holding a paint brush in front of the red blotch on our white house.

Me, the MVP, and the FBI

My father wasn't too upset about the red paint prank—unlike the time I played an unwitting hand in keeping his best player off the field during a pennant race. That was also in 1939 and what I thought was just another innocent childhood prank.

The player was Cincinnati's star catcher, Ernie Lombardi. He was nicknamed "Schnozz" for reasons that were obvious to anyone who saw him. In addition to having a huge nose, he was also extraordinarily slow. Despite his utter lack of speed on the base paths, he led the league in hitting in 1938 and 1942, one of the only catchers to ever do that—the last one to ever do it before Joe Mauer in 2006, as a matter of fact. Lombardi won the MVP award in 1938 and was elected to the Hall of Fame in 1986—the first and only member of the Reds' pennant-winning teams of 1939 and 1940 to be so honored.

Lombardi hit the ball very hard, and the bat looked like a toothpick in his hands. He would often hit line drives off the outfield fence and only get a single. He was such a slow runner that the infielders played 20 feet back on the outfield grass, and the second baseman played behind the pitcher in short center field because he hit a lot of hard ground balls up the middle. He may hold the distinction of being the slowest runner ever to win a major league batting title.

Lombardi wasn't too bad with the glove, either. He was the only catcher I have ever seen who did not turn to look at a foul ball hit over his head. He had an uncanny sense about the ball being playable. He would just look straight ahead and stick his right hand behind him for a new ball if he knew the ball was going in the stands.

One day Lombardi went to my father's office in Crosley Field and left his catcher's mitt on the door handle outside the office. Carved into the leather on the back of the mitt was his other nickname, "Lom." I decided it would be a nice mitt to play catch with, so I took it home. Lom was a very temperamental sort, and he wouldn't play a game without his regular mitt. Though the Reds were in first place, the pennant race was tight, and Lom was refusing to play. So Dad called the FBI and hired the Pinkerton Detective Agency to find the mitt.

I think you know where this is headed.

A few days later I was playing catch in my front yard, and my dad noticed I had an unusually big mitt on my hand. He reached out and asked to see the mitt I was using, and sure enough there was "Lom" carved into the leather. It was the only time my father ever spanked me.

There *Is* Crying in Baseball

The Reds overcame my hijinks to hold off the Cardinals to take the pennant in 1939. They lost in four straight to the Yankees, who earned their fourth consecutive championship and second consecutive sweep. The 1940 World Series against the Detroit Tigers was a different story.

The Tigers were loaded on offense with Hall of Famers Hank Greenberg and Charlie Gehringer, first baseman Rudy York, and the very underrated Barney McCosky. The Series went to seven games, even though Lombardi had suffered a sprained ankle and only caught one game. Cincinnati had no true backup catcher, having lost Willard Hershberger late in the season. Hershberger committed suicide near the end of the 1940 season after dropping a foul pop to cost the Reds a game in the heat of a pennant race. The next day he did not show up for batting practice, and my dad went back to the Boston hotel where the team was staying and found Hershberger in the bathtub covered with blood. The catcher had cut his own throat with a razor. I remember my father telling me later that Hershberger was always very neat and that the reason he cut his throat in the bathtub was so he wouldn't get blood on the carpet or furniture.

After this tragic turn of events, the Reds were forced to use first-base coach Jimmie Wilson as their catcher when Lombardi went down early in the Series. Wilson was amazing. He hit .353 and played great defense in the six games that he caught. The seventh game was won 2–1 by the Reds as Paul Derringer outpitched Bobo Newsom.

As is so often the case, the game's key factor can't be found in the box score. In Game 7 in 1940, the turning point was a defensive play by left fielder Jimmy Ripple. The Reds' advance scout had noticed that York would make a big turn around second base when he got a double, and, sure enough, the slugger doubled late in a very close game. Rather than throw to third as any runner would expect, Ripple threw the ball behind York, who was tagged out trying to get back to second. The Reds rallied to win late in the game.

I attended that game in Cincinnati with my mom and dad. When it ended, I was a little confused by what I saw my father doing.

Tugging on Mom's dress, I asked, "We did win, didn't we?"

"Yes," she answered.

"Then why is Daddy crying?"

A Log Cabin in Cincinnati

My father received a nice bonus for winning the World Series that year and used the money to build a log cabin behind our house. He would entertain his friends there and have steak cookouts for sportswriters covering the visiting teams. Nowadays, I wonder how many sportswriters would be comfortable around a baseball team owner and an open flame.

The relationship between baseball management and the baseball writers was quite different in those days. There were only three or four baseball writers, no regular-season television, and one or two radio broadcasters. The writers were virtually employees of the team since the teams would pay for all their expenses on the road and in spring training. This arrangement did create a conflict of interest. The writers all knew most every secret of the team's operation but had enough sense and loyalty not to print "off the record" information. This relationship began to change during the late 1960s as part of the cultural change in this country and the growth of the media. Today there seems to be more news about what happens off of the field than on it.

Some Very Sad Memories of 1942

In the summer of 1942, before I turned eight years old, my world changed dramatically. My mother and father sent me to Chimney Rock Camp near Asheville, North Carolina. It was a great camp, and I was enjoying myself immensely.

I had asked my dad to have *The Cincinnati Enquirer* sent each day so I could follow the progress of the team and the standings while I was away at camp. One day the paper stopped showing up in my mail. I started to have serious nightmares and became very, very homesick. It got so bad that I told the camp director that I wanted to go home. He talked to my dad, and they both insisted I "hang in there." But I got more and more upset. I could not understand why the newspaper was no longer coming, and I kept begging to go back to Cincinnati.

My father relented a few days later, and he took the train to Asheville to pick me up for the journey home. While we waited for our train to come in to the station, he took me to a restaurant nearby. I was enjoying a dish of my favorite food, red raspberries, when he told me that my mother had died.

He explained that he had been in the hospital with an emergency appendectomy, and my mother set the alarm clock for 6:00 AM to come visit him. When she reached for the alarm clock, she hit her head on the bedside table, causing a blood clot. An ambulance picked her up, and she was wheeled into my dad's room in the hospital. She died shortly thereafter, lying just a few feet from my father.

My mother was very stately and pretty. In my den, I have a big eight-foot picture of my father and mother standing at the bar in our cabin. She always cared a lot about how I dressed. She loved jade, penguins, Southwestern art, and she loved to play badminton. My mother and father would have serious arguments from time to time that really bothered me. I don't recall the content, but I do remember sitting at the top of the stairs listening to them and feeling miserable. To this day I do not like to argue with anyone.

My Extended Family

My Aunt Hazel moved from Moline, Illinois, to stay with my father and me and to help raise me in my younger years. But when I was 14, Hazel went home, and it was just Dad, me, and a maid named Margaret. I slept in the same room as my father, and it was always a challenge to get to sleep before him. He snored very loudly.

A single parent with a demanding job, my father certainly had his hands full. Fortunately for him and for me, he had the extended family of the Cincinnati Reds to help him keep me out of trouble. Well, out of *serious* trouble, anyway.

Before games I would hang out in the dugout once in a while and, when I was a teenager, shag balls in the outfield. After night games my dad always hosted a meeting in the press dining room. The manager, all the coaches, and the baseball writers would drink beer and eat sandwiches while they discussed that night's game and all that was going on in baseball. I had to wait until the bull session was over to get a ride home with my father. Sometimes I would listen in, but often I would make the rounds in the ballpark with the night watchman, whose name was Chuck. He had a homemade blackjack that he kept with him at all times. We would walk to every gate at the park, make sure everyone had left, and then we would lock up. Many times, when I had some buddies with me, we would have races down the ballpark ramps in wicker wheelchairs that were available for the handicapped. There certainly was nothing like being the son of a major league executive.

Train Rides with the Big Club

If you thought that was fun for a kid, riding with the team on the train to Chicago was even better. The train was called the Big Four. It left

Cincinnati at 9:00 PM and arrived in Chicago at 9:00 AM. We occupied a sleeper car with double bunks on each side of the center aisle of the train car. The bunks had drapes that could be pulled shut to create a small private area for sleep. I would get in the bunk with my clothes on, pull the drapes, change into my pajamas, and put my clothes in a net hammock. There was always a club car on the train where the players would hang out, having a few beers before the midnight curfew.

I learned a lot about life listening to the club car discussions. The players would trade baseball stories and talk about their hunting trips and what they were going to do in the off-season. One time in Chicago, three of the players took me to a burlesque house. Fortunately for me—and them, for that matter—my dad didn't know about that.

The team stayed at the old Belmont Hotel in Chicago, which was about a mile from Wrigley Field. My dad and I would always walk to and from the park. My father liked to take me to Marshall Field's department store in the Chicago Loop for breakfast and Don the Beachcomber for dinner. The first time I ever had alcohol was at Don's. They had a rum drink called a Pearl Diver, which tasted like a milkshake. It was so good I had two of them. When I got up to go to the bathroom I was dizzy, but was able to stumble my way there. My father didn't seem to notice. Looking back, I can't imagine why they served alcohol to a 15-year-old, but they did. Of course, those were the days before Mothers Against Drunk Driving and the heightened concern over the effects of alcohol on minors.

With girls and alcohol covered, left fielder Hank Sauer gave me pointers on tobacco. Sauer always gave me gum—Wrigley's Doublemint—and taught me how to wrap it around chewing tobacco so that I didn't swallow it. As anyone who has ever swallowed a plug of tobacco can tell you, that's very valuable information.

Spring-Training Memories in Florida...and Indiana?

As much fun as the regular season was, some of my fondest memories are of spring training. In the spring, I got to hang out with the team down in Tampa, Florida. Before I was old enough to go to school, my mom and dad would take me to the Reds training camp. My parents even brought along a tutor for a year or two when I was in public school. After my mother died, I only went down at spring break—traveling by train from the north to Florida until I was old enough to drive. Once I could drive, my father and I made it a tradition to drive together from Cincinnati to Florida in his big Cadillac. We would always stop near Atlanta, Georgia, so we could have dinner at Aunt Fanny's Cabin. It was a very earthy place with a heavyset woman serving world-famous fried chicken, biscuits and gravy, and greens.

When I was a kid, everyone associated with the Reds—players, coaches, press, and executives—stayed at the Floridian Hotel in Tampa. Everyone except the players' families, that is. While spring training is a real family affair today—with players renting a house or condo for their entire family—players' families were not invited back then.

Spring training is a lot of fun—as anyone who has ever made the trip can attest—but it was an absolute blast for a kid whose father ran the team. I used to drive the hotel elevators, which were manually operated in those days. There was a handle on a big disc in the elevator cabin, and if you turned it left the elevator would go up, right and it would go down, and if the handle was straight up, the elevator would stop. It was a challenge to stop the elevator so that the elevator floor was flush to the proper floor in the hotel.

I have fond memories of my father entertaining guests at the Columbia Restaurant in Ybor City, a neighborhood in Tampa. It was a Spanish restaurant with flamenco dancers. It also had great black bean soup with rice and onions. I still make a visit to the Columbia every spring. In later years, my dad used to entertain at Bern's Steak House, which has become a custom for my family to this day.

SPRING TRAINING...IN INDIANA? OR HOW WORLD EVENTS BROUGHT A SLUGGER TO THE REDS

During World War II teams did not travel to Florida or Arizona for spring training —for both patriotic and economic reasons. During the war, fuel was scarce, attendance was down, and teams were trying to save money. The Reds trained for two years at Indiana University in Bloomington because the school had a large indoor field house practice area with a half baseball diamond and batting cages.

It was at Indiana University that my father got lucky by finding a very special baseball player by the name of Ted Kluszewski. Kluszewski was an exceptional football player who was a defensive end on the Indiana team. He was taking batting practice with the Indiana University baseball team when one of my father's groundskeepers saw him hitting balls a mile. My dad took a look and was so impressed that he signed him immediately to a Cincinnati baseball contract for $25,000, which was a substantial signing bonus in those days. Kluszewski became a very successful big-league baseball player as a hard-hitting first baseman with both the Reds and the Chicago White Sox.

Kluszewski was one of my favorite players of all time. His biceps were so big he had to have his shirtsleeves cut off. "Big Klu" was his nickname, and he was huge. Kluszewski was a very intimidating guy—to most people. His wife was very small, and she used to bring her two boxer dogs with her when she came to pick up Big Klu after the game. This little lady would really yank the big man around like a puppet on a string.

Spring training also has a special place in my heart because it was where I first started to develop genuine friendships with some of the players. Johnny Vander Meer was a left-handed pitcher and the only man ever to pitch back-to-back no-hitters in the big leagues. He achieved that feat in 1938 at the age of 23—two of his three shutouts for the season. He struck out a lot of hitters, but his career record was a fairly ordinary 119–121. Though he'd go on to have some pretty good seasons, it is safe to say he peaked early. I remember "Vandy" not so much for what he did on the field but because he was the first player to be really friendly toward me. In spring training he would make me run laps with him. He called me "puss-gut" and would grab my belly and tell me he was going to run the fat off of me.

Johnny Wyrostek was a good left-hand-hitting right fielder who also befriended me. He would escort me on the team bus rides during spring training, and he would get some of the other players to play 20 Questions with me.

Ewell Blackwell, also known as "the Whip," was the greatest right-handed pitcher I ever saw—even if it was for just one season in 1947. He went 22–8 with six shutouts, but an infection forced him to have one of his kidneys taken out, and he was not nearly as effective after the operation. He was really tough on right-handed hitters because he was 6'6" and pitched sidearm. Right-handed hitters would actually duck away, placing their front feet way out of the batter's box while the pitch would bend over the plate for a strike. He pitched a no-hitter in 1947, and in the next game he had a no-hitter going into the ninth inning. I saw both games and remember Eddie Stanky breaking up the no-hitter with a hard ground ball up the middle for the Dodgers. No one has come as close as Blackwell to matching Johnny Vander Meer's feat. "Blackie," as I called him, would take me to an ice cream parlor every night down in Florida.

Stan the Man and Teddy Ballgame

In addition to getting to know some of the Reds players, being raised in ballparks helped me also get to see some of the other great players from around the American and National Leagues. Two that come right to mind are among the greatest hitters to ever enter the batter's box: Stan Musial and Ted Williams.

Stan Musial, a Hall of Fame player with the St. Louis Cardinals, was my favorite opposing player even though he wore out my dad's team. He had a very unusual stance—crouched over, kind of peering under his right arm at the pitcher.

I still remember the first time I saw him down in spring training in the early 1940s.

"See that kid Musial," said Herm Wehmeier, a pitcher on the Reds. "He'll never hit with that stance."

Wehmeier wasn't the only one who thought that. Long before he got the last of his 3,630 career hits, assessments of Musial's stance were being revised all over the National League. Stan Musial was one of the smoothest hitters and defensive players I have ever seen. He was the first National League player to earn $100,000 in a season. After he retired, I attended a number of social functions with him, and he would entertain the party by playing the harmonica. He was pretty good at that, too.

He is truly one of the nicest players I have ever known, and he might be one of the most underrated. When the All-Century Team was named, the fans somehow left him off, leaving a special "panel of experts" to correct the oversight. Considering that he has the fourth-greatest number of hits in history, nearly reached 500 home runs, batted .331 for his career (and .330 at the age of 41), and won three MVP awards and seven batting titles, one can see why they felt the need to step in.

Ted Williams—the great "Teddy Ballgame"—is widely regarded as the greatest hitter of all time, and I got to personally witness one of the reasons why. I attended a spring-training game between the Reds and Boston Red Sox in the late 1940s. Kenny Raffensberger was pitching for the Reds and struck out Williams with three straight fastballs. After the game, Dad and I were having a Coke in the hotel when Williams came storming into the coffee shop.

"Where's Raffensberger?" Williams demanded. "I need to see that SOB!"

"Why?" my father replied.

"I want to know what the hell was going through his head today."

"What do you mean?"

"What's he doing throwing me three straight fastballs? That bastard throws 90 percent curveballs!"

Mind you, this was a spring-training game. Ted Williams was one intense hitter!

But of all the great players I saw play, I can't remember any of them having the impact Jackie Robinson had when he came to town. Robinson, as we all know, was the first African American player to play major league baseball in the modern era. The first few years he played in Cincinnati, the ballpark was always sold out as fans would take trains up from the Deep South to see Jackie play. He was a very talented and exciting player—one of those very rare players for whom enshrinement in Cooperstown is not tribute enough. In recognition of his role as the pioneer in the integration of major league baseball, Robinson's jersey number—42—has been retired by all big-league teams and is on display in every ballpark.

Re-Creating Road Games in the Radio Studio

Getting to see these players up close and personal was certainly a treat, but working behind the scenes was pretty fun, too. Although I served in many functions with his team, my father never let me be a batboy. He felt it might intimidate the players to think the boss's son was spying on them. When I was 14, I did get to work a few games from the radio studio. Because teams didn't get much money for their broadcast rights back then, many would opt to save money on travel expenses by not sending their announcers to road games. Instead the announcers would re-create the games by reading a ticker tape.

A ticker tape was the "information highway" in the '40s and '50s, like the Internet is today. It was a spool of paper about one inch wide with various news items, stock prices, and ball scores dispatched on the tape. My father constantly read the ticker when other games were in progress to see how the contending teams were doing. For "in progress" ballgames, the ticker tape would only say "1K" for strike one or "2B" for a double. The announcer would have to make up the rest. For example:

"Here's a curve ball low and inside, and McCormick gets it and hits the ball hard to left field. It bounces against the left-field wall as McCormick goes into second standing up with a double."

For all he knew, it could have been a blooper down the right-field line that bounced sideways into the seats.

During these reenactments, I was the sound-effects guy. My job was to hit a two-by-four piece of wood with a wooden mallet every time the announcer would say, "Here's a base hit." It's too bad that I later discovered I could hit that two-by-four with a wooden mallet better than I could hit a moving baseball with a bat.

The team's radio broadcaster was Waite Hoyt, and he remained a voice of the Reds until 1965. Hoyt had pitched for several clubs, most notably the Yankees, before becoming a broadcaster. He won 237 games over 21 seasons, pitched for the Murderers' Row Yankees of 1927–28, and was elected to the Hall of Fame in 1969.

Waite was well liked, but he was not particularly well-prepared, nor was he a very good broadcaster. He would often have the wrong player at bat or on the bases and would even have the score wrong once in a while. When I was listening to road games on the radio and there was a long delay, I always knew that some runs had scored because Waite was busy trying to think up what to say.

Hoyt was great during rain delays, though. He told stories that kept the fans entertained, often about Babe Ruth and his days with the Yankees. When Gabe Paul took over the Reds, the first thing he did was fire Hoyt because he despised his broadcasting. But there was such a public outcry that Gabe had to hire him back.

Life Lessons from My Godfather and My Father

Though he wasn't on the playing field or in the broadcast booth when I was growing up and I never got to work with him, my recollections of my ballpark upbringing would not be complete without mention of my godfather, Branch Rickey. Rickey, a longtime baseball executive and a member of the Hall of Fame, has long been considered the game's most astute and innovative baseball executive. He was my father's mentor and had a lot to do with my father's success in baseball. He also gave neat Christmas gifts. "Mr. Rickey," as I always called him, gave me a Boy Scout knife one Christmas that I thought was so cool because it had a screwdriver, a pick, and a knife all in one metal case.

Mr. Rickey also dispensed gifts in the form of valuable advice. He told me two things when I was a kid that stuck with me all my life: "Luck is the residue of design," and "Determination is the link between ability and capacity."

Rickey was the man who essentially invented the farm system as we know it. The Cardinals had quite the farm system back in the

1930s when my father was running their Triple A club in Rochester. In fact, it was the first of its kind and the model to follow (or not, if you were the Chicago Cubs) for years.

Prior to Rickey coming up with the idea of a major league baseball team owning its own minor league affiliates, the minor leagues were separate entities that existed to find, develop, and sell talent to the highest-bidding major league team. If the bidding didn't go high enough, the minor league team would simply hold on to the player. That's what Jack Dunn, owner of the minor league Baltimore Orioles, did with a pitcher named Lefty Grove. Grove won 97 games in the minor leagues over four dominant seasons with the Orioles until the Philadelphia Athletics finally ponied up more than $100,000 for the rights to the pitcher who would go on to win 300 games in the big leagues.

Rickey knew that the small-market Cardinals would never have the funds to be able to outbid 15 other teams for the services of the best free agents (although the terms *small market* and *free agent* weren't used much back then). But St. Louis did have the funds to invest in minor league teams, which could generate revenue for the big club while also developing players. In fact, the St. Louis minor league system became so successful that it could afford to be the one selling off players to other big league teams. It had so many players at one point that Commissioner Kenesaw Mountain Landis ordered 70 of them to be released. It had gone from owning teams to owning entire leagues.

Rickey believed in signing a large number of young players who could run and throw because he believed you could teach a kid how to hit, but you could not teach arm strength or speed. In 1940 his St. Louis Cardinals had 600 players under contract. The average number is now 170.

Simply put, Rickey put the St. Louis Cardinals on the major league baseball map. Under his leadership, they went from being the only franchise in the National League to never appear in a World Series to being world championships in 1926, 1931, and 1934. He moved on to the Brooklyn Dodgers in 1942, while the Cardinals team he assembled went on to win three more championships in 1942, 1944, and 1946.

Inventing the minor leagues as we know them was "pretty good," but Rickey made his greatest contribution to baseball with Brooklyn. I personally believe that Rickey's decision to bring Jackie Robinson into the major leagues did as much as anything to begin the move toward racial integration in America. His front-office leadership, along with Robinson's outstanding play, made the Dodgers the most dominant team in the National League from 1947 to well into the 1950s, even after Rickey had moved on to Pittsburgh.

Rickey's influence can still be felt today. *Baseball America* published a general manager "genealogy" in December 2005. It was able to trace the "family tree" of 27 of the 30 current general managers all back to Rickey.

Given my father's position as a team executive and later the president of the National League, Rickey was just one of many celebrities I met growing up. I can still remember one event in particular. My father and I were having dinner at the '21' Club in New York and who should walk in with a beautiful redhead on his arm but Frank Sinatra. My father introduced me to Sinatra, and Sinatra introduced us to his guest, "Miss Smith."

Sinatra and Miss Smith sat right next to me, and I could hear their entire conversation.

"Why don't you hop on a plane with me tonight and fly out to Los Angeles?" Sinatra kept suggesting. "We'll borrow some clothes from the set of *Anchors Aweigh* and then go to my yacht at Catalina Island and spend a few days."

Miss Smith kept saying no.

After her fourth martini, she said to Sinatra, "What time do you want to leave?"

My childhood was not just fun and games at the ballpark and dinner with movie stars. Growing up so close to my father, I learned many things from him. The best thing my dad taught me was to make decisions. When we traveled or went out for dinner, he made me pick the restaurant, hotel, and the route to where we were headed. Probably because of that I have always been able to make quick decisions. That certainly helped me the time I went to Italy to buy a circus—but I'm getting ahead of myself.

My father also made me go to a large public high school instead of a private school, even though I had passed the entrance exam to the latter. He explained to me that in the real world I would be working with all kinds of people—not just with rich white kids. The public school I attended, Withrow, was very integrated. I have always been able to get along well with just about anyone—not just people who look like me—and I thank Dad for that.

When I was concerned that I wasn't a good enough student in high school or college, my father helped me then, too.

"With my grades, I'm not going to get a good job when I graduate," I said.

To which my dad replied, "A students become professors, B students become lawyers, and C students make the big money."

Looking back on what career path my college friends took proved my father correct.

Since I was an only child, my father was quite proud of me and wanted me to do well in sports. "Play any sport you enjoy, but work hard to be the best at whatever you choose," he would say. "And don't play in the band!"

It was also very important for me to make him proud. So when I entered college at Denison University, I decided to do just that by making the college football team. I worked out all summer prior to my freshman year with one of my best friends—Jim Brockhoff, who was a great quarterback at Xavier University—so that I could impress my college coach.

I only lasted one week. In fact, the only reason my football career lasted that long was that the locker room showers weren't working, and the team just studied the playbook for the first week. On the first day of real physical workouts, I was gung-ho to show the coaches that I really wanted to make the team. I was the first guy out of the locker room, and I sprinted up a big hill to the practice field in full pads. I did not realize that once I got to the practice field I had to continue running around the perimeter of the field.

Twice.

So much for pacing myself. As I continued on my journey around the field, my legs got weaker and weaker, and the rest of the players kept passing me.

"Giles, you better not be last!" Coach Karl yelled.

Well, I was last, and by the time I had finished the running, the rest of the team was in tackling practice. Some guy tackled me in the stomach, and I threw up all over the back of his jersey. It was not pretty—grape juice for breakfast.

Between the morning practice and afternoon practice I went into Coach Karl's office. "To play football well you really have to like it," I said. "And I don't like it. So I think I'll stick to tennis."

The next day my father drove up from Cincinnati to watch his star football son. He went to the practice field and did not see me. "Where's my son?" he asked.

"I think you will find him in the downtown pool hall," one of the coaches replied.

The coach was right, and my dad was not real proud of me on that day.

But I did have better days to come.

My Dream to Run a Baseball Team

My Mentor, Gabe Paul

When I was 15 years old, I realized that my dream of becoming a big-league baseball player was not going to happen. So I set out on a plan to go to a small university, meet a beautiful girl, get married, join the air force, have two or three kids, buy a station wagon, live in suburbia in a nice house with a dog or two, work in baseball administration, and become general manager of a major league baseball team by the time I was 42 years old. My goals were very specific.

Besides following in my father's footsteps, another important reason that I wanted to be a GM by age 42 involved a man named Gabe Paul. I read in *The Sporting News* that Gabe had become the youngest GM at the age of 42. I wanted to accomplish that same goal.

Gabe is another of the great front-office men in baseball history and someone who was instrumental in my life and career. Gabe started out as a batboy for my dad's team and at the age of 16 became my father's assistant as publicity director and ticket manager. He worked for my father both in Rochester and in Cincinnati before taking over as president of the Reds when my dad became National League president. He was also the man who gave me my first full-time baseball job in 1959, for which I received an annual salary of $4,000.

He bought me my first razor, too—and whenever we were in other people's company, he'd proudly announce that fact. The entire Paul family—Gabe, his wife Mary (who helped raise me), sons Gabe Jr., Warren (named after my father), Henry, and daughter Jenny—were like an extension of my own family. They would have Thanksgiving and Christmas Eve dinner with my dad and me in our log cabin just about every year during the 1940s and '50s.

GABE PAUL

Even though Gabe Paul was involved in professional baseball for 60 years, his name is probably not as well known among baseball fans as it should be. That's surprising, given all that he accomplished and how good he was at what he did.

When Gabe took over the general manager duties in Cincinnati in 1951, the Reds were struggling a bit. After winning back-to-back pennants in 1939 and 1940, they had dropped all the way to sixth place. Cincinnati steadily improved over the next five years, topping the 90-win mark in 1956. By 1961 the Reds were back in the World Series. Gabe had moved on before that season, so he was not there to see firsthand the success of the team he'd built through shrewd trades (first baseman Gordy Coleman, third baseman Gene Freese, outfielder Wally Post, starting pitcher Bob Purkey) and great signings (Negro Leagues stars Vada Pinson and Frank Robinson).

The Cleveland Indians also showed steady improvement in the 1960s under his front-office leadership. They finished in third place in 1968—despite not having a single hitter with either 15 home runs or 60 RBIs. And if you don't think third place is all that big of a deal, you don't know what it was like to be an Indians fan in the 1960s, '70s, and '80s. It would be their highest finish until they won the pennant in 1995.

But it was in the mid-1970s, past the age of 60 and nearing his 50th year in professional baseball, that Gabe had his greatest run as a deal-maker. He was hired by a Cleveland businessman, one George Michael Steinbrenner, who had spearheaded the purchase of the Yankees from CBS for $10 million after a deal to purchase the Indians had fallen apart at the last minute.

One of the reasons the Yankees were on the market at all was the fact that they really weren't the Yankees anymore. They'd been out of the World Series since 1964 and were enduring their worst stretch of baseball since before Babe Ruth came to town. Gabe was named president and general manager and immediately set to work changing all that with a series of remarkable trades. By the time he left the Yankees after the 1977 season, they'd been in back-to-back World Series and had won their first championship in 15 years.

That 1977 championship team was known as the "best team that money could buy"—what with a total annual payroll that approached the outlandish figure of $2 million—but it was Gabe's old-school deal-making that brought the Yankees back to the top. Not just shrewd trades, but gutsy ones.

In April 1974, he traded nearly half of his pitching staff to Cleveland for Chris Chambliss and Dick Tidrow. Tidrow was an invaluable swingman for the Yankees, while Chambliss became a fixture at first base, going on to hit one of the most dramatic home runs in major league history to end the 1976 American League Championship Series and put New York back into the World Series.

In December 1975, Gabe traded a pitcher named Doc (Medich) for a pitcher named Dock (Ellis), and got a young second baseman named Willie Randolph from the Pittsburgh Pirates as part of the bargain. Randolph would go on to become the best Yankees second baseman since Bobby Richardson and would hold down the position for 13 seasons.

And, on the very same day in December, he traded right fielder Bobby Bonds—whom Gabe had acquired the year before for the enormously popular Bobby Murcer—for Angels center fielder Mickey Rivers and starting pitcher Ed Figueroa. Gabe now had his leadoff hitter, the fastest player in pinstripes since another guy named Mickey, as well as a pitcher who would go on to win 55 games over the next three seasons.

All these deals paid off. At the trading deadline in June 1976, Gabe's Yankees team was back in first place. Though they were up by four and a half games and had not lost more than three games in a row until the first week of June, that didn't stop Gabe from pulling the trigger on a nine-player deal—with the Baltimore Orioles, a team in his own division.

In late April 1977, Gabe put the final piece in place when he acquired starting pitcher Mike Torrez from the Oakland A's for a player nearing the end of his career (Dock Ellis) and a prospect who never panned out (Larry Murray). Torrez would be on the mound for New York when the last out of the World Series was recorded, the author of a complete-game victory.

Gabe left the Yankees after that tumultuous season and went back to Cleveland to serve as president. He eventually retired from professional baseball in 1985 at the age of 75, having seen Babe Ruth in his prime, having watched Hank Aaron from start to finish, and having traded for (and dealt away) Barry Bonds's father. Not a bad run.

Early Indications That the Front Office Would Be a Better Fit Than the Pitcher's Mound

Like most boys growing up in the '40s and '50s, my baseball career started on the sandlots. I played knothole baseball, an organized version of youth baseball, which is similar to Little League, plus a lot of sandlot baseball. For me, sandlot baseball was four or five kids playing on some empty lot in Cincinnati, making up various rules depending on the number of kids and the size of the field. I would often use taped-up bats that had been broken by some of the Cincinnati Reds players.

In high school I was not good enough to play on the baseball team, so I played for the Wasaka Boys Club—I played third base, first base, and did some pitching. Back in those days, there was no lacrosse or soccer in school, so the competition for making the baseball team was much more difficult than it is today.

My best sport was tennis, which I started to play when I got cut from the Withrow High School baseball team. I won a lot of tennis tournaments in both high school and at Denison University. I was Ohio Conference doubles champ in my freshman year at Denison, so I decided to play baseball in my sophomore year. You can't be too predictable.

Unfortunately, as a baseball player I was not very good. Neither was the team. And, alas, neither was the coach. Keith Piper was his name, and he didn't know much about baseball. He was the assistant football coach. As baseball coaches go, let's just say he was a decent assistant football coach.

While pitching at Denison, I started a game at Kenyon College, and there were two major league scouts from the Detroit Tigers in attendance—and, of all things, they were there to scout me, a guy who couldn't make his high school team! Spike Briggs, the owner of the Tigers, was a great admirer of my father. So, when he heard that Warren Giles's son was a college pitcher, he sent two scouts in to see if I was any kind of a prospect.

In the first inning, I allowed four runs. In the second inning, I was on first base when the next batter hit a ground ball to short. In an attempt to break up a double play, I went into second with my arms above my head. The second baseman's relay hit my raised arm, and the umpire correctly called both of us out. By the third inning, both scouts had left, having seen enough. I don't know what they wrote on their reports, but I doubt the words "can't miss" were used.

As a pitcher, I had good control and a decent curve ball, and though there were no radar guns in those days, I probably didn't throw 80 mph. I had great control, however. I could hit a bat with a pitched ball from 60'6" with the best of them. It was back to tennis the next year.

During my days in the military, I also played baseball at Harlingen Air Force Base in 1957 and at Lincoln AFB in 1959. The last game I ever played was at Columbus, Ohio, at the tournament for all air force teams. I managed and pitched for Lincoln AFB because I was the only guy who got the ball over the plate, and we only had 10 players on the team. I pitched the entire game, losing 13–1.

The real bad news was that my father and three of my best friends—Lou Rice, Larry Kleinfelter, and Harry Andreadis—had driven up from Cincinnati to watch the debacle. They never let me forget it. So much for my career as a baseball player.

I also learned down in Harlingen that I would not have much of a career as a duck hunter. My next-door neighbor at the base was an avid duck hunter who even went so far as to hand carve his own duck decoys. He invited me to join him on a duck hunt and, having never done it before, I readily jumped at the opportunity to try something new. We got up at 3:00 AM and drove to a lake near Corpus Christi, Texas, where he put out his decoys. We got into the blind with our shotguns, and my neighbor made a few duck calls. A flock landed on the lake, and I started shooting. No one had told me that you were actually supposed to wait until the ducks were back in the air. I ended up shooting and killing about half of his decoys. For some reason, I didn't get a second invitation.

I also wasn't exactly knocking anyone's socks off as a scout. When I was stationed in Texas, my father asked me to go look in on a hot third-base prospect down in Corpus Christi. I've watched a few young players in my day and have made some pretty good calls on more than a few. Not this time. I watched the kid play and wrote up a report that he was good enough to hit in the big leagues but would never be able to field his position.

That was my first impression of Brooks Robinson.

As you probably can tell already, I'm no spin doctor. If I were, I guess I'd just tell you that I scouted Brooksie and was one of the very first to recognize his underappreciated offensive capabilities.

Starting on the Bottom Rung of the Ladder

In the summers of 1949, 1950, and 1954, I worked in the front office of the Cincinnati Reds. My first year I was an assistant to Hank Zurieck, the Reds' publicity director. I mostly folded and mailed news releases and did other grunt work. My second year I worked in the ticket office handling all of the out-of-town requests for tickets.

In 1954 I was an assistant to the farm director, Bill McKechnie Jr., the son of former Reds manager Bill McKechnie. My primary responsibility was to organize and file scouting reports. Here are two scouting reports that stood out:

"Not much power, fair speed, heavy legs, big butt—will only make it as a catcher."

"Too wild to make the big leagues as a pitcher, but he can hit and might make it as a first baseman."

The first one? Pete Rose.

The second one? A pitcher–first baseman for the University of Cincinnati named Koufax.

As you can see, scouting a baseball player is not an exact science. As I was going through the reports, I noticed a history of a player named Cookie Rojas who had played for eight years in the minors, never making more than $4,000 during any given year. At the time, I wondered why a guy like that didn't retire and get a real job. That's just one of many great things about baseball—patience and persistence are often rewarded.

Cookie got drafted the next year by the Phillies, became an All-Star player for a few years with the Kansas City Royals, and ended up with a major league career batting average of .263. He was also one of very few players who played all nine positions during his major league career—all 10, if you count designated hitter. He even finished a game for the Phillies in 1967, pitching one inning and giving up only one hit and no runs.

My first big job in baseball occurred that same summer. The Reds had a farm team in Morristown, Tennessee, in the Class D Mountain States League. The team was in deep financial trouble, and the man running the team was an alcoholic. Not sure which of those was the cause and which was the effect, but I have my suspicions. So Gabe Paul sent me, at the tender age of 19, down to Morristown to run the team. It was quite an experience.

The Mountain States League was supposed to be a league for young players with fewer than two years of professional baseball experience. In reality, there were a lot of Latin players who had played minor league ball for many years, but they changed their last names every two years so that the official records showed they were much younger than they really were.

My office and home consisted of one room in a small, crummy hotel in downtown Morristown. It had one double bed, a desk, a closet, a bathroom, and a ceiling fan. There was no air-conditioning despite the fact that the temperature was never lower than 90 degrees—day or night. The ceiling fan switch gave you the option of low, medium, or high—but no matter where you turned the switch, the fan would only rotate once every 10 seconds or so. Boy, was it hot.

Such was the glamorous life of a budding baseball executive.

The day after I arrived, the Reds sent a young catcher named Pete Wragg to join our team. Wragg received a big bonus after playing at the University of Illinois. He could not find a place to stay when he arrived, so I invited him to share my room. We would often wake up sweating in the middle of the night and head for the municipal pool, climb over the locked gate, and go for a swim.

The ballpark was a rickety wooden structure with one shower in the locker room. Box seats cost 25¢, and you could rent a cushion for an extra 25¢. One of my duties was to collect all the cushions after the game and store them under the stands. The third day there I gave a speech to the Rotary Club and told them what the town needed to do to make Morristown a successful operation. The next day the local paper printed a headline on the front page in very bold print: "27-Year-Old Son of Warren Giles to Save Baseball in Morristown."

Of course, I was only 19 years old, and within 10 days, the entire league folded, and I drove back home to Cincinnati. So much for being a savior.

Making It in Nashville—without a Guitar

After graduation from Denison University in 1956 and spending three years in the Strategic Air Command as a navigator, my first real full-time baseball job began. In the fall of 1959, Gabe Paul, still the president of the Reds at the time, asked me to become business manager of the Nashville Volunteers in the Southern Association.

A civic group led by Hershel Greer owned the team, and country singing great Eddie Arnold was on the board. One of the rewards for working in baseball was meeting lots of interesting people and many celebrities. Because my father frequently socialized with celebrities, I'd essentially grown up around them and always felt fairly at ease in their company.

I enjoyed my time in Nashville, but I have to say that where I worked was about as far from Frank Sinatra and the '21' Club as you can get. Anyone who thought that my tight ties to the president of the National League guaranteed me a cushy life in the family business never spent much time in a place called Sulphur Dell.

The Nashville Vols played in Sulphur Dell, a park that held about 8,000 people and was called "Suffer Hell" by those who spent much time there. Because it was near to—and downwind from—a city refuse site, it was also called "the Dump." The Cumberland River was nearby, and it frequently flooded the ballpark. A railroad track ran right by my desk, and whenever a train came by, black soot would end up in my office.

Even though the ballpark might have left something to be desired, my wife and I enjoyed our time in Nashville very much. We made a lot of nice friends there, and we still stay in touch with many of them. We celebrated the first birthday of our oldest son, Mike, there. I loved the grits, red-eyed gravy, and hot cakes (a small corn pancake served instead of rolls or bread).

The playing field at Sulphur Dell is something else I'll never forget. It was one of the strangest I ever saw. The entire outfield had terraces, and I don't mean the kind that Crosley Field had. These were 45-degree slopes that extended 20 to 40 feet into the playing field in the outfield. Though the dimensions to right field were very short (262 feet), the hitter and the right fielder had to contend with a very high fence, an embankment that started at 224 feet from home plate, and—when there were overflow crowds—fans seated on the incline behind ropes. Outfielders who braved these elements were rewarded with the nickname of "mountain goat." I once saw an outfielder named Chico Alvarez fall down on one of those inclines and catch a fly ball lying flat on his back.

Jim Turner, who had been a successful pitcher with the Boston Braves, Cincinnati Reds, and New York Yankees, was the general manager and manager. He would go on to be the pitching coach for the New York Yankees for many years.

It was my job to handle all public relations, promotions, and advertising, as well as ticket and concession sales. In the winter I spent most of my time selling fence and scorebook ads.

To build and maintain interest in Vols baseball, I started a "Hot Stove League" on Saturday mornings: a breakfast meeting during the winter at a downtown restaurant where fans could talk baseball with Jim Turner and me. I also purchased a second car—a used black Volkswagen Beetle—to get me to and from the park and to my sales calls. As you can see, life for me in Nashville was more than a few steps up from pool hopping to escape a ventilation-free hotel room.

Once the season started, my main job was to promote ticket sales and run the concessions. I would sell out the park to corporations for $3,000 a game, and they could give out as many tickets as they wanted. A couple of times there were 20,000 people trying to get into 8,000 seats.

I created a picnic area with tables and chairs under the stands, learned how to pour six beers at one time, ordered all the food, and hired all the people. When my father came to the park on Opening Day in 1960, he didn't find me with my feet up on the desk; I was carrying five dozen hamburger buns to a concession stand.

He probably would have been more impressed if he'd seen me pouring those beers. This is one trick you *can* try at home. You line up six open bottles and six cups, then bring your hands palms down through the line of beers until you've got a bottle neck between each finger. Then, moving calmly, quickly, and efficiently, you flip your hands, upending the beers into the lined-up cups. Like a well-turned double play, timing is everything—though you should know that Nashville beer patrons are much less forgiving than second-base umpires of the alcohol-pouring equivalent of a phantom tag. Not quite as impressive as Ernie Lombardi holding seven baseballs in one hand, but none too shabby, either.

You had to be on your toes, hustling, and always selling to keep a minor league team in the black. It helped to pay attention to the details, too. Which I did—but most every game, I would come up about 20 hamburgers short when I did the inventory. I could not figure out why until I caught my assistant—a big man named Sparky who had just one eye—taking hamburgers from the freezer and giving them to his sister, who was waiting in a car by the back door. I should have fired him, but I really felt sorry for him and his family. I just reprimanded him and told him not to do it again.

I also got into trouble as a member of the front office at Sulphur Dell. I had a promotion called "Baseball Bingo," where every fan received a bingo card as he or she entered the park. The cards had baseball situations such as "two-base hit" or "sacrifice" instead of letters and numbers. I was on the public-address system running the bingo game, and I had a big bell sitting beside me that I would hit with a wooden mallet if anyone got a bingo. Toward the end of the game there had not been a winner, and the umpires had been making very bad calls, so I got on the PA system and made the following announcement: "If there are no bingo winners tonight, we are going to give seeing-eye dogs to all the umpires."

The Associated Press ran a story the next day with a headline: "Warren Giles's Son Blasts Umpires."

Not so good, considering that my father, as president of the National League, was in charge of the umpires. This turned out to be the first time—but by no means the last time—that I got in trouble for teasing the men in blue.

As much as we enjoyed our time in Nashville, my wife, Nancy, son Mike, a black poodle dog named Toddy, and I moved back to Cincinnati in September 1960. I believed that my goal of being a general manager by the time I was 42 would be further advanced if I worked for a major league team. Gabe Paul wanted me to be a traveling secretary for the Reds starting in the 1961 season. He had been one and thought that the experience would be invaluable, that it would help me get to know the players and how they acted. As I'd later learn, getting to know the players and how they acted truly was invaluable—and entertaining, as well, filling me on more than one occasion with shock and awe.

We moved into our new house in Mt. Washington, a suburb of Cincinnati. We'd been living in the house only a few weeks before my baseball career changed dramatically.

Moving on to Texas

The Baseball League That Never Was

It was a significant move that Gabe Paul made in late 1960 that gave me an opportunity that changed my life. But little did I know at the time that I was essentially running off to join the circus.

Houston and New York were awarded expansion franchises by the National League and officially were to begin play in 1962. Paul was named the new general manager of Houston and asked me to join him as a "jack of all trades." My dad, Nancy, and I all thought it might be a good opportunity to start a baseball operation, so my wife and I packed up and moved to Texas. Mr. Paul also asked Tal Smith, who was working in the Reds farm department, to join us. The move didn't work out all that well for Gabe—who lasted only a few months in Houston for reasons that will soon become apparent— but it wasn't too bad for Tal and me. Tal is still there, and now he runs the place.

Major league baseball ending up in Houston in 1962 had, ironically, less to do with Texas and more to do with New York and California—and a baseball league that never was. In perhaps the last credible threat to major league baseball's "monopoly" hold on the national pastime, the mayor of New York had suggested the formation of a third league. Mayor Robert F. Wagner Jr. advanced this concept in 1958 in response to the relocation of the Dodgers and Giants to California after the 1957 season.

On July 27, 1959, New York attorney William A. Shea—a name that should be familiar to any fan of the New York Mets—announced the formation of the Continental League. Shea reported that it would have franchises in New York (the largest metropolitan area in the country at the time), Houston (seventh), Minneapolis–St. Paul (ninth), Denver (23rd), Toronto (larger than all but 14 U.S. cities), and other cities to be named later. Franchise owners of the original teams would be required to invest $3 million plus the construction costs of new stadiums. The president of the league was to be none other than my godfather, Branch Rickey.

Now keep in mind that Major League Baseball in the late 1950s was on nowhere near the financial footing that it is on today. Attendance, which had peaked in the postwar years at 20.9 million and nearly 17,000 per game, had dropped to 17.5 million and roughly 14,000 per game in 1958. It wouldn't fully rebound until 1977. Many teams were playing in aging structures in decaying urban neighborhoods—the same factors that contributed to the Dodgers leaving Brooklyn and the Giants leaving Upper Manhattan. A rival league led by a brilliant baseball man like Branch Rickey and poised to enter some of the largest markets in North America had to be taken seriously.

My father was scared to death. He feared that the Continental League—if it were to actually happen—would greatly water down the product on the field. In January 1960, three more markets were announced: Atlanta, Dallas–Fort Worth, and Buffalo. Then, after much discussion, consternation, negotiation, and threatened congressional involvement (some things never change), the league reached an agreement with Major League Baseball in August 1960 to disband before a game had ever been played.

The folding of the Continental League came with the understanding that four franchises (Houston, New York, Toronto, and Minneapolis) would be admitted into the existing major league structure. That changed when the Senators moved to Minnesota before the 1961 season; the American League expansion teams for that season would be the Los Angeles Angels and the new Washington Senators, who would eventually move to the Dallas–Fort Worth area to become the Texas Rangers. By 1993, with the formation of the Colorado Rockies, every Continental League market except Buffalo had become big league.

I was the second person hired by the management team of Houston's new major league baseball franchise. This management team consisted of majority owner R.E. "Bob" Smith, part owner Judge Roy Hofheinz, president Craig Cullinan, and vice president George Kirksey.

Smith—a big, strong man of about 60 with bushy silver hair who had earned his money in oil wells and land development—was majority owner and chairman of the board. Though he was the "real money" in the deal, he had very little to say about the operation of the team. The man who really ran the team was Judge Roy Hofheinz— a truly unique individual and one of the most creative and intelligent men I have ever known.

Here Comes the Judge

The life story of "the Judge," as he was known, could be filed under "Only in America." His parents came to the United States with no money on a boat full of Greek immigrants. Hofheinz's father drove a laundry truck and died when his son was only 15. Hofheinz went to work to support his mother, enrolled at Rice University, and graduated from the University of Houston law school at age 19. He was a member of the Texas state legislature at 22, became Harris County judge at 24, and then was elected mayor of Houston in 1952 at the age of 40.

As successful as he was, the Judge's career was not without controversy. At one point, the city council voted to impeach him, but the Judge simply ignored them, stated so publicly, and they caved.

It was during those years as mayor that he formed a partnership with Bob Smith. Mayor Hofheinz knew in advance where new roads were going to be constructed, so he and Smith would purchase as much land as possible around the roads. They would then sell the land after the roads were constructed for a big profit. With interests in radio and TV stations, land, and slag, as well as his law practice, Judge Roy Hofheinz was a millionaire. The Judge was flamboyant and controversial, and he lived by his motto: "Success comes in cans, not can'ts."

If the Judge had another motto, it was, "Never put anything in writing." He always had a stack of pink telephone slips on his desk, and he did as much business as possible by phone. When he sold Gulf Oil on a sponsorship of the ballclub's scoreboard, there was no written contract—and this was for a seven-figure deal.

Hofheinz always worked in a black suit with a black tie, though the white shirt was never buttoned to the top and the coat was rarely on. He almost always had a cigar in one hand and a glass of Scotch in the other. And he insisted on complete loyalty. If he even suspected you were talking behind his back, you were gone.

A Plan to Beat the Heat

It was Judge Hofheinz who convinced my father and the owners of the National League that baseball would be successful in Texas. At that point—with the exception of Los Angeles—there was no major league baseball south of St. Louis and Cincinnati. Even though Houston by 1960 had a population of nearly 1 million and was the seventh-largest metropolitan area in the nation—up from 45,000 and a rank of 85th at the turn of the century—there were still significant obstacles to be overcome. Remember, this was before the days of lightweight uniforms and climate control, back when most games were still played in the heat of the day. At the time, the southeastern region of the United States was for minor league baseball and, in Florida, for spring training.

I was not in those discussions, but I do know the people involved, and I'm sure they went something like this.

"Judge, major league baseball just can't work that far south."

"Sure it can."

"What about the heat? The humidity? It's brutal in St. Louis in July. What's it going to be like down in Houston?"

"That can be taken care of."

"Taken care of? How do you take care of the weather?"

"We'll just build a domed stadium. The world's first indoor, air-conditioned baseball park."

"A dome?"

"It'll be like the Coliseum in Rome."

It tells you something about the Judge that he could offer up such an idea and not be laughed out of the room. You don't get where he got as fast as he got without being able to sell. The Judge was eloquent, articulate, a showman, a ringmaster, a motivator, and, above all else, a great salesman. Along the way, he would need to sell not just baseball people, but everyone from local officials, architects, and builders to voters and employees. And he did just that. After all, as Tal Smith put it, "You could be in his company for only five minutes and find yourself a great believer in whatever he was espousing."

Hofheinz always liked to have a lot of people around him—and because he had such energy and a great sense of humor, it made most people *want* to be around him. All kinds of people. He was just as comfortable talking to his chauffeur as he was to the president of the United States.

When Houston was granted its expansion franchise, it was due in large part to the Judge's vision and confidence. This ownership group had the money and design to "take care of the weather" by building an indoor, air-conditioned, domed stadium—and the audacity to actually be able to pull it off. If you're looking for the end of the baseball era that I grew up in, you could point to that moment.

The other members of the ownership group were an interesting bunch, but nowhere near as outlandish as the Judge. Craig Cullinan, wealthy and a good guy, was presented to the public as the "boss" and was named president because he was very popular in and around town. I really liked him. When Houston was awarded the National League franchise by my father, the Houston franchise was known as the "Cullinan Group."

As time wore on, however, you heard the name Hofheinz more and more. In fact, at the very first league meeting that Houston attended, it was the Judge representing the team—and doing a lot of talking. He spent a fair bit of time at the first meeting telling all the other owners what they should be doing. My father had to take him to dinner afterward and coach him, which is a nice way of saying that he told him you're given two ears and only one mouth for a reason. To the Judge's credit, he heeded my father's advice.

Another member of the Cullinan Group was vice president George Kirksey. He was the energy behind converting the Continental League bid into a major league franchise for Houston. He advised Cullinan and Hofheinz about the baseball part of the operation, having been the former baseball editor of the United Press International news agency.

When I first arrived in Houston to work for this group, my job description was to do anything I was asked to do and to "remain flexible." How true that turned out to be. When I was eventually named publicity director, I worked directly under Kirksey. He taught me how to write news releases as well as how to get them printed in the newspaper, and he introduced me to all the key news people.

The Odd Couple: Gabe and the Judge

While I found it fairly easy to blend in with the Houston ownership group, it was not as easy a transition for the man who brought me there: general manager Gabe Paul. About six months after arriving in Houston, it became clear to Gabe and everyone else that Judge Hofheinz, and not Cullinan, was going to be running the show. Gabe did not agree with most of the Judge's plans or methods of operation. The Judge was a real risk-taker and did everything in a big and sometimes expensive way. It didn't take long for Gabe to leave Houston to become general manager of the Cleveland Indians.

Knowing Gabe as well as I did, I could understand his discomfort with the Judge. Gabe was very conservative when it came to finances—though some of his employees through the years might say tightfisted instead. He used to pay kids $10 to retrieve baseballs hit over the fence in batting practice at Crosley Field so they could be reused. It wasn't all that different outside of the office. He lived in a nice but simple ranch house in Houston—nothing fancy. Gabe and the Judge had very different opinions about money and what to do with it, to say the least.

Unlike Gabe's living arrangements, Hofheinz had three homes—his residence in River Oaks, a beach house that contained all sorts of wild furniture and bizarre decorations including stuffed elephants, zebras, and giraffes, and a hunting lodge out on Katy Freeway west of Houston. The hunting lodge became the meeting place for the Judge and his staff. He frequently had his secretary call his assistants on a Friday morning to tell them there was a command performance Friday night and Saturday at the lodge. The lack of notification was a bit upsetting to the wives of the married guys. When you arrived at the lodge it was always the Judge who cooked all the meals. He loved to cook chili and other spicy Tex-Mex food. Sometimes we would debate important issues, but many times it was just the Judge wanting to get away, have a few drinks, play pool, and cook.

MAJOR LEAGUE BASEBALL AND DESEGREGATION

I have always believed that the arrival of major league baseball in Houston did more than just bring big-league ball to an untapped and rapidly growing market. It also had a lot to do with promoting desegregation throughout the South.

When my family and I moved to Houston in 1960, legal segregation under Jim Crow laws was still in effect. African Americans could not stay in the "good" hotels or go to the "good" restaurants. There were even separate restrooms for "colored" people in public places—including the existing minor league ballpark.

With major league baseball integrating before the rest of the country, teams sometimes had to get creative to ensure that their players were treated equally when they were down South. This was particularly an issue during spring training in Florida. The Dodgers went to Cuba to train after Jackie Robinson joined the club because it was an integrated country. The Cardinals bought a hotel in St. Petersburg so that all their players could be housed in one place. I quickly learned that we would have to address this issue in Houston, too.

Being very involved with the Houston Sportswriters Association—an organization consisting of writers, broadcasters, and other sports enthusiasts to promote sports in Houston—I participated in an annual sports banquet that was held each January at the Shamrock Hilton. After the 1961 season, they honored a great St. Louis Cardinals pitcher—Bob Gibson—who also happened to be black. Gibson was a very proud man and was outraged when he walked into the Hilton and the hotel would not give him a room. He immediately sought me out because I was the one who had invited him. He really lit into me about discrimination. I eventually made arrangements for him to stay in the special suite that Judge Hofheinz rented on an annual basis in the Hilton.

George Kirksey and I met with the hotel and restaurant association and convinced them that if Houston was going to become a truly "Major League City," they had to allow the visiting teams to stay in the good hotels and eat in the fine restaurants. After all, most big-league teams by then had at least two or three black players and some a lot more. Some of these men were among the biggest stars in the National League. Were opposing teams going to allow star players like Frank Robinson or Hank Aaron—or any of their players, for that matter—to be treated like second-class citizens when they came to Houston?

The Shamrock Hilton, built by oil magnate Glenn McCarthy, was the first to integrate. Eventually all the hotels and restaurants joined the Hilton, in time for our first games in 1962.

Paul Richards Works All the Angles

It didn't take long for George Kirksey to persuade highly regarded Orioles manager Paul Richards to "join the circus" as Gabe Paul's replacement. Richards was a good judge of talent and was a very good baseball man. He preached the fundamentals:

You cannot win without good pitching.

You have to have good defense up the middle—catcher, shortstop, second base, and center field.

Repetition in catching ground balls and fly balls is completely necessary to have a good defense—each infielder should take at least 50 ground balls every day and each outfielder should shag at least 50 fly balls every day.

Richards also believed that your first impression of young players is the correct impression and that a general manager should not be afraid to come to a quick judgment on a young talent. Though Richards wasn't the character that Hofheinz was, he did have his own idiosyncrasies and certainly kept things interesting—to put it politely.

Richards certainly had an odd sense of humor. His idea of "funny" was to sit in a room with six colleagues and ask five of them to join him for dinner, conspicuously leaving one person out. Given that there was no way in hell that Richards would pick up the check, maybe being left out was not the worst thing in the world.

Richards hated to fly, so we took trains whenever we could. Because he insisted on blind loyalty from his staff, he liked to have his old cronies around to wait on him or play golf with him. Clint Courtney, a former catcher with Baltimore, was hired as a bullpen coach—but his role was really to be Richards's valet, catering to his every whim and carrying his golf clubs. When Richards, who was about a six-handicap golfer, played golf with Courtney—who was nowhere near as good as Richards—Richards would give him one throw on each hole. Anytime Courtney felt like it, he could pick up the golf ball and throw it.

Although Richards was smart and interesting, he was a man of questionable character. When he played golf, which was frequent, he would have two putters in his bag—one with short leather and one with long leather. When he was measuring a "gimme putt" for him or his partner, he would measure with the long leather, but he would use the short leather when he was measuring his opponent's putt. And he always made sure that someone else in his foursome would pay the green fees—I always had to pay using my expense account when I was playing.

Richards and either Dizzy Dean (the great Hall of Fame pitcher and colorful broadcaster) or Alvin Dark would often play high rollers from out of town for the big bucks—sometimes for $5,000. They would always lose the front nine on purpose, and then double the bet, winning 90 percent of the time on the back nine.

With Richards there was also a fair bit of grandstanding. He was more than a little bit of a self-promoter, so it was hard to separate fact from fable when it came to the innovations he was credited with—like the oversized catcher's mitt that made its debut in Baltimore to help Gus Triandos catch Hoyt Wilhelm's knuckleball. That's probably fact. But when there was a lot of interest from the Orioles and other teams in a young stud pitching prospect—future Hall of Famer Jim Palmer—Richards made it a point of letting us all know that he was out in Arizona personally trying to land Palmer for the Astros. He even went to elaborate lengths to make it appear that he was at a hotel in Arizona. We later discovered that he was actually in Texas the whole time.

Richards would often have me set up dinners for the writers and coaches and have me pay the bill while he was putting the amount on his personal expense account to make a little extra cash. He would also have me or the clubhouse man pay for his laundry, again putting it on his expense account. He was so proficient and innovative at this that he was able to rise from mere double dipping to triple dipping. More serious was the possibility—suspected, but never proven—that he was receiving kickbacks from young players who received what some felt were unnecessarily high signing bonuses.

Richards certainly had a moral compass that was not calibrated with mine. When Houston was getting ready for the 1962 expansion draft, Richards asked me to sneak into my father's National League office to make copies of all the waiver claims so we would have an advantage. It is one thing to pad your expense account, but it is quite another to use unethical means to gain a competitive advantage.

I refused. Richards was livid and said some pretty harsh things to me. I stood my ground—I knew I was right.

Richards tried to find a way around just about every rule he encountered. Major League Baseball had a rule back then that if you paid a high school or college amateur player more than a certain amount of money to sign a contract, then that player immediately had to be put on the active big-league roster and not "farmed out" to the minors. That rule was intended to correct the "competitive imbalance" problem created when wealthy clubs tried to buy up all the young talent. Richards circumvented the $12,000 limit by giving employment contracts to members of a kid's family or signing a brother to a player contract even if the young man could not play. When Houston signed the highly sought after Rusty Staub to a contract, Richards gave Rusty's brother a $12,000 bonus even though he was not a good player and signed Staub's father as a scout for $30,000. My father realized that the integrity of the game was being challenged and convinced the owners to eliminate the $12,000 limit on bonus payments.

THE WILDEST TRADE EVER PROPOSED

Prior to the 1967 season, Houston made the most unique baseball offer I've ever heard of. Paul Richards told me at the Shamrock Hilton that, with the blessing of Bob Smith, he'd offered Houston's entire 40-man roster plus $5 million for the entire Detroit Tigers 40-man roster. Detroit was probably tempted to take the offer. Obviously the trade didn't happen. The 1967 Tigers went on to win 91 games, finishing second in one of the wildest pennant races in major league history, and the 1968 team went on to win the World Series, rallying from a 3–1 deficit. The Astros wouldn't top the .500 mark until 1972.

If Detroit had taken the offer, Houston probably would have gotten to the postseason before 1980 and to the World Series before 2005—but it wouldn't have been as lopsided a deal as you might think. The 1967 Astros had a lot of young talent. Paul Richards might have had some issues, but he was a pretty good judge of talent.

Mike Cuellar (age 30) would go on to become part of one of the greatest pitching staffs in baseball history with a Baltimore Orioles team that went to the World Series in 1969, 1970, and 1971. Dave Giusti (age 27) was a key member of the Pittsburgh Pirates bullpen when they won it all in 1971. Jim Wynn (age 25), the "Toy Cannon," was a power hitter who had a terrific career with Houston and later with the Los Angeles Dodgers. Rusty Staub (age 23) could roll out of bed in the middle of winter and get a base hit, putting up solid numbers for the Astros, Expos, Mets, and Tigers and winding up his career back in New York as one of the greatest pinch-hitters to ever play the game. Joe Morgan (age 23) was simply one of the best second basemen in baseball history. Don Wilson (age 22) was a talented and troubled pitcher who would go on to throw two no-hitters for the Astros before taking his own life. Bob Watson (age 21) was another very talented hitter who put up some big numbers in Houston before moving on to play in the World Series with the New York Yankees and becoming the first African American general manager to win a World Series—also with the Yankees. Larry Dierker (age 20) was one of the best pitchers the Houston organization has ever produced, and he went on to manage the team to several postseason appearances in the 1990s.

You could certainly have done a lot worse than that core of young players.

All of which assumes Paul Richards was telling me the truth about the offer in the first place.

Richards was eventually axed by the Judge when Hofheinz became aware that his general manager was talking badly about him behind his back. He was replaced with the more loyal, but less astute when it came to baseball, Spec Richardson—who spent much of his eight-year tenure being relieved by his fellow general managers of the burden of all that young talent Houston had been stockpiling.

Finalizing a Few Minor Details— a Place to Play and a Name for the Team

With Houston's domed stadium not scheduled for completion until the beginning of the 1965 season, the question became where to play during the 1962, 1963, and 1964 seasons. The original thought was to purchase the Houston Buffs Triple A team in the American Association and enlarge their ballpark, Buff Stadium.

We did purchase the Houston Buffs, and we operated the team during the 1961 season. That was actually what ended up driving the fiscally prudent Gabe Paul right out of town. He came back from spring training to find that Buffs Stadium had been decked out in streamers and bunting as if it were about to host a World Series game. To Gabe, this was both garish and a colossal waste of money for a stadium we'd be operating for one season.

"It looks like a used-car lot!" he exclaimed.

I served as publicity director for the Buffs that season and then continued that role when Houston joined the majors in 1962. However, in 1961, the Judge thought it would be a better idea to build a temporary ballpark next to the area where the domed stadium was to be constructed rather than enlarge Buff Stadium.

"Get the fans used to the area," he would say. "Let them see the domed stadium going up—it'll whet their appetite."

Within nine months, a 30,000-seat ballpark was constructed for only $2 million. The stadium was built on a light steel framework with wooden plank flooring. The reserved seats were aluminum bleachers, and the box seats were metal folding chairs. Though it was only a temporary stadium, the Judge made certain that we dressed it up to hide its limitations. It was bright, clean, and lively, with streamers everywhere. There was a Stadium Club called the Last Chance Corral, one of the first of its kind in a major league stadium. The club had a wooden floor with sawdust on the floor, and it had the longest bar in Texas and served Tex-Mex food. We had a press room behind home plate where the manager, coaches, news media, and I would gather after each game to have a beer and analyze the game.

Paul Richards wanted it to be a pitcher's park, so we made the dimensions big—360 feet down the lines and 420 feet to center field. We also made the grass very high on the infield and the lights not too bright—both of which also benefited the pitchers.

We now had a place to play, but we still didn't have a name to play under. One of my first important duties as publicity director was to select a nickname for the team. Kirksey and I conducted a public contest to pick the name. We had more than 10,000 entries and more than 300 different names. The four most popular names were:

1. Ravens
2. Texans
3. Bayous
4. Colts

Kirksey, a few others, and I all liked Colts the best, but we gave it a twist to Colt .45s so that we could have a gun as the insignia instead of a young horse. There was a malt beverage called Colt .45 with a young horse as its logo, so we did not want to get into any copyright debates. We had the logo drawn with the word *Colt* incorporated into a picture of a Colt .45 pistol with smoke coming out of the barrel. We picked orange and black as the team colors and put ".45s" on the front of the cap. Unfortunately, we did eventually end up in a copyright dispute—but with the manufacturer of the Colt revolver, instead.

The Next Mickey Mantle

We were permitted to sign amateur players and play in the Arizona Instructional League in the fall of 1961, six months before we played in the big leagues. Houston entered two teams in the league—one called the Colt .45s and the other the Colt .22s. We wanted to get as many young players as much experience as possible. We had a lot of promising players, but only three wound up doing well in the major leagues: outfielder Rusty Staub, catcher John Bateman, and shortstop Sonny Jackson.

One of the more memorable players on the Colt .22s who didn't end up doing much in the big leagues was John Paciorek. He was an 18-year-old high school superstar from Detroit who was sought after by many teams. Richards, a few of our scouts, and I took him to dinner at Gibby's Steakhouse in Chicago. I have never seen any person eat as much as John did. He had 56 ounces of sirloin steak, two big plates of home-fried potatoes, vegetables, and two half cantaloupes with double scoops of vanilla ice cream.

The next day we signed him to a $55,000 bonus, and we thought we had signed the next Mickey Mantle. He looked like Mantle—big and strong, played center field, could run fast, and hit the ball more than 500 feet. In batting practice he was awesome—hitting three out of four pitches well over the fence in all directions. Unfortunately, his performance in batting practice didn't translate to big-league stardom. He could handle his steak and his ice cream, but he couldn't hit a breaking ball or any pitch thrown faster than 90 mph. This was one of those cases where Richards's first impression didn't serve him well.

John Paciorek played one game with the Colts, on the last day of the 1963 season against the Mets. At the age of 18, he went three for three, drove in three runs, and scored four. Fortunately for him, the Mets didn't have many pitchers who could throw anything hard or with movement over the plate.

An injury the following year during spring training ended his career, and you can now find John at the top of the list for career batting average at 1.000. John was the biggest disappointment of my young baseball career. Ironically, his younger brother Tom, who played football at the University of Houston and was not considered much of a baseball prospect, signed a baseball contract out of college and had a pretty decent 18-year career in the big leagues with the Dodgers and others.

Heat, Humidity, Mosquitoes, Cowboy Hats, Cow Dung, and Booze

The first team that the Colts put on the field left a bit to be desired, but keep in mind that we were picking from the players the other teams didn't want. In the winter of 1961 the Colt .45s and New York Mets selected their players in the expansion draft, each team paying $125,000 for the first four players, $75,000 for the next 16 players, and $50,000 each for the final three players. Unfortunately, but not unexpectedly, almost every available player had some sort of a problem—lack of talent, excessive fondness for alcohol, anger management issues, and sometimes all of the above.

Though the players we had to work with had been bench players elsewhere, we made sure they stood out in other ways. Judge Hofheinz, a guy who never seemed to run out of ideas, came up with a notion that the traveling party had to wear fancy cowboy suits when we traveled as a team. The outfit was quite sharp— a Columbia blue suit; blue cowboy hat; orange, blue, and white cowboy boots; orange and white shirt with an orange string tie. We were the talk of the league, and we would take a lot of kidding from fans when we pulled up to a ballpark in our team bus wearing our cowboy suits. In addition to their somewhat unusual appearance, the suits were quite hot in the summertime. The players complained so much that we ended up wearing them for only half of the season.

These outfits made their debut in January 1962, when I started an off-season promotional caravan, an initiative that would continue throughout my entire career in Houston and in Philadelphia. We traveled with the manager, six players, announcers, some support personnel, and myself. We would make two stops per day, meeting at Rotary clubs and the like, followed by a press conference with the news media in towns throughout Texas and Louisiana. We sometimes flew on a chartered DC-3 plane, but mostly we traveled by bus and always wore our blue cowboy suits.

The first day out in 1962, our bus broke down heading to Corpus Christi. When the driver and a few others got out of the bus to check the engine, a big truck carrying cows drove by. A couple of the cows relieved themselves as the truck passed, leaving us with cow dung all over our nice cowboy suits. Not a good omen.

As with everything else surrounding this team, the spring training experience of the Houston Colt .45s was also decidedly not run of the mill—it was quite a different experience than it had been with Cincinnati. The team trained in Apache Junction, Arizona, for a couple of years. Apache Junction is about 30 miles east of Phoenix. It was not much—a one-block-long shopping area, gas station, the baseball field, and the hotel where everyone stayed: Superstition Hotel at the foothills of Superstition Mountain. The locals called it

Superstition Mountain because it was believed that anyone who went up there trying to find the Lost Dutchman Mine never came back alive.

My wife, my son Mike, and I stayed in an efficiency apartment in the hotel. It was a fairly new hotel—pretty nice with a big swimming pool. The hotel bar had an old guy with a beard who looked like an old gold miner, and he played a guitar. He went by Superstition Joe, and he was a real local favorite. I had Joe throw out the first ball when we opened up the new Geronimo Park in Apache Junction.

While today's players ride up to the spring training site in a fancy SUV or perhaps a chauffeured limousine, the Colt .45s had more basic means of transportation. One of our more colorful pitchers, Dick "Turk" Farrell, would walk the half mile from the hotel to the park with his .22 pistol, shooting snakes and rabbits along the way.

The South and Southwest were still pretty segregated in those days. Manny Mota, a dark-skinned Dominican, tried to rent an apartment in Apache Junction, but no one would rent to him because his skin was dark. So Nancy and I went out and rented an apartment in our name and then gave the keys to Mota and his family.

The Houston Colt .45s won the Cactus League title that first year. Winning the Cactus League title meant that you had won the most exhibition games in Arizona. Based on the reaction of our new fans in Houston, you would have thought we had won the World Series. When the team flew home from Arizona to Houston there was a big celebration at the airport with bands, banners, and thousands of people celebrating our "championship."

That same year, I made what was probably Houston's best signing. He was a young CBS weekend TV reporter who I hired for $13 a game to be the public address announcer. How many baseball teams can say that their PA announcer would go on to make more money in one year than the team's entire starting lineup made in a career?

Dan Rather made his mark in TV reporting on Hurricane Carla and the John F. Kennedy assassination and of course went on to become one of the most-watched and highest-paid TV news anchors in the history of broadcasting. The names that Rather called out most frequently in 1962 were not exactly Murderers' Row. How many names do you recognize?

C   Hal Smith
1B   Norm Larker
2B   Joey Amalfitano
SS   Don Buddin
3B   Bob Aspromonte
LF   Al Spangler
CF   Roman Mejias
RF   Jim Pendleton

Not a single one of those players had ever come to bat 500 times in a season before coming to Houston—and few played well enough to get 500 at-bats with us either. Key pitchers included Hal Woodeshick, Dean Stone, Dick Farrell, Jim Owens, and Ken Johnson. Only one of those fellows—Jim Owens—had ever pitched more than 200 innings in a season, which he did once for the Phillies back in the 1950s. Harry Craft, a very fine man, was the manager. Cot Deal was the pitching coach. Two of Paul Richards's disciples—Luman Harris and Jimmy Adair—were coaches.

We played our first game on April 10 in Houston, on the Judge's 50th birthday. We beat the Cubs that day and went on to sweep the three-game series from them. Despite the team's collective lack of experience as big-league regulars, we were getting pretty good at pitching, and Roman Mejias was fourth in the league in home runs at the All-Star Break with 21. He hit only three the rest of the season. The Colt .45s ended up losing 96 games, but did finish ahead of the Chicago Cubs and Casey Stengel's New York Mets. It took Houston seven years to get to the .500 mark, while it took the Mets seven years to get to the World Series. Although Houston finished ahead of the Mets in 1962 and 1963, Houston never made it to the World Series until 2005 and then lost to the Chicago White Sox in four straight games. The Mets not only got to the World Series, but won world championships in 1969 and again in 1986.

That season I got to see one of the strangest plays I have ever seen in the more than 8,000 baseball games I have watched. It was at Forbes Field in Pittsburgh. Knuckleballer Bob Tiefenauer was pitching for the Houston Colt .45s, and Hal Smith was catching. Bill Mazeroski of the Pirates was on third base, and, with one out, a fly ball was hit to right field. Right fielder Jim Pendleton caught the ball and threw to home as Mazeroski headed for the plate. Tiefenauer went to back up the throw behind home, and along the way he switched his glove for catcher Smith's oversized mitt used to catch knuckleball pitches. Smith caught the ball from Pendelton and did a swipe tag to get the out.

Unfortunately for us, we became known less for "heads-up" plays like this and more for where we played. Colt Stadium quickly became famous not for the quality of play on the field but for heat, humidity, and very large mosquitoes. Both dugouts had cans of bug spray, and we sold them at the concession stands, too. One Sunday we played an afternoon doubleheader against the Los Angeles Dodgers before a standing room crowd of 33,000 people. More than 100 fans passed out from heat exhaustion. As a result of this, we received permission in 1963 from the National League to play all of our Sunday games at night during the months of June, July, and August. The upshot of this is that we traded unbearable heat during the day for mammoth mosquitoes during the evening—or some other factor, like the time we got "fogged out" in a night game against the Reds.

Despite our relative lack of success on the field when the real games started and the difficult climate in Houston, I enjoyed my first year serving as both traveling secretary and publicity director. Taking the news media, manager, and coaches to the finest restaurants and talking baseball was a lot of fun and very educational as well. I also established a custom whereby the manager and coaches would come to my suite after a road night game to have some food and beer, discuss the game, and tell baseball war stories. And I got paid for this!

Occasionally I would pitch batting practice on the road, taking advantage of my ability to hit the fat part of the bat with a pitched ball. I also often played bridge on the plane trips with Norm Larker,

Al Spangler, and Hal Smith. On one trip, Larker, who was famous for having a bad temper, was getting very bad hands, so he picked up the cards, tore them in half, and threw them all over the plane. This wasn't anything new for Norm—he once threw the entire bat rack on the field in Milwaukee because he was angry about balls and strikes.

In the '60s, the team planes had an open bar, and we had a group of big drinkers on the team. Alcohol consumption was much more prevalent in the era from 1960 to 1980 than it is in the 21st century. Today's players do not seem to drink as much, and, when they do, they usually consume wine and beer instead of the hard stuff that was prevalent years ago.

Of course, free-flowing alcohol created some problems. For example, Jim Owens, who was known for being a tough guy and a hard drinker, slugged me in the Stevens Hotel lobby in Chicago while I was passing out the room keys. Turk Farrell and a couple of other players jumped on Owens to prevent further difficulties. Owens had no real reason for doing it, and he did apologize to me the next day.

Turk Farrell—our resident snake shooter—was one of my favorites. He drank about as much as Owens but didn't throw as many punches. He was a big, fun-loving guy with a huge heart, but he did like his booze, women, and staying up late—often all at the same time. One Saturday night in Philadelphia, I returned to the Warwick Hotel around 2:00 AM to find Farrell coming out of the elevator all dressed up and heading out.

"Turk, don't you have to pitch tomorrow afternoon at 1:00 PM?" I asked.

"Yes."

"Shouldn't you be in bed?"

He shook his head. "Come with me, and I will show you the after-hour spots of Philadelphia."

He took me to Sinatrarama, where they played Sinatra records all night, and then to the CR Club, which was rumored to be Mafia connected. We got back to the hotel at 6:00 AM, got up at 9:00 AM, and Turk pitched a four-hitter, winning 4–1.

One night in Milwaukee I got a call from the police at 4:00 AM. They informed me that Farrell was in jail for disturbing the peace. I went to the police station and bailed him out. As you can see, I was taking that part in my job description about being flexible seriously.

One year the team stayed in the Marina Hotel in Los Angeles because the guy who owned the place was a big honcho with one of our television sponsors, the Schick razor company. The players hated the hotel. It was in a deserted area with nothing to do but hang out in the bar—which we all did. One night there was some heavy drinking going on, and a ruckus occurred. I turned around to find Farrell pushing a man high up a synthetic palm tree. It turned out to be the big shot from Schick who also happened to own the hotel.

That sponsorship lasted only one year.

Not all the action was taking place off the field. There were several memorable on-field experiences during my three years at Colt Stadium. For example, our pitchers managed to throw two no-hitters and not end up with a shutout in either one. Don Nottebart pitched a no-hitter, beating the Phillies 4–1 and allowing one unearned run. Ken Johnson pitched a nine-inning no-hitter but lost 1–0 when Nellie Fox made an error—the first pitcher to ever achieve such a feat. On a sadder note, pitcher Jim Umbricht, the only Houston pitcher with a winning record in both 1962 and 1963, contracted throat cancer and died. His ashes were scattered in the Astrodome.

Bob Aspromonte—who had been stuck in the Dodgers farm system until we got him—was Houston's best player back then and hit some of the most significant home runs in the team's early history. In 1962, a nine-year-old boy in a local hospital asked Aspromonte to hit him a home run. He did. In 1963, when the boy returned to the hospital for more surgery, he asked for another one. He got a game-winning grand slam. The two crossed paths once more, and Aspromonte was asked to deliver one more time. Did he finally fail to deliver? Hardly. Another game-winning grand slam, this time to beat the Mets.

Along the way, we also managed to lose 17 straight games to the Philadelphia Phillies. I decided that we needed something extra to break the streak after 15 games, so I hired an Indian "witch doctor" to sprinkle good-luck dust at home plate and a local character named One-Eyed Kelly to sit by the Phillies dugout. Kelly claimed that if he stared at the Phillies pitchers, they would pitch poorly. Neither the good-luck dust nor the one-eyed stare worked, as Houston lost both games of a twi-night doubleheader.

Houston finally snapped the streak the next day behind the "slugging" of our number eight hitter and our pitcher. Gene Mauch, the Phillies manager, was so mad after losing the game that he stormed into the clubhouse and threw the players' postgame dinner all over the clubhouse.

Our witch doctor must have had his good-luck dust on time delay.

The Astrodome

"We are building something that will set the pattern for the 21st century. It will antiquate every structure of this type in the world. It will be an Eiffel Tower in its field."

—*Judge Roy Hofheinz*

Getting Out the Vote

If job one for the Judge had been to convince the National League that the Cullinan Group could make a modern-day Roman Coliseum work financially, then job two was to actually find a way to make a modern-day Roman Coliseum work financially.

It became obvious to Judge Hofheinz that job two required a change in how the stadium bonds would be financed. The original plan called for the bonds to be backed by stadium revenues, but the revised plan called for the bonds to be backed by city revenues, resulting in much lower interest expense. In order to do this, however, it would be necessary to hold a public referendum that would have to be voted on and passed by the citizens of Houston. This proved to be quite a challenge.

Hofheinz put together a committee whose job it was to make sure the referendum passed. Trying our best would not be good enough for the Judge. I was on the committee along with the Judge, George Kirksey, and a bright, good-looking, short guy named Jack

Valenti. Valenti ran an agency in Houston that did all of our advertising, and he later became president of the Motion Picture Association of America.

One of our most important tasks was to get the chamber of commerce, along with county, state, and city politicos, to support the referendum. We decided to arrange a four-day, first-class trip to Los Angeles and San Francisco via charter flight to take all the dignitaries to visit both Dodger Stadium and Candlestick Park. It was called the "Rain-or-Shine Trip," and I was in charge of the whole thing. I arranged cocktail parties with a few movie stars—such as actress Jayne Mansfield—dinners, shows, and then meetings with the mayors of Los Angeles and San Francisco. We also made sure to get them in front of club officials from the Dodgers and Giants who told them how valuable a great ballpark would be to the development and growth of a metropolitan area. By the time we returned to Houston, we had the full support of the city fathers and politicians. The trip went so well that the Judge hiked my salary from $6,000 to $7,000 per year, which was a significant raise at the time.

Now the next task was to get the citizens of Houston on board. Hofheinz had run many political campaigns, including Lyndon Johnson's campaign for the senate. He pointed out to us that the key to getting the referendum passed would be to convince African Americans to vote for it and to make sure they were able to get to the polls. It would be a desegregated facility that would bring jobs to the area, so I recruited Willie Mays, Hank Aaron, and Ernie Banks to do radio and TV spots promoting a positive vote on the referendum. Having played at Colt Stadium, you can see why they wanted to help.

To ensure that anyone interested in voting for our referendum found his or her way to the voting booth, I drove through the city with a loudspeaker attached to my car announcing, "Vote 'Yes' on the stadium bill. Turn your porch light on, and we will take you to the polls."

I had a team of employees following me who would pick up anyone whose porch light was turned on. When all was said and done, the referendum passed—with less than a 1 percent majority.

The Roof

Now all we had to do was build the place. The opportunity to be involved with constructing the world's first domed stadium was very special. We broke ground on January 3, 1962. Tal Smith, who at the time served as a player personnel guy, was appointed to be the owner's representative. He worked with architects and contractors to make sure the stadium was constructed properly for baseball. Tal had a photographic memory and was very bright and dedicated. He did a terrific job. We both took visiting managers and other dignitaries through the facility as it was being constructed, and the overwhelming reaction—even from baseball folks who would be considered staunch traditionalists—was nothing short of awe.

Our greatest construction challenge was the roof. At the time, most people thought getting a roof that massive to stay up was going to be the hard part. After all, its span—at more than 600 feet—would be twice that of anything ever built at the time. However, it turned out that it wasn't the size of the roof that was the problem.

The roof had to be built to allow enough sunlight to get through so that the grass would grow. Because the light would be passing through Lucite panels—4,596 of them—it had to be diffused. Otherwise, the grass would grow unevenly, and shadows would be created that would make the field look like a waffle iron. The roof ended up being constructed with prisms between two pieces of plastic—which worked, but only for a short period of time, as we would soon discover.

We opened the Astrodome by playing five exhibition games in three days, three games against the Yankees and two against the Baltimore Orioles. A stickler for details, the Judge drove the hallways of the stadium in his golf cart in the wee hours before the grand opening, checking that there was toilet paper in all the restrooms.

President Johnson was in attendance to throw out the first ball. One of the highlights was Mickey Mantle hitting the first home run in the dome, in front of more than 47,000 people. The lowlight, almost literally, was discovering during these games that the outfielders could not track fly balls during daylight hours or in twilight.

Nevertheless, the games went on. When we opened the regular season a couple of days later, I had one of my most successful "first ball" ceremonies. There were 28 United States astronauts at the time, and they all lived in the Houston area because NASA headquarters was nearby. I invited them to participate in the opening ceremony. I arranged for all 28 astronauts to line up in a row behind the Houston dugout and then put our 25 players plus three coaches in a line on the field in front of the dugout. The astronauts threw out the first balls simultaneously—it was quite a show. The Phillies won the opener 2–0 when Dick—who at the time went by Richie—Allen hit the first official home run in Astrodome history.

Obviously, the visibility in the dome was just as bad during the regular season as it was during the exhibition games. We tried to solve this new problem by painting the southwest quadrant of the roof. As was becoming a somewhat disturbing trend, that solved one problem while creating another. The good news: the outfielders could now follow the balls. The bad news: the grass died—particularly on the infield.

Trying to Grow Grass Indoors

What to do? We tried orange-colored baseballs, but they were too slippery. Paul Richards suggested we play on a dirt infield like they did in Japan. The ground crew ended up having to paint the dying grass green, but the paint ended up on the baseballs. Neither Abner Doubleday nor Judge Roy Hofheinz envisioned baseball this way.

Basically, we'd managed to fund and build the world's largest baseball stadium, but we couldn't really play baseball in it. Ultimately, Judge Hofheinz concluded that the solution was to create a new kind of playing surface. With our grass problem well documented, the Judge began to receive all sorts of "solutions" in the mail—some from credible businesses, others from crackpots. He passed these to Tal Smith, who eventually ended up with an office full of samples. The most promising turned out to be from the Monsanto chemical company, a carpet manufacturer that convinced us they could make a synthetic grass. In fact, their Chemstrand lab had been working on it for a number of years and had even tested it at the Moses Brown School in Providence, Rhode Island, the year before— replacing the dirt floor in their gymnasium with something they called Chemgrass.

Tal Smith went up to Providence to look at it and gave it a favorable report: it was green, had fibers, and looked like grass. Hofheinz didn't need much convincing, so we met with the Monsanto folks in the Judge's office overlooking right field to hammer out an agreement.

"How much will it cost?" Hofheinz asked.

"One million dollars," was the reply.

"That's exactly what I was thinking of charging you for the promotional value," the Judge replied. "We can split the difference, and you can give us the grass free."

"Free?"

"Sure. You give us the grass free," Hofheinz said, "and I will let you call it AstroTurf. Then you can sell it all over the world and make lots of money."

They agreed, and AstroTurf was born.

That was November 1965. The manufacturing process was slow and painstaking, so when the first test came in January 1966, it was with a fairly small number of strips that created a square of turf. Unfortunately, when we tried it out, the balls were bouncing all over the place at bizarre angles. That got fixed when they figured out that the direction of the fibers on the strips had to be aligned. With that out of the way, now all we needed was three acres of the stuff.

In two months.

It required a Herculean effort on Monsanto's part to have it ready for our first exhibition game on March 19, but they did it. There wasn't a lot of time to spare, however. The turf was finally laid out in the infield early that morning, only a few hours before the first pitch.

The Dodgers won that game, with each team piling up a lot of hits. The infielders had not yet adjusted to the speed of the field, so many ground balls made it into the outfield.

"We can work on slowing the field down," one of the engineers said.

"Forget about it, son," Hofheinz replied. "Give me nothing but three-base hits."

The investment Monsanto made in artificial turf for the Astrodome turned out to be quite significant. We had originally installed the AstroTurf on the infield, but soon the outfield grass deteriorated. Out of necessity, the Astrodome became an all all-AstroTurf field. And because the Astrodome hosted events other than baseball, Monsanto also had to manufacture the stuff so it could be moved back and forth on huge rollers to accommodate the rodeo and other events held on good, old-fashioned, nonsynthetic dirt.

Over time, popular opinion would turn almost uniformly negative toward domed stadiums and AstroTurf. When first introduced, however, they were recognized as great feats of engineering and progress. Billy Graham referred to the Astrodome as a "tribute to the boundless imagination of man." The Judge loved it, too, but his concerns were on much more pragmatic issues—namely, making it pay. That's why we ended up cutting up the AstroTurf strips we'd tested back in January and selling them for a buck apiece.

Finding creative ways to generate revenue was all in a day's work. Marketing and promotions were very important to the creation, development, and sustainability of the Astrodome. I was involved in all the marketing decisions and, since this was Texas, we were expected to do things in a big way. Artificial turf was just one of many ways we were making our mark in Houston. We had a scoreboard that was 474 feet wide, and we had the longest dugouts in the majors. The Judge wanted the longest dugouts in baseball because he believed fans wanted to buy tickets that placed them behind the dugout, so we designed the Astrodome accordingly. At 120 feet, we had lots of extra behind-the-dugout seats for which premium prices could be charged.

A team name that was a throwback to the Wild West didn't really fit with a team that played inside a nine-acre flying saucer, so we changed the name of the team in 1965 from the Colt .45s to the Astros in a nod to the burgeoning space program and nearby NASA head-quarters. And we officially changed the name of what had been the Harris County Domed Stadium—catchy it wasn't—to the Astrodome.

Once we decided to tie the names of the team and the stadium to a space theme, it was important that everything be tied to that theme. For example, we designed uniforms for the daily game employees that featured usherettes (aka Spacettes) in gold lamé space suits with space boots, and the ground crew (also known as Earthmen) in space helmets. To first-time fans, when the ground crew ran out to fix the field, it must have looked like a science fiction movie. In addition, we gave all the eating areas space-oriented names such as the Countdown Cafeteria. But, no, we did not make the team's traveling party wear anything lunar-related on road trips.

A NEW SPRING-TRAINING HOME, TOO

The Judge hated the team's spring-training home in Apache Junction and decided to build a training complex in Cocoa Beach, Florida, near NASA's Cape Canaveral facility. He wanted to replicate Dodgertown in Vero Beach and felt it was good marketing to have Houston train near the astronauts' launch site. Maybe so, but we didn't draw many people at the little Cocoa Beach ballpark—though we did have our fair share of snakes in the outfield. I operated the scoreboard and handled the public address announcing at the same time.

The Cocoa Beach complex was quite different from the Apache Junction training site because the Judge always liked to do things in a unique way. The players, staff, and press lived in a dormitory with a ballpark and some practice fields nearby. Everyone had a roommate, and for the two years I was there I roomed with the manager. One year it was Grady Hatton, and one year it was Harry Walker—the same guy my father had traded Hank Sauer for. I served as both traveling secretary and publicity director at the time.

The year that I roomed with Harry "the Hat" Walker was most memorable. I often drove about 45 minutes to Orlando to go to the dog track with base-ball writer John Wilson. When I would return around 11:00 PM, Harry would be waiting up for me to tell me about the movie he had just watched on TV. I was dead tired, but he would sit on his bunk bed just five feet from me with only a pajama shirt on describing to me this great movie he had just seen. Within minutes I was sound asleep, and Harry kept on talking and talking. Harry the Hat could talk about almost anything, but what he really loved to talk about was hitting.

Harry may have cost me some sleep, but I would never have had the good fortune to end up as a part owner of a major league team had Walker not told Phillies owner Bob Carpenter that I was a great marketing guy.

The Eighth Wonder of the World

I wrote all the promotional pieces on the Astrodome and declared it the "Eighth Wonder of the World." It always amazed me that the news media used that term for many, many years. The stadium—and that term—certainly captured the public's imagination.

The Astrodome proved to be such an attraction that we began to offer tours of the facility. I designed a glossy, four-color brochure that we sold for $5 to visitors. I also wrote the speech for all the tour guides. We hosted tours four times a day when there were no games, and we averaged about 3,000 people per day for many years.

People are attracted to the first-of-a-kind—especially when it remains a one-of-a-kind for as many years (10, to be exact) as the Astrodome did. It was not just the roof, the plastic grass, and the longer-than-a-football-field scoreboard that set the Astrodome apart. The Judge had another brainstorm for the stadium that was novel at the time but commonplace today—and some would say as essential to a baseball team as turf, light, and left-handed pitching.

The original design of the stadium included about 2,000 seats at the highest seating area of the dome. They were to be sold as general admission tickets at a cheap price. The Judge remembered that the Roman Coliseum had special boxes for the royalty of Rome to chitchat and socialize while watching the gladiators and other extravaganzas.

Halfway through the construction, the Judge decided to turn that level into skyboxes by building rooms adjacent to the seats with a bar, sofas, tables, and restrooms. We sold them on an annual basis for a steep price. Luxury boxes are now a major ingredient of every new ballpark built since 1970—and one of the driving forces behind nearly every renovation of a ballpark built before 1970.

Now if you thought those skyboxes were nifty, you should have seen where the Judge lived. The Astrodome had become his fourth home, with Hofheinz building the most unique office and living quarters I've ever seen. Located in the rafters in right field, there were two bedrooms, an office with a view of the field, and a saloon area that had a slanted floor and a beer mug that you could slide from one end of the bar to the other. It would never slide off the bar because it had a magnetic base on the mug. There was a spittoon in the corner; if you pretended to spit into it, the spittoon would shake and rattle. There was a secret button under the bar that made this happen.

A man of very eclectic tastes, the Judge also had:

a bowling alley
a putting green
an antique pool table
a barbershop
a movie theater
a patio complete with fake trees
a matching set of teak Thai temple dogs as tall as me
a marble-topped desk with a gold telephone
a gold-plated bathroom complete with velvet toilet seat
a boardroom with carpet on the walls
a chapel with a crucifix that could be turned to display a Star of David
a place for President Lyndon Johnson to sleep

Yes, the Judge and LBJ went back a ways and were fairly tight. They would stay up drinking and telling the worst, dirtiest jokes you could imagine. Spending time with the Judge certainly offered you an interesting perspective on the world.

Having a Lot of Fun (and Sometimes a Bit Too Much) Operating the World's Largest Scoreboard

Given his version of an owner's box, it should come as no surprise that the Judge would not settle for the mere, manually operated variety of scoreboard that was prevalent throughout the big leagues at the time. The scoreboard in the Astrodome was really something special, and I was the man in charge. It took four people to operate it; Tony Siegle, Wayne Chandler, and Herb Elk were my key assistants. The big board in center field had the usual baseball information, but it also had two features that had never been constructed before. One was a very large video board in the middle where we could show animated clips. We had animations for the national anthem and some serious features, but we also had a lot of humorous clips. One of the most popular showed a very dejected pitcher walking into a shower, slipping on a bar of soap, and falling on his butt—we used this every time we knocked the opposing pitcher out. Forty years later, the Astros still use this cartoon in their Minute Maid Park.

The other unique feature of the board was the home-run spectacular. At the push of a button, a 45-second animated show would explode with horses, snorting bulls, cowboys, fireworks, and lots and lots of noise. The scoreboard was very colorful and everyone loved it.

Well, almost everyone.

Several incidents involving the scoreboard embroiled me in some personal controversy. One year, umpire John Kibler kicked a Houston player out of the game in four consecutive games. After the fourth ejection, I offered up an editorial comment on the scoreboard: "Kibler did it again."

Naturally, the home fans started to boo Kibler and all the other umpires, which did not please the men in blue. The next day I received a phone call from my father, who was still president of the National League at the time and in charge of all the umpires. The conversation went like this:

"Bill, who put the message on the board about the umpires?"

"Gee, Dad, I'm not sure who it was, but I'll be sure to tell him not to do it again."

"Well, when you find out who it was, tell him his allowance is cut off."

In an unusual display of remorse, the next game I put "I shall not write messages about the umpires" 50 times on the message board.

Another incident involved baseball commissioner Bowie Kuhn, who did not have the same sense of humor that my father did. At the time, Kuhn also happened to be very unpopular in Houston because of his ruling on a controversial trade we had made with Montreal. We dealt Rusty Staub for Don Clendenon, but Clendenon refused to play for us; he retired instead. The commissioner forced us to rework the trade—so we still lost the very popular Staub, but did not get Clendenon. To make matters worse, Clendenon "unretired" and went to our expansion rival, the Mets, and played a major role in their 1969 "miracle" championship.

Kuhn was at the Astrodome for a game soon after that decision, and I put a multiple-choice question on the board: "Who is the most unpopular person here at the game tonight?" The answers I listed were:

A. Frankenstein
B. Hitler
C. Pete Rozelle (the NFL commissioner who had recently announced that Houston would not get the Super Bowl)
D. XXXXX XXXX

Then I flashed: "The answer is XXXXX XXXX."

The next day Kuhn called me and told me to fly to his office in New York City. He was not a happy camper about me making fun of the Office of the Commissioner of Baseball, and he put me on a year's probation. A lot more than my allowance was at stake on that one.

Another time we had a night game with the Mets that lasted 24 innings and did not conclude until 1:37 AM. Earlier I had put on the board: "I told you sex would never replace baseball"—which probably would have gone over better if it hadn't been Boy Scout Night.

I also had several run-ins with Leo Durocher when he was the manager of the Chicago Cubs. Durocher hated the Astrodome and just about everything about it—particularly the AstroTurf field ("a giant pool table") and my scoreboard antics. I would kid him a lot with messages and cartoons I put up on the board, and he got so mad that one night he phoned me from the dugout, called me every dirty word imaginable, ripped the phone off the wall, and threw it on the field.

The next day I had a red phone installed with a sign that said "For Leo Who?" When you picked it up, a loud siren would go off.

Durocher was quoted in the paper saying the AstroTurf infield was so bad that you had to wear tennis shoes. So when we took up the grass in the outfield to make way for even more AstroTurf, I figured he deserved a memento. I packaged the last piece of sod and a pair of tennis shoes and sent it to Durocher's office in Chicago.

Though not everyone appreciated how I used our electronic marvel out in center field, Houston fans were real novices about the nuances of baseball back then, and the scoreboard was a help to them. We would put up "Charge!" and "GO" quite frequently on the scoreboard to get them involved. There was a direct telephone line from the Judge's perch in right field where he watched the game to my seat in the scoreboard booth. He would call me periodically to put up special messages. When he was drinking and had guests in his box, he would call even more—over and over again—telling me to put up "Charge!" or "GO." During one game he called me so much that I yelled at him and hung up the phone. I thought I would be fired the next day, but he never said a word about it.

Perhaps because of our growing reputation for being willing to try anything and everything—something that would keep the Judge from ever winning any popularity contests among his fellow owners—we were suspected of using some other unique aspects of the Astrodome to our advantage. One particular conspiracy theory—that we were playing games with the air-conditioning to aid fly balls while Houston was up and to hinder them when the visitors were at bat—gained enough credence that my father even had to come to town to investigate the allegations and put the controversy to rest.

In addition to the scoreboard and the air-conditioning, another unique feature of the Astrodome was the very large speakers hanging down from the roof. The ground rules dictated that if a batted ball hit a speaker in fair territory, then the ball was in play. If it hit a speaker in foul ground, it was declared a foul ball and a dead ball. The only player who I saw hit a speaker in fair territory was Mike Schmidt. He got robbed of a home run when a towering smash hit a speaker and fell to the ground. For that effort—probably one of the hardest balls he ever hit—the ground rules held him to a single.

The roof of the Astrodome was 208 feet high at the apex, and there was a circular set of lights about 40 feet in diameter that could go up and down like an elevator. We would occasionally have pregame "Fungo-Hitting Contests" to see if anyone could hit a ball against the top of the roof. Dodgers pitcher Ed Roebuck and St. Louis pitcher Joe Hoerner were the only players I ever saw do it.

The Astrodome also had a gondola that hung from the roof, which could be used for photographers. Mets announcer Lindsey Nelson announced a game from there. When Casey Stengel asked the umpires what the ruling would be if Nelson were hit with a batted ball, he was told that any ball hitting Nelson would be in play.

"My man is a ground rule," Stengel replied. "That's the first time my man was ever a ground rule."

Our announcers were initially Loel Passe and Gene Elston. Elston was a very good and solid announcer, but Passe was a real cornball who knew nothing about baseball. Nobody liked him except the Judge. In the mid-'60s, we replaced him with a young blond kid from Iowa who had been broadcasting the Hawaii Islanders baseball games. The kid's name was Harry Kalas, and I guess you could say he worked out all right. Harry and I have shared many, many great baseball moments.

THE AMAZIN' CASEY STENGEL

You could fill a book with Casey Stengel stories, but a personal favorite of mine is one I got to see firsthand. When the Mets first opened for business and

Stengel was their manager, I made it a point to gravitate toward him any time we were in the same room because he was so much fun to be around.

I watched him as he helped make the job of reporting on perhaps the worst team ever assembled a fun experience. There was a beat reporter in New York by the name of John Drebinger who had a hearing aid. Stengel conspired with the other writers to play a trick on him.

Stengel stood in front of a large group of writers, waving his hands and moving his mouth—but no words came out. Meanwhile, all the writers other than Drebinger were scribbling furiously. And there's Drebinger, looking confused, fiddling with his hearing aid, and banging the side of his head.

When you considered all the success he had as a manager—five consecutive championships with the Yankees and 10 pennants in 12 years—and combined it with the gibberish that came out of his mouth when he spoke, you were often left to wonder whether the man was really smart or really dumb. A few years later in Philadelphia, I asked Richie Ashburn what he thought.

"Whitey, was Stengel smart or dumb?"

"Bill, I played for him for a whole season in 1962," Ashburn replied, "and I have no idea."

My Memories of Rocket Man, Muhammad Ali, and the John Kruk of Bullfighting

In addition to handling the publicity, running the scoreboard, and endangering the lives of announcers, I was in charge of the promotions geared to attracting more fans. This was where I built my reputation for doing some crazy stuff to make people smile and have fun. Some stunts were tame, others were a bit strange, a few were epic, and more than a few were never to be repeated.

Louisiana Weekend was always a big success. We paid tribute to celebrities from Louisiana like Al Hirt and Pete Fountain and had pregame musical shows. Country Western Night always went over well, too. Every year we would hold a pregame or postgame concert with a well-known country singer. Our singers included, among others, Roger Miller and Eddy Arnold.

In 1965 George Kirksey and I organized an Old Timers Game that had to be one of the greatest arrays of players ever assembled—most of whom were in the Hall of Fame. Some of the all-time greats who played in the game included Joe DiMaggio, Satchel Paige, Carl Hubbell, Bobby Thomson, Bill Dickey, Duke Snider, and Ernie Lombardi.

Long before Roger Clemens, we had our own Rocket Man. This guy would dress like a spaceman with a jet pack on his back and "fly" all around the dome, getting up as high as 150 feet. This was a perfect promotion for a team and a stadium with a space theme. It went over well, and we had him back a couple of times.

Fireworks nights are popular at events all throughout America, but usually the fireworks are set off *out*side, not *in*side. We had to explode the fireworks in the parking lot outside of the Astrodome because of the roof, so all the fans had to walk outside to see the show. This did not work particularly well, so I only did it one year.

Like our attempt at fireworks night, I had a few other promotions that did not work well at all. One was a Flag Day pregame show where the local Shriners, all decked out in white tuxedos, gave a description of each of the 13 flags that had flown over our country. However, I did not realize that they would play the national anthem after each presentation. The 40,000 fans had to stand up and sit down 13 times as the anthem was played. Even for the patriotic fans we had in Houston, 13 proved to be a bit much.

The other bomb was a trick-shot expert who hit golf balls from a bunch of different positions. The problem? The balls were breaking a bunch of lights on our expensive scoreboard. Ten minutes into the show, Judge Hofheinz called me on the phone.

"Get that guy out of here!" he roared. "He's destroying our board!"

We pulled the plug on that one.

Spurred on by all the excitement being generated by the dome and the crazy stuff going on inside (planned and unplanned), ticket sales shot up in 1965. After drawing only 725,000 fans to Colt Stadium in 1964, the Astros became only the fourth team in the history of Major League Baseball—after the New York Yankees, Milwaukee Braves, and Los Angeles Dodgers—to draw 2 million fans in a season.

Even though Houston still hadn't found its way into the pennant race, there were a lot of great baseball moments on the AstroTurf. We hosted the 1968 All-Star Game; not surprisingly, in the Year of the Pitcher, it was a 1–0 ballgame. Don Wilson no-hit Hank Aaron and the Braves in Houston in 1967 on Father's Day. Wilson was a real talent but he did have some issues—he threw another no-hitter two years later in Cincinnati in a game in which he was so angry he had to be restrained from charging the Reds dugout after the final out.

The Astrodome proved to be a perfect venue not just for baseball and football (the Houston Oilers and the University of Houston also called it home), but for all sorts of special events. To take advantage of the facility's size, capacity, and all-season comfort—and in order to generate more revenue—I soon found myself promoting quite a number of nonbaseball events.

Jack O'Connell, who became a good friend of mine, was in charge of booking the Astrodome, and we did come up with some fun and interesting events. From prize fights and bullfights to basketball and soccer, with some Dorothy from *The Wizard of Oz* thrown in along the way, we were in the middle of them all.

Prize Fights

We promoted three heavyweight fights while I was in Houston. The first one featured heavyweight champion Cassius Clay versus Cleveland "Big Cat" Williams. One of our strategies to promote the fight was to have Cassius train for 30 days in a ring we constructed in the exhibit hall that had been built next to the Astrodome. As a result, I had the opportunity to spend a lot of time with Clay before and after his workouts. He is one of the most memorable people that I have ever met.

I asked Clay why he "popped off" so much, a style that just wasn't very common back then. He explained that when he was a kid, he would watch a lot of pro wrestling. It was not very popular until Gorgeous George Warner entered the scene and started to brag all the time and wear fancy outfits.

"I wanted to do for boxing what Gorgeous George did for wrestling," Clay explained.

That he did, and then some.

Clay would always sit on the edge of the ring after a sparring workout and talk to the news media and fans. Very personable and clever, he was an engaging combination of sass and sweetness. He almost always spoke poetically, and I got to hear him utter some of his most famous phrases such as "float like a butterfly and sting like a bee." He also offered a prediction, as he so often would: "Big Cat will be on the floor by four."

"Who writes your stuff?" I asked. "You've got a great PR man."

"I write it all myself," he replied.

During his workouts, he would let his sparring opponents hit him 100 or more times hard in his stomach and arms.

"Why do you let your body take so much punishment?" I asked.

"See my face?" he said. "Not a scratch on it. I let them wear themselves out hitting my arms and stomach, but I try not to ever let them hit me in the face."

Clay was wrong about Big Cat being on the floor by four. He knocked him out in the third round. Soon after his fight with Williams, Clay became a Muslim and changed his name to Muhammad Ali. Ali fought Ernie Terrell in the Astrodome, and I was again in charge of the publicity and promotion of that fight. But his personality had changed. He was much more reserved around me, though he continued to pronounce: "I am the greatest!"

On the night of the Terrell fight, I received specific instructions from Ali's trainer, Angelo Dundee. "Bill, when Ali and I walk through the crowd there will be 10–12 well-dressed black men following us," Dundee explained. "When they get to the news media seats surrounding the ring, you are to stop them and tell them to go back to their seats."

When I did exactly what Dundee instructed me to do, one of the members of Ali's Black Muslim entourage pulled out a .45-caliber pistol and stuck it hard into my stomach.

In response, I said, "You're welcome to sit wherever you like."

For me, the actual fight proved less interesting than the events before it. Ali beat Terrell in 15 rounds.

The third fight I promoted was a round-robin tournament of heavyweights to determine the World Heavyweight Champion. The title had been stripped from Ali because of his refusal to be inducted into the armed services.

"I ain't got no quarrel with them Viet Cong," Ali had explained.

Years later, I saw Ali on a flight to the Caribbean, and I was honored that he recognized me. Sadly, however, his mind seemed scrambled. I don't know whether it was caused by Parkinson's or the punishment he took in the ring. During his prime he did not get hit in the head that much, but, unfortunately, he stayed in the ring long past his prime. His three magnificent fights against Joe Frazier, plus the punishment he took from Leon Spinks and Larry Holmes, exacted a heavy toll on him.

There will never be another like him.

Bull Fights

In addition to prize fights, we also promoted two "Bloodless Bullfights." The first one featured matador Jaime Bravo, and the second one featured Paco Camino.

The Camino fight was more classical but not as much fun and did not draw too well because the fans really did not like the "bloodless" aspects of the fights. A "bloodless" fight meant that when it came time to kill the tired bull, the matador would just poke the bull between the ears with his hand instead of a knife.

The Jaime Bravo fight, even though it too was bloodless, was still quite exciting. Bravo—the perfect name for him—was a real showman. He was not your classical matador and more like the John Kruk of bullfighting.

We kept the bulls in a pen outside the Astrodome to build up excitement before the fight, and Bravo would come over and taunt them. In the ring he played for the laughs, too, dropping to his knees to challenge the enraged animal. While matadors are a notoriously macho group of individuals, Bravo made it a point to hop out of the ring when the bulls came after him. As the saying goes, I might be dumb, but I'm not stupid.

Before Bravo went out for his bullfight he spent about an hour in the Judge's chapel, praying for his safety.

The Houston versus UCLA Basketball Game

On the evening of January 20, 1968, the Astrodome was the center of the basketball universe. In one of the most memorable college basketball games played anywhere, the University of Houston, ranked number two and led by Elvin Hayes, hosted the UCLA Bruins, ranked number one and coming off a series of national championships. UCLA was led by Lew Alcindor, who most of you probably know by the more familiar name he would eventually adopt: Kareem Abdul-Jabbar. His Bruins were riding a 47-game winning streak.

At that time, there had never been a basketball crowd of more than 25,000 fans. The Judge wanted to set an all-time attendance record for basketball. At the press conference to announce the game, he began to get a lot of criticism from the media for his attempt to do just that.

"With as many as 55,000 in attendance," a reporter said, "how will the fans be able to even see the game?"

The Judge proceeded to pick up a basketball and hold it next to a baseball. "See these two balls?" he began. "More than 50,000 people have been following this little white ball, so they ought to be able to follow this big basketball."

It turned out to be an amazing night, with Houston capitalizing on Alcindor's subpar play (he had a patch over his left eye because of a scratch on his cornea) to upset UCLA and end the Bruins' winning streak by a score of 71–69 before 52,693 fans. This game also marked the very first national prime-time telecast of a college basketball game.

Soccer

We promoted a soccer match between two of Europe's best teams: Real Madrid and West Ham of England. Five days before the match we had sold only 3,000 tickets, so I delivered 50,000 complimentary tickets to NASA headquarters nearby, and we had more than 45,000 people at the match. Only a few people knew that a mere 3,000 had paid for their tickets.

The Houston Sports Authority (HSA) did join a soccer league that used teams playing in a U.S. league during the normal off-season. Our team was from Brazil. We did not draw too well, so it lasted only one year.

The Judy Garland Concert

The Judy Garland concert we promoted certainly proved to be a dicey situation. We drew only 7,000 people in a stadium set up for 60,000. The promoters were afraid that Judy would walk off the stage if she saw such a small audience.

What did we do? We turned off all the lights so that she wouldn't be able to see how few people were actually there. The show went on as planned.

In addition to these events, I promoted motorcycle races, midget auto races (boy, were they noisy), polo matches, a Billy Graham Crusade, the Democratic National Political Convention, musical concerts, and the rodeo.

All of that paled in comparison to a mission that the Judge sent me on in 1967, which was one of the most memorable events in my life.

A Secret Mission

A Command Performance

The call came while I was at home.

"Do you and your wife have passports?"

It was November 1967. The woman on the other end of the line was Mary Frances Guggenheim, Judge Hofheinz's secretary. Considering where I worked and who I worked for, I was used to getting some off-the-wall questions. But this one was a first.

"No, we don't."

"Then you need to get downtown immediately and get them."

"Why?"

"Because you're going overseas in 48 hours."

"Overseas? Where are we going? What are we doing?"

"I can't tell you where you're going or why you're going there," she replied. "I can only tell you that it's very important and that you should expect to be gone for about two weeks."

Remembering that being flexible was still on my job description as far as the Judge was concerned, Nancy and I were at Houston's Hobby Airport two days later. Our three boys were with our neighbor, Eileen Light. Mary Frances was there to hand us our tickets at the airport. Stack of tickets, I should say. Nancy and I—and a number of other members of the team's front office—were going around the world.

The Secret Is Revealed

We flew to New York and then boarded a plane to Rome. We knew where we were going now, but we still had no idea why. It wasn't until we were halfway across the Atlantic that the Judge got the Houston group all together and introduced the 10 of us to Mr. Irvin Feld and Feld's son.

"Mr. Feld and I are going to meet with John Ringling North," Hofheinz explained. "We're going to purchase Ringling Brothers circus from him. Madison Square Garden is also trying to buy the circus, so we have to move quickly. And quietly."

When we arrived in Rome, we went to the Excelsior Hotel and checked in under false names because the Judge didn't want the news media to know that any of us were in Rome. Sure enough, the phone in our hotel room rang about 3:00 AM, and I asked my wife to pick it up. The caller was a Houston newsman who asked to speak with me.

"I think he's still in Houston," Nancy replied, looking right at me.

A Photo in Every Paper in the World, Plus *Life* Magazine

"Your role," the Judge informed me the day before the acquisition, "is to get a picture of the contract being signed."

That was fairly mundane for Judge Roy Hofheinz, so I was thinking there had to be more to it than that. I waited for the rest of the story.

"And to make sure that picture is printed in every paper in the world," he continued, "plus *Life* magazine."

That sounded more like the Judge. The signing was to take place in an old warehouse in some alley in Rome at 11:00 AM. A picture taken in an empty warehouse with three men in suits was not a good candidate for worldwide attention, so I had to think fast. I remembered where the first circus was ever held, so I instructed everyone to meet at Rome's ancient Coliseum at noon for the photographs. This would be a lot better than a warehouse, but I still woke up the morning of the big day with an uneasy feeling.

"What's wrong?" Nancy asked.

My father shaking hands with Commissioner Landis (top) in the late 1930s, and striking a familiar pose later in his career as president of the National League (bottom). *Bottom photo courtesy of Robert Huntzinger.*

What a life! Sitting in the Reds dugout with my father and coach Hank Gowdy (left), with manager Bill McKechnie (right). *Photo courtesy of the Cincinnati Reds.*

No one ever accused my father of lacking passion for the game. Here he is giving it to the umpires at Crosley Field in Cincinnati. I preferred to keep a low profile. My approach would change over the years, though.

That's me (top: kneeling, third from right) posing with my Wasaka Boys' Club teammates in 1950, and with my dad at Yankee Stadium for the 1957 World Series (bottom).

My dad (left) in a state of undress as he waited for his pants to arrive from the cleaners, consulting with brilliant baseball man and family friend Gabe Paul, who gave me my start in the industry.

Some of the most powerful men in baseball gathered for this photo, with Judge Hofheinz (left), Walter O'Malley (rear), and John Galbraith (right) flanking my gavel-wielding father, Warren Giles. *Photo courtesy of Gulf Photo.*

The idea of a domed stadium seemed almost laughable at the time, but the Astrodome was a resounding success and an innovation that truly changed the landscape of professional sports. *Photo courtesy of Gulf Photo.*

Horsing around in the broadcast booth at the Astrodome in 1965, while running the scoreboard and getting into all kinds of trouble with my great friends Tony Siegle (left) and Wayne Chandler (right). *Photo courtesy of Gulf Photo.*

With my wife, Nancy, at the Coliseum in Rome, the sight of one of my biggest triumphs in the business.

Another perk of the job: shaking hands with the great Joe DiMaggio (top) and the immortal Satchel Paige (bottom) at an old timers game in the Astrodome in 1969. *Photo courtesy of Gulf Photo.*

"We need something else for this picture."

"The Roman Coliseum is not enough?"

"No."

"Well, what else do you have in mind?"

I pondered that for a little while, then told her what I thought we needed.

She didn't ponder that for very long before telling me she thought I was nuts. "Where do you think you're going to find *that*?"

"I don't know," I shrugged. "Maybe we should ask the concierge. They know everything, right?"

Nancy and I went down to the lobby, found the concierge, and told him what we needed to find. And fast.

"I don't understand," he replied in broken English.

Thinking that speaking more slowly might help, I said, "I. Need. To. Rent. A. Baby. Lion."

As confused as he looked, I could only imagine the look on his face if he actually could understand what I was saying.

I did my best imitation of a lion, at which point he directed me to the Rome zoo. We went there—as good a place as any to find a baby lion, right?—and found the zookeeper. I started to play charades again as a way of asking him if we could rent a baby lion.

He took us to see the mama and papa lions, but there were no babies, and I doubt he would have let us leave the premises with one even if there were. Nancy and I were about to give up. Then, leaving the zoo to head over to the Coliseum, we just happened to notice a man with a lion cub sitting on a bench. Not something you see every day, but fortuitous for certain.

The man had a little business going where he would take pictures of children with the cub. After a few minutes of negotiations, we agreed that he and his lion would accompany us for the sum of $80 U.S. I can't recall how much we had to pay the driver to let the lion cub in the taxi.

So there we were—Nancy, me, a photographer, and a lion cub— in a cab driving down the main avenue in Rome. After all we'd been through over the past few years, it wasn't easy to surprise that

Houston group anymore. They'd seen a lot, to say the least. But they had never seen me with a lion cub on a leash.

We posed Hofheinz, Feld, John Ringling North, and the baby lion on a stone shelf in the Coliseum. After the pictures were taken, I still had to rush to the photo store to have prints made and then deliver the pictures and news release to the press.

The next day the picture and a short story about the purchase of the circus appeared in papers all over the world. The next issue of *Life* magazine carried the photo, too. A *full-page* picture. On the inside back cover. The publicity person's equivalent of a game-winning grand slam!

We all celebrated the acquisition of the circus at dinner the next night but decided that if we followed the itinerary as planned we would be spending most of our time in airplanes and airports. So we spent a few days in Rome and Madrid, and then Nancy and I split from the group and flew to London to visit Nancy's sister and brother-in-law at an air base near London.

The Judge was so happy with the picture in *Life* magazine that he gave me a big raise in salary and put me in charge of all publicity and promotions for the entire Astrodome complex. The Judge's aspirations had not ended with the Astrodome. On the drawing board was the AstroWorld amusement park, four hotels, and an exhibit hall.

I also became publicity director of the Houston Apollos minor league hockey team that the Judge's Houston Sports Authority had purchased. I did not know a thing about hockey but learned quickly. The Apollos were a farm team of the famous Montreal Canadiens and a number of the Apollos turned out to be good players in the NHL, including defenseman Serge Savard and goalie Tony Esposito. Esposito set a record for shutouts as a rookie goalie with the Chicago Blackhawks.

My responsibilities were expanding as the Judge kept working on his dream of turning his entertainment complex into a city within a city. We completed the large hall adjacent to the Astrodome and used it for exhibits, trade shows, and conventions. In 1968 we had the Ringling Bros. and Barnum & Bailey circus performing there for 90 straight days. I got to know a lot of circus performers, particularly a man named Gunther Gebel-Williams, who was the tiger and lion tamer. He was a real class act. The rest of the circus performers weren't so nice to have around. They lived like gypsies in small trailers, and they often didn't smell too good. They certainly played it fast and loose. I remember one guy being introduced as "straight from Vienna, Austria," when he was a classmate of mine from Cincinnati.

The next development was AstroWorld—an Amusement Park modeled after Six Flags over Texas near Dallas. AstroWorld was a mini Disneyland with rides and shows located 500 yards south of the Astrodome. Soon after AstroWorld opened, the Judge built four Astrodomain hotels adjacent to the dome and the amusement park. The marketing concept was to have families visiting the area spending the day at AstroWorld and the night at an Astros game. Very few families did both in one day, but some stayed at one of the hotels overnight so they could do the amusement park one day and a game the next.

Another Era Comes to an End

It was becoming obvious to me that I was getting away from being a baseball man. I was becoming more of a marketing man for the Judge's various enterprises, so I started getting a bit restless. Fortunately, I got a call in September 1969 from Bob Carpenter, who owned the Philadelphia Phillies baseball team.

Little did I know at the time that I would end up leaving Houston right before the wheels started to come off for the Judge. Like many visionaries, he ended up overreaching. The high interest rates of the 1970s, coupled with his extensive Astrodomain development efforts, forced him deep into debt and eventually cost him operating control of his empire. He was forced to sell off the pieces, and ownership of the Astros eventually transferred to John McMullen.

Judge Roy Hofheinz, already confined to a wheelchair after a stroke in 1970, died of a heart attack in 1982, survived by his three children and his second wife, Mary Frances Guggenheim.

A Philadelphia Story

September 1969

September 1969 was an exciting month on the baseball field, with the first divisional races in history coming to a close.

In the American League, the Baltimore Orioles—behind the hitting of Boog Powell and Frank Robinson and the pitching of Dave McNally, Mike Cuellar, and Jim Palmer—were finishing up a 109-win season and coasting to a 19-game margin of victory in the East. In the West, the Minnesota Twins of Harmon Killebrew, Tony Oliva, and Rod Carew were finally able to pull away from a very surprising Oakland A's team that had ridden young talent like Catfish Hunter, Rollie Fingers, and Reggie Jackson into the franchise's first legitimate run at the postseason since 1932.

In the National League, Hank Aaron's Atlanta Braves were reeling off a 20-win month to surge past the San Francisco Giants of Willie Mays, Willie McCovey, and Juan Marichal in a tightly contested race in the West. And, of course, one can't think of baseball in September 1969 without thinking of the "Miracle Mets" leaving the "Cursed Cubs" in the dust, dashing Ernie Banks's last best hope for a World Series appearance.

For me, the action in September 1969 was off the field, as I got my best chance yet to achieve my dream of running a major league baseball team. Bob Carpenter, who was a good friend of my father's, explained to me that the Phillies were moving into a new ballpark in 18 months and wanted to hire a good marketing guy to improve their attendance. Philadelphia had drawn only 519,000 fans in 1969, ahead of only the expansion San Diego Padres, and representing the fifth consecutive year of a precipitous decline from the 1.4 million that came to the ballpark during the team's ill-fated 1964 season.

Though I love Philadelphia now, my memories of visits to the area at that time were not too fond. I'm a big fan of restaurants, and while there are many, many great places to eat in Philadelphia now, there weren't all that many in 1969. If there were any top restaurants besides Bookbinder's back in the 1960s, I wasn't able to find them. My impressions of Philadelphia also weren't helped by the fact that Connie Mack Stadium wasn't in the greatest of neighborhoods. On Houston's visits into town, we certainly weren't seeing Philadelphia at its best.

Nevertheless, I decided to fly into Philadelphia for an interview. It took place in Carpenter's home in Montchanin, Delaware, in the "chateau country" north of Wilmington. There is a lot of old money in that part of the world and a lot of beautiful old homes to admire on the drive through—until you realize you're looking at the servants' cottage and the main house is about a half-mile back from the road, usually a sprawling estate about the size of a small college.

Carpenter, his son Ruly, and George Harrison (the Phillies' vice president of finance) interviewed me for a couple of hours. During the interview Carpenter explained that he was going to retire in a couple of years, and he wanted his son Ruly and me to "run" the team when he did. This was starting to sound like my real opportunity to become a general manager.

A few days after the interview Carpenter called to offer me the job of director of business operations with a salary of $17,000. Reporting to me would be public relations, sales, promotions, marketing, stadium operations, radio, and television—basically everybody except the players and the finance guys. I told him I was excited about the job, but $17,000 was only $2,000 more than I was making and that Philadelphia was a more expensive place to live. We finally

agreed on a salary of $18,500, with the Phillies paying all our reloca-
tion expenses. Nancy was not too thrilled, but she was a real trouper
about it.

It didn't take long for Nancy and me to come to love Philadelphia
—the culture, the neighborhoods, the proximity to the mountains
and the shore—and we can no longer imagine living anywhere else.
At the time, however, she had very little desire to move our family
there. I explained to her that it was a great career opportunity and
that we would only be an hour and a half from New York City. We
could go once a month to New York to see a Broadway show. I
guess Nancy should not have been surprised when New York visits
turned out to be more like once a year.

Upstaged by a Trade That Never Happened

The Phillies were to have a big press conference to announce my
arrival in Philadelphia, but my move was delayed a week. Philadelphia
was attempting to make a trade, one that would prove to be very difficult to complete and quite historic.

The Phillies were trading their controversial and temperamental
star slugger, Richie Allen. Allen had been Rookie of the Year in 1964
and was one of the greatest hitters the organization had ever produced, but he had real problems with the Philadelphia media and
fans. In response to his treatment by the fans, Allen had even taken
to spelling out the word *Boo* with his foot in the dirt by his position
at first base. The supremely talented but very unhappy Allen was
going to St. Louis, along with Cookie Rojas and Jerry Johnson, for
Tim McCarver, Joe Hoerner, Byron Browne, and Curt Flood.

There was only one problem: Curt Flood refused to play in
Philadelphia.

Flood—a very talented center fielder and key contributor to the
Cardinals' championship teams of 1964 and 1967, as well as the
1968 team that fell one win short of repeating—felt that he was not
a piece of property to be traded at somebody's whim. He believed
that he should be able to control his destiny, that at the age of 31,

with 12 years of service in the big leagues, he should have some say on where he played. Flood decided to challenge the baseball reserve clause, which essentially granted a team the rights to a player in perpetuity.

With the help of Marvin Miller and the Major League Baseball Players Association, he filed a lawsuit to become a free agent. The case went all the way to the Supreme Court, where he ultimately lost. He did not play in 1970 while the case made its way through the judicial system, but he did return to play the following year with the Washington Senators. He retired after playing just 13 games. Prior to the trade, Flood was in the prime of his career, approaching 2,000 hits, only a few points shy of a .300 lifetime batting average, and an outstanding fielder. It is not inconceivable that Flood's willingness to take on a system that he felt was unfair cost him a legitimate shot at 3,000 hits and induction to the Hall of Fame.

The Phillies acquired two players—Willie Montanez and minor league pitcher Bobby Browning—as compensation for Flood's refusal to report. In November 1970, Flood was dealt by the Phillies to the Senators for three players, none of whom ever made an appearance in a Philadelphia uniform either. Although Curt Flood lost his bid for free agency, he is still considered the pioneer in the players' battle to overturn baseball's reserve clause.

Once the drama of the attempted trade played out, I arrived in Philadelphia to a lot of fanfare. I was introduced as the man to convert the Phillies' stodgy, conservative, and tired marketing strategy into a new era of creativity and risk-taking.

Unlike in Houston, where I was working for a man who was as eccentric and innovative as anyone who ever owned a major league baseball team, my new boss in Philadelphia was a blueblood and a traditionalist. The Carpenter family had a long history in Delaware and was joined by marriage with the state's royal family, the DuPonts. While Judge Hofheinz often reveled in the craziness that swirled through the Astrodome, Bob Carpenter—and George Harrison, too, for that matter—would roll their eyes in disbelief at the stunts we ended up concocting. But with attendance down more than 60 percent in only five years, they knew that we had to try to do some things differently to get folks back to the ballpark.

The Last Days of Connie Mack Stadium

My first year in Philadelphia was 1970, the final season that the Phillies would play at Connie Mack Stadium. Connie Mack Stadium—originally Shibe Park—had been home to the Philadelphia A's and, since 1938 and their move out of the Baker Bowl, the Phillies. In operation since 1909, it had seen eight World Series, two All-Star Games, and countless Hall of Famers from both leagues, and it had been the site of Lou Gehrig's four-home-run game in 1932.

It had also seen better days.

Located in the heart of what once had been an industrial center in North Philadelphia, it was a unique ballpark with lots of character. Center field was very deep (447 feet to the deepest part) and had a lot of sharp fence angles. This produced many triples and inside-the-park home runs. The right-field fence was 32 feet high, and a scoreboard in right center rose to 50 feet. The fence was high for two reasons: one, the dimensions were short and the A's didn't want it too easy to hit home runs, and two, Ben Shibe and Connie Mack, the co-owners of the Philadelphia A's, did not like the fact that fans were watching games for free from rooftops of the row houses along 20th Street just beyond right field. This was particularly true in the early 1930s, when the A's had their great teams. The high fence went up in 1935 and was referred to by the media as the Spite Fence.

Worth noting: though the stadium had seen five world champions and two pennant winners before the Spite Fence went up, from that point forward its occupants would never win another championship and would only reach the World Series once in 35 years.

For the modern fan, Wrigley Field, home of the Cubs and located in a residential neighborhood on the North Side of Chicago, is associated with rooftop seats. That phenomenon really began in Philadelphia, though the Cubs for several years had to deal with the same issue of fans watching games for free from the rooftops. In 2003 the team made a deal with the owners of the buildings to get a piece of the action. Judging from the 2003 NLCS, played soon after that deal was made and featuring an epic collapse by a Cubs team only five outs from the World Series, one has to wonder whether—like the Spite Fence—this was a wise decision.

Sixty years after it was built, Connie Mack Stadium was still a great place to watch a game. You were right on top of the action from almost any seat. The problem was the parking and the neighborhood, which had deteriorated badly in the years following World War II. There was very limited parking, and if you tried to park on the street, kids would approach you and offer to watch your car for a dollar. If you declined, there was a good chance you'd return to find your tires slashed.

The first day at my job in Philadelphia, I worked until 9:00 PM. The next day I read in the paper that a man was shot to death at 9:15 PM at the exact spot where my car was parked outside the stadium.

The offices in Connie Mack Stadium also had character—if you define *character* as "features that are considered quaint and charming by those who don't have to work there every day." The park had a very small elevator—which has since been donated to the Hall of Fame—that handled about eight people and ran from ground level to the rooftop press box. It stopped at two other floors, where the Phillies offices were located, including the floor for my office. My big promotion had not exactly netted me a glamorous corner office— mine had exposed drainage pipes, and I had to bend over to get from the office entrance to my desk.

At least I had my own desk. I had three guys in my sales office sharing one desk—one in front, one behind, and one on the side trying to make do with about a square foot of working area. Let me tell you, it wasn't easy to hire a secretary when her office at her current job was nicer than mine.

When the A's left town for Kansas City after the 1954 season, Bob Carpenter bought the park from the A's for $1,657,000. He did so with great reluctance.

"We need a ballpark as much as we need a hole in the head," he said.

Although I worked there only one season, I will always remember the toothbrush-style light towers; the ground crew rolling the batting cage all the way to the storage area in dead center field after batting practice; park superintendent Andy Clarke sitting at the pass gate admitting for free all judges, policemen, members of the clergy, and women in high boots; the square Longines clock on top of the scoreboard; and the many billboard ads, particularly MAB Paints, Philco, Ballantine Beer, and, of course, ALPO dog food in the power alley in left center.

My job was to get more people into Connie Mack Stadium in its farewell season and generally create more interest in the team so that attendance would be much greater when the Phillies moved to Veterans Stadium in April 1971. When I arrived, there were fewer than a dozen people involved in marketing, group sales, ticket sales, and advertising sales. By 2005, there were close to 100 people involved in those functions. Only one other person has been there longer than me—Larry Shenk, the Phillies' efficient vice president of public relations.

One of my first hires for the sales and marketing team was a young man I was introduced to by Robin Roberts at a baseball clinic he was running at a local private school. This fellow was a freshly minted Wharton MBA who wanted to get into the business side of baseball. It was one of the more interesting interviews I ever conducted—taking place, as it did, in a locker room and lasting all of about a minute. The kid certainly wasn't expecting to be interviewed that day, or he would have worn more than a jockstrap. His name was Dave Montgomery, and he worked out all right. He succeeded me as CEO in 1997.

Bill Veeck Wasn't Baseball's Only Wacky Guy

With the Phillies barely topping 500,000 in attendance in 1969 and hardly any marketing effort being made, I knew there was nowhere to go but up. Nowadays many teams draw more than 3 million per year, and the Yankees drew more than 4 million in 2005—but in those days the goal was to draw 1 million people, which only about half of the teams were able to do in 1969.

I also knew that, if nothing else, I could build attendance by addressing the problem of Andy Clarke's free-pass list. He had the longest such list of anyone in baseball—perhaps ever. After Andy left, we would get letter after letter after letter from folks inquiring about their free season tickets and why they hadn't arrived yet.

Clarke sure was a character. He was a very large man who, though he did not drink, had a garage full of beer cans. He had the ground crew bring them over from Connie Mack Stadium to his house. There they would sit, in his garage, unopened. When they started to rust, he'd have the groundskeepers replace them. With new cans. They would sit in his garage. Unopened. One theory was that he was saving up for a victory celebration when the Phillies finally won it all. I'm not certain there was any rational explanation.

Cutting down on the longest list of free season tickets in the history of Western civilization wasn't the only thing we did to try to build attendance in Philadelphia through the 1970s. We offered a number of promotions that were creative, fun, and usually—but not always—pretty effective.

During one of our six losing streaks in the 1970 season, I met with my staff to discuss the situation. "We can't go out on the field," I said, "but we have to do something."

We decided to hold Turn Things Around Day at the park. We announced the lineups backward and kept the score backward starting with the ninth inning. The batboy wore his hat backward, and we gave Pennsylvania Dutch "hex signs" to the first 10,000 fans in attendance. This was not a good idea, as the fans started pounding the signs on the wooden seats, which created what could charitably be called a very irritating sound. We lost again anyway. I guess we should have tried Reverse Day instead—where the other team's runs counted for us.

I knew the final game at Connie Mack Stadium had to be special, as the fans had a lot of fond memories—good and bad—of the oldest major league ballpark still in use in the country. I decided to give all of the 31,822 fans a certificate verifying that they had attended the final game at the park. Little did I know that they would be finding their own ways to commemorate the occasion.

We also had 5,000 wooden seat slats in storage that would no longer be needed because the seats at the new ballpark were plastic. I thought it would be a good idea to give them away to the first 5,000 fans.

It was not a good idea.

By the fifth inning, fans were pounding the slats on seats and pillars, creating a horrific sound. That wasn't the only sound being created in the stands. Many fans had arrived at the game with hammers, pliers, screwdrivers, and wrenches. During the game, everyone in the park could hear these tools at work taking down anything the fans could pry loose.

The game was delayed often as fans ran on the field to dig up some dirt or grass, or even take one of the players' caps. As the game continued, the natives kept getting more restless by the minute. Seat slats were pounding, hammers were hammering, and the fans were yelling and throwing things onto the field. The press box was shaking, and the team's employees were scared to death.

Unfortunately, the game was tied 1–1 at the end of nine innings, and it was getting dangerous to be on the field. The umpires met with the managers—Gene Mauch of the visiting Montreal Expos, who was familiar with Connie Mack Stadium as manager of the Phillies in the mid-'60s, and Frank Lucchesi—to discuss what to do. The umpires wanted to call the game a forfeit and give the win to the Expos. Mauch, a man who could certainly anticipate the next move on the chessboard as well as anyone, declined the gift.

"You forfeit this game to us," Gene said, "and we'll have a riot on our hands."

Instead, they decided to call the game a tie at the end of 10 innings if no team scored in the tenth. A tie was avoided when Oscar Gamble singled in the winning run in the bottom of the tenth, giving the Phillies a 2–1 victory.

My plan had been to land a helicopter at home plate at the end of the game to transport home plate to the site for home plate at

Veterans Stadium. But when Tim McCarver scored the winning run, fans poured onto the field, grabbing anything they could get their hands on.

Lucchesi tried to hug Gamble after the game-winning hit. Gamble kept moving instead, saying, "Hey man, run. Let's get the hell out of here. We can celebrate later."

I waved the helicopter off, and we moved home plate the next day.

I stood transfixed as fans left the game with all sorts of souvenirs: seats, pipes, wooden signs, concession equipment, you name it. I saw one man leaving the stadium with a urinal! It certainly was a night to remember.

A year later, a large fire gutted the place. It was sad for longtime fans of the A's and Phillies to see Connie Mack Stadium, once a jewel of a ballpark, become a derelict property. At the site now stands Deliverance Evangelistic Church, which seats 5,100 people.

I learned a lot about Philadelphia baseball fans that first year. They were passionate, loud, and a bit rough from time to time, but they were knowledgeable. During a game in San Francisco in May, starting catcher Tim McCarver broke his hand. A few innings later, backup catcher Mike Ryan broke a finger. The Phillies called up catcher Mike Compton from Triple A to catch and activated a coach, Doc Edwards, as the second-string catcher.

Compton got hurt in the first home game after the West Coast trip, and Coach Edwards had to catch. When he threw out a base runner trying to steal, all the fans got to their feet and gave Edwards a standing ovation. At first I didn't understand what was going on. I had never seen a player get a "standing O" for throwing out a runner. Then I realized that the fans were recognizing a 33-year-old man, who had not been active in the big leagues since 1965, for accomplishing a subtle but impressive feat.

I realized then that Phillies fans knew and appreciated the game. Hall of Fame broadcaster and former Phillie Bob Uecker—who could get off a quip about the boo-birds in Philadelphia with the best of them—may have said it best: "The fans there are smart and mean, and you can count on them."

It's no different now, 36 years later. These fans have raised their children to be the same way—which is why in 2006, when Aaron Rowand made the greatest catch I have ever seen, running into the center-field fence at Citizens Bank Park to rob Xavier Nady of a bases-clearing double in a closely contested game with the rival Mets, breaking his nose and fracturing a bone under his eye in the process, he immediately became a legend in Philadelphia. He got a standing ovation as he walked off the field, a bloody towel held to his face. He got a standing ovation when he returned to the lineup two weeks later. And sales of his jerseys at the Citizens Bank Park concession stands went through the roof.

Phillies fans are demanding and passionate, but they are smart, too, and they appreciate effort more than any other group of fans in baseball.

Yes, I had certainly learned a lot in my rookie year about the fans and media and about the Phillies employees, but the time had come to make our big move from the oldest park to the newest park in baseball.

Kiteman, Hugo Zucchini, Benny the Bomb, and the P.T. Barnum of Baseball

Several major league cities decided at about the same time in the late 1960s to build new multipurpose stadiums to replace aging neighborhood ballparks. Philadelphia's new multipurpose stadium, to be called Veterans Stadium, was already about 75 percent complete when I arrived in Philadelphia in October 1969. However, I reviewed the plans for the facility, and I had the architects make two significant changes in the stadium's design.

The first modification was to install 23 "super boxes" between the lower and upper decks on the 400 Level at the Vet. The idea stemmed from the skyboxes in the Astrodome, which were popular even though they were placed in the worst location of the stadium. This type of service had never been available in a Philadelphia sporting venue. And because the Vet would be home to both the Phillies and the Eagles, the owners of the boxes would receive season tickets to both teams, as well as the opportunity to use their suites for other special events such as concerts.

The Vet, unlike other multipurpose stadiums of the same era that were built in a circular shape, was made in the shape of an *octorad*—an architect's word that comes from the Latin words for "eight" and "radius" or "eight points on a radius." Because of this unique, eight-sided shape, the number of seats in the super boxes varied from 18 to 28 seats. A customer had to buy the maximum number of seats for football but only 10 seats for Phillies games—with an option to purchase additional Phillies tickets for their box on a game-by-game basis. We felt the price of the box would be too steep if they had to purchase up to 28 season tickets for the Phillies.

We designed and built the basic "suite" part of the super box but permitted the owners to make their own decisions on decorating the inside and to install a customized door. This proved to be very popular with the suite owners. Continental Bank even installed a door that looked like a bank safe.

The suites became so popular and were such a good source of revenue that the Eagles and the City of Philadelphia joined forces in the 1980s to build 89 more "penthouse suites" at the top of the Vet. The Phillies were also granted permission to build another 26 super boxes on the 400 Level. This was part of the deal to develop more revenue for Eagles owner Leonard Tose so that he would not move his team to Arizona. Sadly, Tose ran into financial difficulties and had to sell the Eagles anyway. The new owner, Norman Braman, did keep the franchise where it belonged—in Philadelphia.

There were, of course, some issues with huge, multipurpose stadiums. One was that the seating capacity was designed to accommodate football. The Phillies had just come from a ballpark with a capacity of only 32,000, so there was a concern that a capacity of 65,000 at the Vet was way too big for baseball. My father suggested that the Phillies install a huge drape over the upper deck in center field. The theory of the drape was to create the impression that most of the seats in the park were filled. My father believed that seeing empty seats in a stadium was psychologically a bad thing for attendance.

Larger venues often use these drapes to create the impression that most of the seats are filled.

I did not always agree with my dad, and this was one of those times. I convinced the Carpenter family to remove the drape from the plans because I expected to do a lot of big promotions where the seats would come in handy and would generate more revenue for the team. In retrospect, however, my father was right. On certain dates, such as Opening Day and for certain promotions, we did draw big crowds of 50,000 and more. But that was not the norm. When we had crowds of 30,000, which was good attendance, the park still looked empty because of all the empty seats in the outfield upper deck. This became a lesson learned for me, and when we built Citizens Bank Park I insisted on a seating capacity of 40,000–45,000.

Now that the Vet was complete, with super boxes and 60,000 seats to fill, my first goal to market the Phillies was to make Opening Day a very special occasion. In Philadelphia, Opening Day was no big deal. The Phillies had been averaging only 15,000 in attendance. They had a small Salvation Army band play the national anthem and some city council member throw out the first ball. Of course, I had to change that. Although I had upgraded the 1970 opener at Connie Mack Stadium from the Salvation Army to a great high school band and had the mayor instead of a city council member throw out the first ball, I wanted to save my most creative ideas for Opening Day at the Vet.

Because I wanted something more exciting than a politician shot-putting a ball to the catcher from the front of the mound—and because I didn't want to have to choose between the mayor and the governor—I came up with a different concept entirely. I knew that balls had been dropped to players from Philadelphia's City Hall before, so I decided that we should drop the first ball from a helicopter.

I also knew that ball drops can be quite dangerous. If you don't spin the ball the right way it will come down like a knuckleball; a player had broken his wrist at one of those City Hall ball drops. So we tested it well before Opening Day—in the snow, as a matter of fact—with the man I would later assign to Kiteman motivation duty: Paul Callahan.

GM John Quinn, Dallas Green, farm director Paul Owens, and I were all on hand to see the effort. Since we didn't know the aerodynamics of the Vet back then, we didn't think the helicopter would be able to hover over the field—so to add to the degree of difficulty, it would be dropping the ball in a fly-by. Our stunt catcher Callahan was not a ballplayer, so he would have benefited from any advice that the Phillies front-office brain trust had to offer.

He didn't get much.

"Get a helmet," Owens yelled down from the press box.

The first ball hurtled down toward Callahan, he short-armed it, and it fell to the snow. Quinn, Green, Owens, and I reacted as any true Philadelphia spectator would react: we booed.

The helicopter flew by again, the ball fell, and Callahan made a diving catch in the snow. That's how he remembers it, anyway— I recall it being more of a stumble and fall than a dive.

"Okay, we're doing it," Quinn said, "but not with McCarver. Use the backup catcher, Ryan."

It was April 10, 1971. Just like the last game at Connie Mack Stadium, the Phillies were playing the Expos. I had spent the night before with Larry Shenk and Dave Montgomery living the life of a baseball executive before the opening of a new park—specifically, unpacking and rinsing the new dishes for the stadium because no one else had done it yet.

Prior to the opener, we had Montreal general manager Jim Fanning arrive by dog sled followed by a dozen colorfully dressed members of the Royal Canadian Mounted Police. The first ball was dropped from the Arco helicopter 150 feet above the field, and Phillies backup catcher Mike Ryan caught the ball on the run after first bobbling it. The entire pregame show, including popular local entertainer Mike Douglas singing the national anthem, received huge coverage on TV and in the print media.

Needless to say, the aborted Kiteman flight in 1972 also got a lot of media attention, so we brought him back for 1973. This time the ramp had a flat area to stand at the top, was three times as wide, convex, and located in center field. On Opening Day, after yet another big buildup, he skied down the ramp without being blown into the seats, but he and his kite collapsed in center field.

The fans booed.

I decided to try something different for the opener in 1974. It was the "Cannon Man," Hugo Zucchini. He *successfully* shot himself out of a cannon near second base to a net behind home.

The fans cheered.

For our next Opening Day, in 1975, we brought in a high-wire motorcycle act with a pretty lady named Monique hanging by her legs upside down from a trapeze under a motorcycle driven by some circus performer named Guzman. As they got near home plate, she dropped the first ball.

The fans cheered that one, too.

I took a little detour in 1976 to honor the nation's bicentennial. I hired a man to ride a horse all the way from Boston to Philadelphia. He carried the first ball and a lantern. We called him Paul Revere. As he entered the Vet he handed the first ball to my friend from Houston, Rocket Man. Rocket Man flew 150 feet into the air, landed near the pitching mound, and handed the first ball to former Phillies pitching great and Hall of Famer Robin Roberts, who did the actual throwing of the ball from the mound to home plate.

Parachute Man arrived on the scene for the 1977 opener as Pat Mulhern jumped from a plane and parachuted to the pitching mound with the first ball. The fans liked that one, too. We were on a roll!

Parachuting in with the first ball became a fairly regular show in years to come because the fans got a big kick out of it. Popular local TV weatherman and avid skydiver Jim O'Brien was Parachute Man in 1983. It was his one and only appearance at the Vet. Sadly, Jim died in a jump a few years later when his chute did not open.

The Golden Knights of the U.S. Army and the U.S. Navy Leap Frogs appeared many times. They always had a team of five to eight individuals, with one carrying an American flag and one with the first ball. Their routines were not only exciting, they were patriotic.

The Phillie Phanatic got in on the first-ball action a couple of times, once by parachute and once on the "Slide for Life." He slid down a wire from the upper deck in right field to the Phillies dugout, delivering the first ball.

With all those great characters to choose from, one of my personal favorites was Benny the Bomb. Benny would enclose himself in a decorative coffin behind the pitcher's mound. The box would explode with a loud noise, shattering all over the field, and Benny would pop out of the debris with the first ball. The noise was so loud for one of Benny's appearances that Dan Baker, who was down on the field to introduce him, was deaf until the third inning.

Kiteman III, IV, and V returned in 1980, 1984, and 1990. The problem in those years was that it worked pretty well. That proved to be less interesting than the fiascos we had had earlier. But at least the fans didn't boo. Well, that's not entirely true. When Baker introduced Kiteman III in 1980, he first asked the crowd if they remembered Kiteman I and Kiteman II. Just being reminded of those failed attempts drew boos.

I knew that it was going to require more than just creative Opening Day festivities to enlarge our fan base for the other 80 home games during the season. I wanted to create a ballpark experience where Mom, Dad, and the kids could come to a Phillies game and say to themselves as they left the park that they enjoyed themselves—even if the Phillies lost, which we were doing a fair bit of in the early '70s.

I had an open-door policy and listened to lots of crazy ideas that my staff came up with as we tried several different things to make it more enjoyable to see a Phillies game. Any time there was some question about what we should do, I had a sure-fire method for getting us to a decision.

"I'll ask my wife," I said, "and see what she thinks."

I constructed a home-run spectacular on the façade of the stands in center field that would go off when the Phillies would hit a home run. Philadelphia Phil and Phyllis dressed in Colonial costumes were introduced as our mascots. In addition to having Phil and Phyllis walking around the stands shaking hands with fans, their replicas were part of the home-run spectacular.

When the Phillies hit a home run, Phil would swing a bat and baseballs of light bulbs would travel along the center-field façade and hit Phyllis in the rear end. She fell backward, pulling a rope. A cannon went off, smoke poured out of the barrel of the cannon, and then the crack in the Liberty Bell stationed nearby lit up. We had to put an end to the home-run show in 1983 because we added more super boxes in the area where the spectacular was located, and the home-run show was blocking the seats. As for Phil and Phyllis, they are now resting in peace at Storybook Land near Atlantic City.

We installed dancing waters behind the center-field fence. Fountains of water would periodically shoot upward and swirl around in time to music. A slight problem would occur from time to time when the wind was blowing toward center field. About 100 fans sitting behind the dancing waters would get very wet. And stained—the dancing waters didn't just dance, they were dyed pretty colors, too.

To further add to the ambiance, we put palm trees behind the outfield walls down the left-field and right-field line. We actually put those in for Ron Stone, an outfielder we had in the early '70s. He tore it up one year in Florida in spring training but did nothing when we headed north. We put in those trees to see if it would help him recapture his Clearwater stroke. It didn't work.

We eventually introduced a baseball-cap-shaped golf cart to bring in pitchers from the bullpen, but before that we'd bring our relievers to the mound in a fire engine and their guys in a gasoline truck.

Nifty bullpen wheels, palm trees, good music, dancing waters, and an exciting scoreboard were important in creating an atmosphere of family fun. One of the most rewarding statistics to me is that 67 percent of fans attending a Phillies game come with another member of their family. This does not happen at a pro football game.

The closest we had to family unfriendly experiences at Phillies games were in the family picnic areas down each foul line. These got removed when we added more seats in the early '80s—which was probably for the best, given that families were not actually the ones buying tickets to those areas and what was going on down there was anything but a picnic. If fans hopped down in there to go after a foul ball, they were taking their lives into their own hands. We ended up having to hire a "goon squad" to maintain order.

We had a bit more luck with the Hot-Pants Patrol, which was the name given to a group of usherettes when the Vet first opened. Our usherettes ranged in age from about 18 to 80, but only 40 were selected to wear the short shorts and white boots of the Hot-Pants Patrol. I'm told that did not exactly do wonders for the clubhouse chemistry of our squad of usherettes.

The members of the Hot-Pants Patrol were all attractive young ladies, and I interviewed and hired most of them. It was a tough job, but someone had to do it. I could claim that I gave everyone who interviewed for the Patrol very extensive tests in English and math, but the truth is that ladies with the best figures got the job. I don't recall asking my wife for her input on that one.

The Hot-Pants Patrol—which actually predated the country's hot-pants craze by about two years—ended up getting us national exposure. Fans got to vote for the member of the Hot-Pants Patrol who would be crowned Miss Schmidt's by our sponsor, Schmidt's Beer. The Patrol participated in countless promotions in their first year of existence—after all, they were better than the team on the field.

I also insisted that we have ballgirls down the left- and right-field foul lines and that they be very attractive. Mary Sue Styles, a beautiful girl with flowing blond hair, became legendary because broadcaster Richie Ashburn would often refer to her as "that beautiful Mary Sue made another great play on that foul ball."

Needless to say, things were different back then.

Another concept of mine is what I called "staircase marketing." The idea was to get fringe or nonbaseball fans to a Phillies game once. Our hope was that they would enjoy the experience so much that they would attend three or four games the next year, and then take the next step by purchasing one of our multiticket plans. The key to all that was to get them to a game for the first time.

How did we do that? We used pre- or postgame concerts with Dionne Warwick, Ronnie Milsap, and others. We also had Crazy

Night (where we brought back all of our goofy Opening Day acts), College Nights, Circus Night, cash scrambles, wheelbarrow races, duck races, toga parties, high-wire acts, ostrich races, an ice skating show, and, of course, giveaway days with hats, shirts, bats—you name it. These were all part of my plan to encourage a potential fan to take that first step up the staircase. I also have always believed that if we could get a child interested in a certain promotion, then that child might talk his or her parents into coming to a game. The giveaway souvenirs with the Phillies logo were also good walking advertisements for us.

Perhaps the best example of what promotions can do was evident in 1972. The Phillies drew 1,350,000 fans despite a dismal 59–97 record. The "Great Wallenda" tightrope walk—which was one of my most memorable promotions—took place that season. The great Karl Wallenda, age 67, was a high-wire legend. His high-wire walk, held on a rainy day between games of a doubleheader on August 13, was absolutely nerve-racking. Wallenda, who had the strongest forearms and hands of anyone I have ever met, was to walk across a five-eighths-inch cable stretched from the right-field foul pole to the left-field pole at the top of the stadium. Because the cable had to be stretched in a hurry between games, there were 12 feet of slack. The fact that the cable was not taut was going to make the walk much more difficult. Wallenda's daughter hysterically protested and demanded that we cancel the show.

What did her father do?

Wallenda was not fazed. He chugged two beers, grabbed his pole, and went up to the wire. He walked about 15 feet onto the wire and sat down, yelling and signaling to the ushers holding guide wires along the way to pull on them to eliminate some of the slack. A crowd of 33,000 fans and every player and coach in both dugouts were staring, mesmerized by the act.

Wallenda finally stood up, proceeded to the middle of the wire, and did a handstand. The fans were awestruck and applauded wildly. He made it to the other side to the strains of "You'll Never Walk Alone" on the stadium organ, where he was greeted and hugged by his hysterical daughter. The walk took 17 minutes, and Wallenda announced afterward that his handstand was for "our boys in Vietnam."

I met him in the press dining room to congratulate him, whereupon he consumed 10 ounces of scotch whiskey in about 30 minutes, explaining that it was the scariest walk he ever made. Bill Conlin, longtime writer for the *Philadelphia Daily News*, heralded the 1972 Wallenda skywalk as "Giles's finest hour as baseball's P.T. Barnum forever enshrined."

I brought the Great Wallenda back for Memorial Day in 1976 as part of the bicentennial celebration and, at age 71, he took a 20-minute walk on the wire in front of 52,000 fans. Even with that many people in attendance, you could hear a pin drop at the Vet. During the second half of his walk, he unfurled a U.S. flag and a 13-star flag at the ends of his pole.

Unfortunately, a few years later, Karl plunged to his death sky walking between the twin towers of the Condado Plaza Hotel in San Juan, Puerto Rico, on March 22, 1978, at the age of 73, done in by high winds and poor rigging. He will always be remembered fondly by Phillies fans for the spectacular shows he put on at Veterans Stadium.

Animal Trouble

Some of my "P.T. Barnum moments" were not as heralded.

The ostrich race was one of my promotions that didn't work out as planned. Having already pitted the Phillies' two most popular announcers—Harry Kalas and Rich Ashburn—against each other in a tricycle race, it seemed only logical to have them race ostriches around the warning track. Harry and Rich were seated in sulky carts like you see in a harness race—except pulled by ostriches instead of horses. We'd soon learn that there's a reason why harness racing is done with horses and not ostriches.

When the race started, the birds went ballistic. Both Harry and Rich were scared to death. Ashburn, whose nickname was "Whitey," literally turned white. They both jumped out of the carts. The ostriches ran around like crazy, and one of them jumped into the stands.

No more ostrich races.

My duck race was just as bad. That was one of Paul Callahan's suggestions, having been to some bar in San Francisco that was standing room only for turtle races. The idea was to have 16 live ducks lined up between second and third base. One of our Hot-Pants Patrol was assigned to each duck. The usherette had a number on her back corresponding to the duck's number. The ducks would race to the first-base line with the girls enticing them with breadcrumbs. Unfortunately, at the precise moment that the race was to start, a clap of thunder boomed out, and the ducks all ran into the third-base dugout in terror. We eventually found them hiding in the tarp.

No more duck races.

My ground crew really hated any promotion that featured animals because they almost always involved significant cleanup efforts. And if you think Frisbee-catching dogs can make a mess, imagine what can come out of a pregame show featuring the elephants from the Ringling Bros. and Barnum & Bailey Circus. That promotion ended up with two elephants urinating quite aggressively in the Phillies dugout. One of them—who must have been a Mets fan—appeared to be trying to fill the entire dugout all by himself. Boy, did that stink for a while. I was asked what kind of grief I got from the players when their dugout got defiled. The truth is that I stayed away from them for a while after that one.

When we saw that we had a game on Easter Sunday in 1973, we knew we would need to do something special to draw a crowd on that holiday. We planned to present Steve Carlton with his 1972 Cy Young Award before the game, but it would take more than that to fill the place. One of the original suggestions that my open-door policy produced was a softball game between the local media and the Playboy Bunnies, but I nixed that. Instead, we decided to have the world's largest Easter egg hunt—with thousands of plastic Easter eggs taped under the seats—and a promotion called the "Highest-Jumping

Easter Bunny." The plan was to have someone dress up as a bunny, get into a hot-air balloon at home plate, take off, and fly to who-knows-where. The person who found the bunny would win $1,000 and season tickets for the whole family.

"Let's get one of the local morning DJs to be the bunny," I said. "We'll get lots of free promotion. Those guys are so egotistical, that's all they'll talk about for a month."

So we lined up one of the disc jockeys and were ready to go when something tragic happened. Down in one of the Carolinas a DJ in a hot-air balloon doing a station promotion got blown into an electrical wire and was killed. Our DJ heard about it and bailed on us. Try as we might, we couldn't find a single taker to replace him.

But as with the Kiteman, promotional efforts had been heavy, and the show must always go on. We went to the bullpen and called on our ball-drop guinea pig, duck-race guru, and Kiteman aide-de-camp, Paul Callahan. Callahan—who must have been given the same "be flexible" speech when I hired him as the one I got in Houston—was down on the field watching the flight of the trial balloons. Thanks to the aerodynamics of the Vet, each test balloon got sucked up right into the light stanchions.

Needless to say, Callahan was a bit nervous when the big day arrived. But he had mustered up his courage and donned the very large full-body bunny costume, complete with bunny head. That's when our finance VP, George Harrison, paid him a visit.

"I need you to sign this release," Harrison said, pushing an insurance form at him.

Not exactly what you'd call a rousing pregame speech.

Callahan looked at the waiver, thought about his fiancée, and shook his head. "I'm not signing that."

"You need to sign it."

"I don't mind dying, George," Callahan said, "but I want to get some money out of it if I do."

"You have to sign this," Harrison said, getting agitated.

"Fine," Callahan said, handing him the bunny head. "You do it then."

Harrison angrily handed him back his head—literally—and stalked off.

Callahan came to see me, showed me the form, and told me what happened.

I read it and said, "Well, Paul, I wouldn't sign it either."

Fortunately for Callahan, the hot-air balloon did not behave as the trial balloons did. Unfortunately, every time the balloon got 10 feet off the ground, it came crashing back down on the field. The downdrafts in the Vet were too tough for it to overcome.

After the third attempt—and the third crash—the balloon basket tipped over and landed sideways on the turf. Callahan felt the heat on his back from the balloon's open flame and panicked. And all the little kids on hand to see the Easter Bunny got to see him rolling around on the turf, convinced he was on fire.

Needless to say, the fans booed.

Promotions involving animals—even fake ones—did not seem to be my thing.

I didn't do all that well with college students, either.

On one of our College Nights, I decided to have a mattress-stacking contest. We invited about 15 universities to participate. The idea was to see how many students from each university could stack on one of several mattresses we had down on the field. It was really quite interesting to watch. The engineering students at Lehigh University won by a wide margin because they really had a plan.

But there was a problem. A big problem. Many students on the bottoms of the piles were injured, three or four seriously, and lawsuits followed. Some of the kids on the bottom of the pile, under all that weight, were "losing control of their bodily functions" as one of my groundskeepers put it. Yet another promotion they had to clean up after, as they frequently reminded me.

No more mattress-stacking contests.

We had a Disco Night that featured some since-forgotten group that was on the charts in the mid-'70s. We had a portable dance floor on the field for the group and their backup dancers to do their thing in their one-piece, sequined jumpsuits. We didn't have to clean up after that one, but we did see some dance moves that were far more adult than the "family entertainment" Phillies were looking for.

They didn't get invited back.

A different kind of heat down on the field caused problems for some of our promotions. On a hot summer day, the field at the Vet could get to be 120 degrees on the playing surface. When we did a Diane Furs promotion with our usherettes in August, the company wasn't too thrilled with us when they saw—and smelled—their furs when they got them back.

In the early years of the Vet, we would have a giveaway for kids almost every Sunday. We also sold child general admission tickets for only $1. On a few occasions, we sold 60,000 tickets, but it looked like we only had 30,000 people in the park. We finally figured out the problem. Youth baseball teams would come in busloads. They would buy their $1 tickets, get the giveaway items, leave the park, give the items to a coach or parent, purchase another $1 ticket, and go get another item. One team of 20 kids could leave with 50 to 100 shirts, bats, or jackets. The first time we had Jacket Day we had 90,000 people trying to get in the park. It was a parking and traffic disaster. Needless to say, we soon changed the system so that kids had to pay the full general admission price of $4 when we had a giveaway.

In the Astrodome in 1973, tennis star Billie Jean King defeated Bobby Riggs in a match that was billed as the Battle of the Sexes and televised nationally. In 1974 I decided to do a takeoff on the Battle of the Sexes by promoting a tennis match between a doubles team of Richie Ashburn and me against Julie Anthony, the number four ranked female player in the world at the time. Richie and I had to hit the ball in the singles court and Julie could hit into the doubles court that was laid out on the AstroTurf infield. I thought for sure we would win, but Julie cleaned our clock, 6–2 and 6–2.

Another of my favorite promotions was the cash scramble. The concept was to spread $10,000 in cash—crunched up dollar bills ranging from $1 to $100—on the infield. We would pick six fans at random to come on the field to collect as much of the cash as possible in three minutes.

The "at random" part was a bit misleading. I told our sales guys to always pick two attractive young ladies, two kids, and two older folks—someone for everyone. The cash scramble was fun to watch, and the fans loved it. While my team went to great lengths to find pretty ladies in halter tops for the cash scramble—even breaking out field binoculars to scan the park row by row—it was a nun who actually ended up being the most famous participant we ever had. She was able to use the large sleeves and pockets of her habit to pretty much clean out the infield. A picture was taken of her in action that got picked up by all the wire services. When she got back to the convent in California, the mother superior wanted to know where the money was.

A View from the Ground Crew

Some of the most memorable moments at the Vet had nothing to do with the marketing and promotions folks and everything to do with the folks who truly do it all and see it all—the ground crew.

They were the ones who had to take care of things when the Vet's water system went south in the middle of January and turned the entire 400 Level into a skating rink.

They were the ones who had to clean up the worst-smelling mess in the history of the Vet—which, surprisingly, involved no animals. A beer truck backing down the ramp behind the outfield—in an empty park, fortunately—lost its brakes, took out an overhead door, crashed through the right-field fence, and overturned on the warning track. This was before the warning track was synthetic, so the beer saturated the dirt and reeked for the better part of a year. Not many things can make a major league groundskeeper cry, but this came close. The smell was so bad some folks swear that it affected whether some fly balls got caught.

The groundskeepers were also the ones who had to watch while the city workers attempted to pilot the Zamboni machine, a contraption that sucked water off the artificial turf. It has been said that no city worker ever drove a Zamboni sober and, judging from some of the results, I can't really argue. One recurring episode was the wrong button being pushed when it came time to dump the water that had been collected. The way this play got drawn up on the chalkboard: park the Zamboni on the warning track, press *this* button, and spray the water *down* into the drain alongside the outfield fence. The way it often happened: park the Zamboni on the warning track, press *that* button by mistake, and spray the water *up* over the outfield fence and into the stands.

Ironically, they actually discovered that shooting the water over the fence was more efficient than using the drain—and, if executed in center field, could be done without shooting the water *into the crowd*.

Rain was the bane of my existence in my role as operations director—especially when it was raining late in the season on a team's last visit to town. In those situations, if you can't get the game to five innings, you'll lose the game and a fair bit of the associated revenue. To help us get our games in, we used a local guy who was incredibly accurate with his forecasts. I relied on him heavily to make decisions about calling the game—which earned me quite a reputation with the players and the umpires.

Greg Luzinski and Larry Bowa, in particular, *hated* playing in the rain. As soon as it started raining, they wanted to go home. They'd give the ground crew all sorts of grief to relay on to me.

"Giles needs to call this bleeping game," they'd say. "Is he blind? Can't he see it's pouring out here?"

The ground crew would do their best to defend my honor. "Bill's weather guy is telling us there's a break in the storm."

Which would only prompt more grumbling and cursing from Bowa and Luzinski.

Eventually the ground crew started answering the players' complaints with a phrase that our weather guy often used to describe a break in the storm to our west. "There's a window at the airport," they'd say.

"You tell Giles that we're not playing at the bleeping airport," the players would reply.

One time, when we were playing a game that we really wanted to get in, we got a call from our guy. "There's an unbelievable storm heading your way, and it'll be there soon," he said. "But it will only last 15 minutes. You've got to make certain that you get the field covered at the first drop of rain."

Unfortunately, when we called down to the ground crew, they were shorthanded. Anyone who thought that handling a tarpaulin is easy got to see a vivid demonstration of how difficult it actually is—because we had a bunch of front-office guys down on the field trying to roll it out onto the infield in a stiff wind.

It didn't work too well. When we lost our future CEO, Dave Montgomery, under the billowing tarp, we knew we weren't getting that game in.

Such is the life of the ground crew—taken for granted until the one time you desperately need them and they're not there. "The pay is not much," as the saying goes, "but you're a part of it." Our ground crew members earned about $6 a game back in 1972—which they were fine with until they learned that the ballgirls were getting $10 a game. Two of the crew—one of whom, Mike DiMuzio, is now the director of ballpark operations at Citizens Bank Park—complained to then-owner Ruly Carpenter.

Carpenter thought about it for a day, then came back to them and said, "You guys are like the manager, the ballgirls are like the players. No one comes to see the manager. That's why you don't make as much."

But because these two had the guts to ask, they got bumped to $8 a game.

They had no problem getting that meeting with Ruly to discuss their pay because he would watch the game with them. He liked to sit in the ground crew area behind home plate, banging on the glass when he thought the ump blew a call. The owner and the ground crew got to know each other pretty well.

"From where we sat, we got a great view of how all the high rollers got treated," DiMuzio said. "We pointed this out to Ruly, and he made us a promise that if we ever won the division, he'd have the usherettes come down and serve us champagne. And the man was true to his word."

The crew also got to know Ruly's brother Keith, who was the first video guy the Phillies ever had. He would film the games from the ground crew's station behind home plate. Unfortunately, Keith wasn't the most dedicated film man baseball has ever seen.

"The hell with this," he said in the middle of one session. "I'm hungry. I'm going to get a hamburger."

Keith's videos from the press box weren't much better, as the camera would frequently stray from the pitcher to some blonde walking up the aisle behind home plate.

Party Time

In the same spirit of fun we were creating around the Philadelphia Phillies, we ended up throwing a lot of parties in Philadelphia during the 1970s. Some were planned and some were spontaneous, but nearly all of them were a blast. To celebrate the 1980 championship, we threw a party at the Franklin Plaza Hotel before it had even opened. We threw a going-away party for one of our administrative staff down in Atlantic City that was so much fun, she took back her resignation on the bus ride home.

I always loved to throw a party. I loved to see people having a good time.

In high school I was in charge of the senior prom that historically had been held in a hotel with a four- or five-piece band with about 300 kids in attendance. I decided to go big time by hiring Stan Kenton and his band, and I rented out the largest dance hall in the Cincinnati area—Castle Farm. It was a huge success, with 1,500 kids dancing into the wee hours.

When Philadelphia hosted the All-Star Game in 1976, I wanted to break new ground just as I did with my high school prom. I decided to dramatically change the philosophy of the social life at the All-Star Game. I believed the All-Star Game should be more than just a game and a buffet dinner at a hotel on the evening prior to the game.

After all, I thought to myself, baseball was showcasing the 50 or so best players in the entire world.

So in 1976 I rented the Judge Lewis Quadrangle in Independence Park at the doorstep to the Liberty Bell and Independence Hall. There was a big awning over the area, and I constructed a bandstand and dance floor in the center of the quad. I hired a great dance band from New York and a Mummers band to perform. We transported the 1,500 guests from their hotel to the quad in the city's cable-car-type trollies. When the guests arrived, they were greeted by the Phillies' Hot-Pants Patrol holding trays of wine and gin and tonic. There were plenty of bars and sumptuous food stations distributed throughout. At about 10:00 PM, a spectacular fireworks show exploded overhead.

Everyone had such a great time that succeeding All-Star Game parties kept getting bigger and better, and eventually the All-Star Break turned into a three-day celebration with a "futures game" on Sunday, a home run derby on Monday followed by a gala party, and then a pregame party on Tuesday. The attendance at the social functions grew to 5,000.

Our party for the 1976 All-Star Game extended all the way to game day. We really decked out the stadium for the event, going well beyond the standard red, white, and blue bunting. We even had "Happy Birthday America" and the skyline of Philadelphia put on the outfield wall.

To keep true to my tradition of offbeat pregame activities, we had elaborate festivities lined up, which included a group of Hare Krishna. Evidently, the Hare Krishna took their participation very seriously and rehearsed their performance for about three days in the bowels of the Vet. The nonstop humming nearly drove my ground crew out of their minds.

Fat, Green, Indefinable, and Lovable

As you can see, in all facets of baseball you must learn to expect the unexpected. You never know what's going to happen next, what's going to hit and what's going to miss, and when the law of unintended consequences is going to kick in. Perhaps the best example of this is the story of the Philadelphia Phillies mascot.

Personally, I never believed mascots would work in baseball. However, in the mid-1970s the San Diego Chicken became very popular at Padres baseball games. The Chicken was not an employee of the Padres, but rather a promotions guy for a San Diego radio station.

Denny Lehman, the Phillies director of marketing, periodically traveled with the team. He saw firsthand how much fun the Chicken could create. For two or three years, Denny badgered me to have a real mascot to replace Phil and Phyllis. He explained that the Chicken was creating more of a family atmosphere at Jack Murphy Stadium and that the number of fights in the stands had decreased dramatically.

In 1978 I relented and asked our promotion director, Frank Sullivan, to contact the people who designed Big Bird on *Sesame Street*. I asked the designers—Bonnie Erickson and Wade Harrison—to create something fat, green, indefinable, and loveable.

Their first rendition was not to my liking. I asked them to make him fatter and make his nose bigger. They did. The Phillie Phanatic was born.

"How much will it cost?" I asked.

"Twenty-nine hundred, and we own the copyright," they replied. "Or $5,000, and you can own the copyright."

I did not believe the Phanatic was going to be a success, so I decided to save the $2,100. What a mistake! Of course, the Phanatic has become one of the most recognized and most popular aspects of the Phillies. A few years and one lawsuit later, I bought the copyright for $200,000.

Once we had the costume, the question was who was going to wear it. A young man named David Raymond was working part-time as the mailroom man. He was a football player on the University of Delaware team coached by his father, Tubby Raymond. Dave was kind of a wise guy, but he showed a lot of self-confidence. His mother was deaf, so I figured that he'd probably had to learn to communicate with his hands and body. Raymond took the job and was immediately a big hit as the Phillie Phanatic. We sent him to mime school, where he learned how to talk with his body. We didn't want the Phanatic to ever talk.

The plan was to have him perform with some of the pregame shows, appear in the stands in the third and seventh innings, and do a short skit on the field in the fifth inning. His popularity continued to grow each year, and he eventually became a true Philadelphia icon, appearing in the city's marketing brochures and advertisements. Raymond retired after the 1993 season, but Tom Burgoyne, the back-up Phanatic, took over and didn't miss a beat.

The Phanatic has made thousands of personal appearances at charity functions, birthday parties, bar mitzvahs, and almost any other gathering of people wishing to have a little fun. Every one of these numerous public appearances has helped to publicize the Phillies—even the one where he knocked a dignitary off a platform and we got sued for $250,000.

Nearly everyone who has ever encountered the Phillie Phanatic has come away with a smile—with one very notable exception. That would be Los Angeles Dodgers manager Tommy Lasorda. Lasorda was a lifetime member of the Dodgers family, first as a player, then as a coach, and finally as a manager. He still serves the team as a member of their front office. He frequently claims to "bleed Dodger blue." His loyalty to the franchise is legendary and probably without equal in this day and age.

Though Tommy is a wonderful ambassador for the game and is known for having a great sense of humor, he also has a temper, and his outbursts are legendary. The Phanatic got to see that firsthand. It was a tradition for the Phanatic to poke fun at umpires and opposing players, and most of them took it in good fun. Most people assumed that Lasorda was taking it in good fun, too—even when baseballs came firing out of the Dodgers dugout toward our mascot's big green head. Those fans close enough to the dugout to hear the words coming out of Lasorda's mouth as he threw those brush-back pitches knew better than anyone what he really thought.

You have to give the Phanatic credit for being a gamer—though he got hollered at and dusted, he kept coming back for more. And after a few years of this, it was Tommy who finally snapped. When the Phillie Phanatic used his ATV to run over a dummy in a Lasorda uniform—a dummy complete with a pot belly stuffed under the shirt—Tommy complained to our front office for such an inappropriately "violent display," and I guess we did not tell him what he wanted to hear. And when the Phillie Phanatic dressed up a dummy in Lasorda's uniform and did it again, Tommy came charging out of the dugout, grabbed the dummy, and started beating the Phanatic with it, knocking our mascot to the turf. I guess body slamming a real person who happened to be in a costume was an *appropriately* violent display.

"At first I didn't know if he was joking or not," Dave Raymond said later. "But then he punched me, and I thought, 'You know, maybe Tommy doesn't think this as funny as I do.'"

I later learned that one of his own players—Steve Sax—was the insider who got the Phanatic a Tommy Lasorda uniform. Evidently, all the Dodgers players knew how much Lasorda hated the Phanatic. *Hated.* It's a long season, and you've got to stay loose to get through it. They figured it would be fun to see Tommy get all worked up by something fat, green, and indefinable turning a potbellied dummy in a Dodgers uniform into turfkill.

"Work Hard and Have Fun"

And, hey, fun is what it's all about. We must have been doing something right because the Vet is one of a very select group of baseball stadiums that drew more than 1 million fans in every year of its existence.

When I first came to Philadelphia, I hired a bunch of young people to help me build interest in the ballclub. I brought in a lot of women, too—which was not at all common in baseball back then. It became a very close-knit group, with friendships that have lasted to this day. My marching orders to them were to "work hard and have fun"—and that they did.

They helped me develop and implement some great ideas to build excitement around the Phillies during the early '70s. It could have been a chore coming to work every day for a losing team—a team that had never won a championship in its nearly 100 years of existence—but they were indeed determined to work hard and have fun. And when the Phillies finally did break through, clinching the NL East title in Montreal in 1976, the staff celebrated just like the ballplayers. Though they were at the Vet, miles away from the team, they broke out the champagne, too. Still wanting to continue the celebration, but trapped in champagne-drenched clothes, they headed down to the locker room and changed into the players' home uniforms, which they wore out on the town late into the night. They even managed to get them back in one piece the next day.

My mantra might as well have been to "work hard, have fun, and meet your future spouse" with all the marriages that took place within the Phillies family—too many to count, but probably more than two dozen. The Phillies always were a "family business." We were very loyal to our employees, and they returned the loyalty and then some. Our manager in the early 1970s, Frank Lucchesi, once observed how fervent the employees were. "When we win," Lucchesi said, "the secretaries type faster."

I'd even hear stories about our employees being out in public and getting into violent arguments with anyone who said anything bad about the Phillies or the folks who ran the team. It just wouldn't have been the same—neither as successful nor as fun—without them.

MY FAVORITE MOMENTS AT THE VET
- three World Series
- two All-Star Games
- 66,700,288 passionate fans
- Pete Rose breaking Stan Musial's National League hits record
- Tug McGraw and Mitch Williams closing games
- Mike Schmidt and Greg Luzinski hitting mammoth home runs
- the huge American flag on the field for special events
- Terry Mulholland's no-hitter in 1990

- Paul O'Neill of the Cincinnati Reds kicking a ball from right field that actually ended up holding the winning run at third in the ninth inning of a game the Phillies eventually won two batters later
- the dogs and horses on the field in Game 6 of the 1980 World Series—only in Philadelphia!
- the Zamboni machine—only on turf!
- watching five Hall of Famers play for the Phillies: Jim Bunning, Steve Carlton, Joe Morgan, Tony Perez, and Mike Schmidt
- organist Paul Richardson—in the days before blaring music recordings, he was a perfect accompaniment to baseball
- the ground crew
- rain delays—great times to socialize and talk baseball
- the Hot-Pants Patrol—one of my best promotional ideas…at the time
- Jackie Donnelly—an ancient ballboy who served before the Beautiful Mary Sue
- Yoyo—a grand old guy who danced in the stands and was a fixture at all of the sports venues in Philadelphia
- the Liberty Bell
- Phil and Phyllis
- monkeys sweeping the bases
- elephants "fertilizing" the AstroTurf
- the streakers
- the Mummers
- the standing ovation for Ozzie Smith when he played his last game at the Vet
- the special nights Larry Shenk produced to honor Tony Taylor, Mike Schmidt, Steve Carlton, Richie Ashburn, and Harry Kalas
- Richie Ashburn and Harry Kalas in the broadcast booth
- Dan Baker in the public-address booth—a wonderfully distinctive voice that was as much a part of the Philadelphia baseball experience as Harry and Whitey
- owner Ruly Carpenter on a ramp behind home plate, sitting with the ground crew so he could badger the umpires

- the wonderful people who worked for the Phillies and the city
- the tears in Larry Bowa's eyes on September 17, 2001—the first game played after 9/11
- the final weekend and the closing ceremony—pure emotion for everyone who participated and one of the great events of my life

Putting the Pieces Together

"That team's got talent. All they need is a leader."
—*Pete Rose to Joe Morgan during the 1976 NLCS,*
describing the Phillies

The Losses Begin to Pile Up—and So Does the Young Talent

The Phillies had a new $49.5 million stadium, but it was not translating into much success on the field.

1971: The team lost 95 games, second most in the National League and fourth in the majors. They were dead last in the NL East, 30 games off the pace.

1972: Things got worse, with the Phillies losing more games (97) than the year before—in a strike-shortened season, no less. They were 37.5 games off the pace in the East, the worst team in the National League, and won more games than only the Texas Rangers.

1973: Dead last again, more than 90 losses, and one of the worst records in the majors.

If you looked closely, however, you could see some cause for optimism, even as the losses piled up. Larry Bowa solidified his hold on the shortstop position in 1971, leading the league in fielding percentage for the first of six times. In 1972 Greg "Bull" Luzinski took over left field, and Steve Carlton won 27 games. In 1973 Danny

Ozark—whose hiring I championed—took over as manager. Two more of our minor league products took over starting positions: a very smart third baseman-turned-catcher and second-generation major leaguer, Bob Boone, and a shortstop-turned-third-baseman by the name of Mike Schmidt.

The Pope, Uncle Hughie, and the Witch Doctor

How did the Phillies begin to turn things around? Though it was a team effort—not just on the field but in the dugout and the front office—a critical turning point came in 1972 when Bob and Ruly Carpenter named Paul Owens the team's general manager.

Owens, known as "the Pope" because of his likeness to Pope Paul VI, was a wonderful judge of player talent. The Phillies had been struggling since the disaster in 1964. Pope started to build up the farm system when he took over as farm director in 1965. In addition to turning over the scouting staff, he convinced the Carpenters to build a state-of-the-art spring training complex in Clearwater, Florida. It featured four fields radiating out from a clubhouse in the center. An observation tower was built on top of the clubhouse, with views of all four fields—a feature that has been copied at other spring training sites ever since. The Carpenters loved it so much that when it was completed they told Owens how much they'd wished they'd done it years ago.

Most importantly, Owens made some very astute acquisitions. The two most brilliant moves the Phillies made actually took place before he was named general manager. At his urging, the team drafted Mike Schmidt in the second round of the 1971 amateur draft and traded Rick Wise for Steve Carlton.

As farm director, Owens personally scouted Schmidt, who was a shortstop at Ohio University. Owens loved Schmidt's arm, power, and athleticism but knew immediately Schmidt's position would be third base, not shortstop. Schmidt struggled early but is now regarded as the greatest third baseman to ever play the game.

Owens never doubted him. My sales director, Paul Callahan, tells a story of going with Owens to see a young Mike Schmidt play in

Reading, Pennsylvania. Callahan watched Schmidt crush a home run on a fastball in his first at-bat, then wave at breaking balls the rest of the day. Based on that performance, Callahan was thinking Schmidt would have huge problems in the big leagues. When asked what he thought of Schmidt after this game, Owens didn't share that belief.

"If his knees hold up," Owens said, "he'll be in the Hall of Fame."

Even when Schmidt failed to hit his weight in his first big-league season, the Pope stood by his assessment.

Owens knew a thing or two about pitchers, too. After the 1971 season, both Rick Wise of the Phillies and Steve Carlton of the Cardinals were coming off successful seasons, but both were having difficult contract negotiations with their team's owners. The Pope suggested to Bob Carpenter and general manager John Quinn that they should trade Wise for Carlton. Though Wise and Carlton were the same age, had the same amount of big-league experience, and had won almost the exact same number of games to that point in their respective careers, Owens felt Carlton could be the more dominating pitcher. He certainly called that one right.

Rick Wise would go on to win 113 more games in a very respectable 18-year career. Steve Carlton would go on to win 252 more games and four Cy Young Awards, establishing himself as one of the greatest pitchers the game has ever seen.

In the first season after the deal was made, Carlton had the most remarkable pitching year in baseball history. In 1972 his 27 victories represented 46 percent of the Phillies' 59 victories. Whenever Carlton pitched in the second half of that year, attendance would be 10,000 to 15,000 greater than the average.

Little did we know at the time, but we were on the verge of the franchise's golden decade (1974–1983), which was a very fun time for Phillies personnel, the fans, and me. I was in all the meetings when "the gang of six"—Ruly Carpenter, Paul Owens, Dallas Green (Pope's handpicked replacement as farm director), super-scout Hugh Alexander, Danny Ozark, and me—would discuss player trades, manager and coaching changes, and draft picks. I often made suggestions, and Owens actually took my advice a few times. But it was not easy to keep up with the group because several of them were heavy drinkers and thought nothing of staying up all night discussing player trades.

Owens was a wonder to behold at the winter baseball meetings. He would create a command center in his suite with record books and scouting reports on all major and minor league players throughout baseball. Not just their "tools" were scouted, but their "makeup"— how they handled adversity, what kind of teammate they were, leadership characteristics (or lack thereof), and other things like that. While tools are on display for anyone to see, a player's makeup must be supplemented with inside information that you glean from opposing players and managers—and, perhaps most useful of all, from the trainers and clubhouse guys who are around them a lot outside of the public eye and often know better than anyone else what a player is really all about.

Owens would assign each of our top scouts five or six teams to investigate. The scouts would go to the lobby of the hotel or to the suite of their assigned teams to find out which players might be available in a trade and which of our players they liked. Once Owens got a rundown on each team, we would sit around the command center creating trades among ourselves until the Pope heard one he liked. When he heard one he wanted to make, Owens would tell the scout to have the opposing general manager come to our suite. The Pope and Alexander would take the GM aside to try to negotiate a deal—usually by Owens asking for a player he knew he could not get and then "settling" on the player he really wanted.

Owens wasn't afraid to offer prospects—and lots of them— if that's what it was going to take to add a key piece. This was especially true in the late 1970s, when we knew we had a window of opportunity to bring a championship to Philadelphia. I can remember him going back to Pat Gillick of the Blue Jays over and over again, trying to pry loose one of their two young starting pitchers, Jim Clancy or Dave Stieb. Each time we showed up at their hotel room we added another player to the deal. We ended up offering a five-for-one deal, but the Blue Jays never bit.

While all of these "games" were going on, Owens was drinking his Jack Daniel's and ginger ale. He was amazing. He could be up all night making a trade, finalize the deal at 7:00 AM, and then—without the benefit of either food or sleep—shave, splash on some cologne, put on a coat and tie, and hold a 9:00 AM press conference looking fresh as a daisy.

Owens certainly never found himself in the predicament that his predecessor, John Quinn, found himself in one morning in December 1970. Quinn had worked through the night with Harry Dalton, the general manager of the Orioles, on a deal for prized Baltimore prospect Roger Freed. Quinn woke up with a hangover, a press conference scheduled to announce the team's acquisition of Freed, and no recollection of whom he had traded to get him.

The Phillies made a lot of trades during the golden decade, and I am still not sure whether Owens or Alexander deserved the credit. After all, when a trade was heralded by the fans and media as a good one, Alexander would always come up to me and tell me it was his deal, not the Pope's! It was probably a case where their talents were very complementary—Owens setting the high-level direction, Alexander doing the detail "grunt" work, and the two of them working together to seal the deal.

Alexander, known as "Uncle Hughie," was truly one of baseball's great characters. Given how many characters baseball has had through the years, that is definitely saying something. Hughie was a promising outfielder in the Cleveland Indians organization until he lost the full use of his left hand in an accident. He loved to tell stories and jokes, and the story about how he got injured was fascinating. As he told it, he was working on an oil rig in Oklahoma when his shirt got caught in an oil pump and his fingers got smashed in the pump. He wrapped his fingers with his shirt and had to walk five miles to find an Indian witch doctor. The Indian gave Hughie a bottle of whiskey and told him to drink half of it and pour the rest on his mangled fingers. The doctor then picked up an ax and cut off all his fingers.

He told that story hundreds of times, even though it wasn't even in the same area code as the truth. My son Mike wrote a book on

"Uncle Hughie," and in his interviews with some of Hughie's six wives (yes, six, one of whom he married twice), he discovered that Alexander lost his fingers at a church picnic when his shirt got caught in a pump that was used to put cold well water on watermelon. The hospital was a half block away and had no witch doctors on staff.

Hughie claimed he was the only white man to run a faster 100-yard dash in high school than Jesse Owens. He hit .346 with 17 home runs in Triple A, but only managed one hit in 11 at-bats in the big leagues with the Indians.

I really liked Hughie—he was very entertaining and kept people laughing even though most of his stories turned out to be greatly exaggerated. He also had very strong opinions about players and was usually right.

Phillies on the Rise…but Falling Just Short

By 1974 some of those late nights at the winter meetings were really beginning to pay off. With Dave Cash at second base—joining key players like Jay Johnstone, Ollie Brown, Bill Robinson, Del Unser, Gene Garber, and Jim Lonborg, who were also snagged from other organizations—the Phillies were an 80-win ballclub for the first time in seven years and within hailing distance of first place for the first time in eight years. Cash didn't just bring talent to the ballclub, he brought an upbeat attitude. Coming from the best team in the division, the Pirates, Cash was a winner who loudly proclaimed, "Yes, we can."

In 1975, with Dick Allen back in town, Garry Maddox now patrolling center field, Larry Christenson in the rotation, and Tug McGraw in the bullpen, we were a legitimate contender that gave the neighborhood bullies—those "lumber company" Pittsburgh Pirates—a real scare.

The stage was set for the best stretch of baseball in the Phillies' history. In 1976 we won 101 games and took the division by nine games as Schmidt led the league in home runs for the third consecutive season. In 1977 we won 101 games again and held off the Pirates again as Carlton topped 20 wins for the fourth time in his career. Even though we won "only" 90 games the following year, we captured our third consecutive division title in 1978. There was only one problem—we kept falling short in the playoffs.

In the 1976 playoffs we were just happy to be there...and it showed. We got swept by the Reds as they reeled off seven straight wins to sweep through the postseason and repeat as champions. In 1977 we fell to the Dodgers in four as we suffered through two of our worst losses ever: a Game 3 we should have never lost and a Game 4 that should never have been played.

Game 3 was the most excruciating loss I ever witnessed. The teams split the first two games in Los Angeles, with the Phillies taking Game 1 after blowing a 5–1 lead and then being stymied by Don Sutton, 7–1, in Game 2. The team felt very confident, given how dominant we'd been at the Vet that season. After dropping our first five home games, we had gone 60–16 in Philadelphia.

In the third game in Philadelphia, the Dodgers took a 2–0 lead against Larry Christenson in the second inning, with umpire Harry Wendelstedt blowing a call at home on a play where Steve Garvey scored a run without ever touching the plate. In the bottom of the second with two outs, Dodgers pitcher Burt Hooton got wild—though Dodgers fans, manager Tommy Lasorda, and Hooton himself will tell you that it was Wendelstedt who was the first one to lose his hold on the strike zone. But when Hooton made the mistake of losing his cool and pointing at the umpire after getting squeezed on a call, the die was cast. I will never forget the fans behind home plate yelling and going crazy after every Hooton ball from that point forward. It was so loud and vicious, you almost couldn't hear the television announcers. The Phillies fans actually caused a veteran pitcher to have a meltdown on the mound. He had to be taken out in the second inning after walking four in a row—three of them, including the pitcher, with the bases loaded.

The Phillies plated two more in the bottom of the eighth after the Dodgers tied it 3–3 to take a 5–3 lead going into the top of the ninth. We were three outs away from taking a stranglehold on the series, with our ace, Steve Carlton, rested and ready to put the Dodgers away in Game 4.

I have had nightmares in my life, but none have hung with me longer or more vividly than the nightmare of Friday, October 7, at Philadelphia's Veterans Stadium. Gene Garber gets Dusty Baker and Rick Monday to ground out. Up by three with no one on and two outs, we are in total control. A pinch-hitter, the ancient Vic Davalillo, gets a bunt base hit—at the age of 41. The next hitter, 39-year-old pinch-hitter Manny Mota, down no balls and two strikes, hits a deep fly ball to left field. Left fielder Greg Luzinski backs up to the wall to catch it, and it hits off his glove, off the fence, and back into his glove for a double.

All season long, manager Danny Ozark has put Jerry Martin in left to protect a lead. Not today. He wants "the Bull" in for the last out—even though few if any players nicknamed "Bull" have ever been known for their glovework.

As painful as that play is, it's the next one that is imbedded in my mind forever. Davey Lopes hits a shot at Schmidt at third. It takes a wicked hop off a seam on the AstroTurf and caroms off Schmidt toward short, where Larry Bowa makes a miraculous play, barehanding the ricochet and throwing to first in one fluid motion to end the game.

But umpire Bruce Froemming calls Lopes safe.

All the TV replays show Lopes was out. Bowa, Ozark, and first baseman Richie Hebner go ballistic, but to no avail. Maybe because he knows he blew the call, Froemming doesn't toss any of them from the game.

Garber then picks Lopes off first, but a bad throw sends the runner to second. Bill Russell singles in the go-ahead run. Mike Garman gets the Phillies out in the ninth—though, as if to rub salt in the wound, he does hit Luzinski with a pitch, which prompts Ozark to lift him for a pinch runner: the aforementioned designated defensive replacement, Jerry Martin. I'm so upset, I go back to my office and break my right hand slamming it against my office door.

The next night is another disaster as Carlton loses 4–1 to Tommy John in pouring rain. A rainout could push a Game 5 out to Monday night, and ABC already has *Monday Night Football* holding down that slot. It is a very eerie, gloomy night, but National League president Chub Feeney sits in his box without a raincoat as if to tell the world that it really wasn't that wet. I thought at the time the game should not have been played, and I still feel that way today.

Many people, including myself, believe that the 1977 team was the most talented team in the history of the franchise.

Things didn't go that much better in the 1978 postseason. The Dodgers were our opponents again—though neither Wendelstedt nor Froemming received a return invitation to umpire in the series. We dropped the first two games in Philadelphia, then got off the deck to win Game 3 in Los Angeles and rallied to send Game 4 into extra innings. We ended up falling to the Dodgers again, though, as the normally sure-handed Garry Maddox dropped a line drive in the bottom of the tenth inning.

The Missing Ingredient

We had a great team—with a number of All-Stars and two future Hall of Famers—but there was still something missing. Many people had their theories about what that missing piece was, including me. All I had to do was think back to 1976 during the first game of the National League Championship Series in Philadelphia against the Cincinnati Reds. Pete Rose led off the game against Steve Carlton. He hit a routine single to center field, but he decided to try to stretch it into a double. It was a big gamble, but with sheer guts and determination he slid easily and safely into second base. Though Rose didn't end up scoring, that play intimidated the Phillies and set the tone for the entire series as the Reds handled us fairly easily.

I said to myself then that if the Phillies ever had a chance to get Pete Rose, we needed to do it. With the advent of free agency after the 1976 season, that time would come sooner rather than later.

Free agency significantly changed how a team went about adding talent to their roster. Back in the late '70s, the gap in revenue—and therefore payroll—between teams was much smaller, so there was a much more level playing field for the acquisition of free agents. The Yankees, then as now, were certainly a key player in the free-agent market, but they had much more competition for the top free agents than they do now. And by reaping immediate dividends in their signing of Reggie Jackson before the 1977 season, the belief was widely held across major league baseball that free-agent signings were the key means to propel one's team to a championship.

Simply put, front-office men now needed to do more than "just" make shrewd trades and smart draft choices. Selling established stars on joining your team and outbidding other ballclubs for their services was now part of the job description.

After the 1978 season, Pete Rose became a free agent. Even though he would have preferred to stay in Cincinnati, it was obvious that Bob Howsam and Dick Wagner, the key executives of the Reds, did not want him back. They even went so far as to take out an advertisement in the local paper defending their position. Since Pete was one of the most popular players in the game—not to mention a native of Cincinnati, a member of the 3000 Hit Club, and only a few months removed from a 44-game hitting streak—I wondered what was really driving their thinking. Was it because he was 37, or was there more to it than that? After all, Pete was a great ballplayer, but his off-the-field activities were well known in baseball circles and raised some concerns. Was it his gambling? Was it his womanizing? Did Howsam and Wagner know something that we didn't know?

I went to Phillies owner Ruly Carpenter and general manager Paul Owens with two questions: would they like to have Pete Rose, and could the club afford him? They both gave me the same answer—they would love to have him, at the right price. Rose was making less than $400,000 a year and was looking for a very significant bump. We put aside any concerns about why the Reds were willing to part with a player like Rose and went after him.

I was the point man to try to make it happen because I knew Pete and his agent, Reuven Katz. The mere possibility that we could be courting Pete Rose was already generating a lot of media attention, so we wanted a low-key meeting in a quiet place. At my invitation,

Pete and Reuven flew by private jet from Cincinnati to Philadelphia in November 1978. I picked them up at the airport and drove them about 45 minutes to Ruly Carpenter's house in Delaware.

Ruly, Paul Owens, George Harrison, and I sat down with Pete and Reuven in the Carpenters' living room. After the normal pleasantries, Katz pulled out a videotape of Pete's field accomplishments.

"We don't need to see the tape," I said. "We know what kind of player he is."

Reuven then proceeded to elaborate on how much Pete could help a team promote itself by making public appearances and being colorful with the news media.

"We understand that," Ruly said. "How much money do you want?"

We knew there was going to be a lot of competition for a batting champ and MVP like Rose and that this could drive the price for his services past the $600,000 that Reggie Jackson had gotten on the open market. The stakes were raised even higher by our belief that a lot of the competition for his services would be coming from within our own division. The outcome of this negotiation could very well have a major impact on the balance of power in the NL East.

We heard that the St. Louis Cardinals, owned by Gussie Busch, had offered Pete a Budweiser beer distributorship. The Pittsburgh Pirates, owned by John Galbraith, a noted horse farmer, had offered racehorses. Both of these added perks were in addition to a four-year contract.

Reuven went on to add, "We've been offered seven figures a year for four years by an American League team."

Seven figures!

Ruly, a graduate of Yale University, started counting on his fingers and exclaimed, "My God, that's a million dollars a year! Let's have lunch."

Until Nolan Ryan in 1979, no player had ever been given a salary of $1 million per year. This was almost double what we gave Mike Schmidt in 1977, when we signed him for $3.3 million for six years. The American League team going after Rose was, to the best of our knowledge, the Kansas City Royals. We'd heard that their owner, Ewing Kauffman, might be sweetening the pot with stock in his pharmaceutical company. Like the Phillies, the Royals had built a very solid team that was snakebit in October, losing to the Yankees in the playoffs each of the past three seasons. Like the Phillies, the Royals had probably come to the same conclusion—they were one player away and that player's name was Pete Rose.

Over a very quiet lunch in the Carpenter dining room, Ruly announced, "The highest we can go is $600,000 a year for four years."

Later that day, we held a press conference at Veterans Stadium. More than 100 media types were there to hear Pete Rose and the Phillies announce that he was *not* going to sign with the Phillies. How often do you see that?

I wasn't ready to give up. After the press conference, I took Pete and Reuven back to my office. I gave Pete a dozen red roses for his wife, Karolyn, and Phillie Phanatic dolls for his two children. As I drove them to the airport, I gave Pete my best sales pitch. Since we'd been told by his agent that he had a million-dollar offer on the table from an American League team, I started by explaining to him why he really should stay in the National League.

"Pete," I explained, "if you don't stay in the National League it will kill your good friend, my father."

My father, even when president of the National League, still spent most of his time around his old team, the Reds—especially during spring training—and had struck up a friendship with the ballplayer.

Pete didn't say a word.

"Pete," I said, handing him the National League "Green Book," which I had opened to the records section, "look at all those NL records. You are second in almost every offensive category."

No comment.

"If you change leagues you won't have a chance to be first."

Still nothing, but I could tell he was listening.

"Don't you want your kids and grandkids to know you were first?"

Pete Rose knew his own statistics better than any player who ever played the game, so I was fairly confident this would resonate with him.

"Pete," I said, shifting gears, "your good friends Larry Bowa, Mike Schmidt, and Greg Luzinski really want you as a teammate."

Not a word.

"We all believe we can win a world championship in Philadelphia if you join us."

We had arrived at the airport. As I was walking them to their private jet, Reuven whispered to me, "If you can get Ruly up to $800,000 a year, I think I can talk Pete into signing with you guys."

Nowadays, an $800,000 salary and a $200,000 increase seems like nothing. Hell, the league *minimum* in 2006 was $300,000. But it was real money back then. At $800,000, Rose would be the highest-paid player in baseball history. And that $200,000 increase Katz wanted—that was a 33 percent increase over where we wanted to be. Add a couple of zeroes to it if that helps you understand what kind of hill we had to climb. Any team today—even the Yankees— would have to swallow hard before upping a four-year guaranteed offer from $60 million to $80 million.

Heading back to the office, I had a brainstorm. If Pete Rose signed with the Phillies, our flagship TV station would benefit tremendously with high ratings and more advertising revenue. We could get them to pay us $200,000 more a year for broadcasting rights. I presented my idea to Ruly, and he blessed it. I contacted WPHL-TV, the station that served as the local network for Phillies' telecasts, and presented my idea to them. Within a couple of days they agreed, and we upped our offer to Pete to $800,000 a year. We were at the winter baseball meeting in Orlando, Florida, when the deal was finalized. On December 5, 1978, we held a press conference announcing that Pete Rose was now a member of the Philadelphia Phillies.

The reaction of the fans to the news was amazing. We sold more than $3 million worth of tickets in 30 days. For the 1979 season, we sold more than 3 million tickets for the first time in the 96-year history of the franchise.

Pete Rose: The Good, the Bad, and the Ugly

Rose certainly held up his end of the bargain in 1979. He hit .331 and topped 200 hits for the 10th time in his career, breaking Ty Cobb's record. Mike Schmidt thrived with Rose as his teammate, hitting what was then a career high of 45 home runs. Unfortunately, Rose and Schmidt did not get much support, as a number of key players went on the disabled list. In fact, we lost three pitchers on one day, the Fourth of July: Larry Christenson and Dick Ruthven from arm problems, Randy Lerch from a Center City mugging. We won 84 games and finished in fourth place, 14 games behind the Pirates.

The following year—1980—it all came together. The Phillies won their one and only world championship. Pete was a key player and the leader of the team, inspiring those around him in many ways. When Mike Schmidt was inducted into the baseball Hall of Fame, he gave Pete Rose credit for making it happen. Though he was thought by many to be the best third baseman to ever play the game, Mike didn't realize how good he was. Almost every day Pete would tell him, "You're the best player in the game." Mike always felt that Pete's confidence in him gave him the boost he needed.

During the 1980 season, the *Philadelphia Inquirer* ran an editorial, "Peter Rose for President," extolling Pete's work ethic, determination, and hustle. Once, after returning to Philadelphia from a long road trip at 4:00 AM, he went to the batting cage to take hitting practice because he had gone 0-for-4 in the previous game.

The Phillies converted him from a third baseman to a first baseman, and he would work an hour longer than any other player to hone his defensive skills at first base.

Rose had tremendous concentration and the ability to block out everything except the task at hand. On the day his first wife filed for divorce, Pete went 5-for-5.

Richie Ashburn, the Phillies announcer, wrote in his newspaper column, "It is almost impossible to play every game with intensity. Rose plays every game, every at-bat, and every pitch with intensity. He is a player for all season, all decades, all time."

In 1981 Rose tied Stan Musial's National League hit record of 3,630 on June 10 off of Nolan Ryan. The next day the players went on strike. When baseball resumed 60 days later, Pete broke Musial's record in the first game he played with an eighth-inning ground-ball single to left. One of the 60,561 fans in attendance was Stan Musial, who stepped onto the field to congratulate Pete as the game was stopped. "He's been a credit to baseball," Musial said. "He would have been a great player for the Gas House Gang."

Pete was also great in front of a microphone and with the news media. He had a sharp mind and a quick sense of humor. On the night he broke Musial's hit record in Philadelphia, we had a press conference. We had arranged to have President Ronald Reagan call Pete at the beginning of the conference. Our switchboard operator, Kelly Addario, was having trouble getting the call through, so there was a delay of a few minutes.

While waiting for the call with the cameras rolling and a live feed going out over the radio, Pete said, "Tell him I'm busy." Then, in a reference to one of the president's current headaches—the federal air traffic control operators who were on strike—he added, "The phone operators must be on strike, too." Rose wasn't through, however, observing with a smile, "It's good there's not a missile on the way."

The president's call finally got through. "This is Ronald Reagan."

To which Pete replied, "How you doing? I was going to give you five more minutes."

Despite his many heroics on the field, the sports world found out later that Pete Rose was far from perfect. For one thing, he was a notorious womanizer. During the 1980 season he left free tickets for both his wife Karolyn and his girlfriend Carol (eventually to be his second wife) at the same game. Karolyn, a very good friend of my father's and a friend of mine, stormed into my office.

Karolyn, already knowing about Carol's relationship with her husband, complained, "She's got better seats than I do! You need to do something about it."

She was in tears because, to make matters worse, Pete's girlfriend had hired a plane to fly over the park with a sign that read, "Pete, I love you."

I called Pete into my office and said, "Everyone, including your wife, knows about your girlfriend, Carol. But why do you flaunt it so much?"

He said, "Bill, here's the way I look at it. There are four primary vices: drinking, smoking, gambling, and womanizing. I don't know if you chase women, but I do know you smoke, drink, and gamble. I do not smoke or drink. My only vices are gambling and womanizing. So I'm a higher-moraled [*sic*] person than you."

I really did not have an answer for that.

KAROLYN ROSE

Karolyn Rose was a very memorable person. The first time I met her was in an elevator at the International Hotel in Tampa, Florida, where the Reds held their spring training. Their son Pete Jr. was with her, and my father was with me.

My father introduced Karolyn to me and commented to her, "Petie is really growing up, and he looks like such a nice boy."

Karolyn responded, "Yeah, but he cusses too goddamn much."

I will always remember her kindness. In 1979, when my father was in a coma, dying in a Cincinnati hospital, Karolyn Rose came to his room and held his hand for an hour every day for a month.

Gambling, Pete's other main vice, caused him a lot of trouble.

I went to the St. Petersburg dog track many times during spring training, and Pete was always at the track betting $500 in quinellas. One time he invited me to sit with him and his friend, who was also his handicapper. I bet on the same dogs as Pete—although only $60 a race compared to his $500—and we did not cash one winning ticket. He had a friend, Mario, who would run bets for him at horse tracks, at dog tracks, and with bookies on basketball games. Pete lost more than he won, and eventually he was in serious debt. The bookies started to come after him for their money.

One way that Pete financed his gambling was through paid public appearances I arranged for him. He enjoyed the public adulation as well as the money. However, he always told me he wanted to be paid in cash so his agent wouldn't know about it.

"Bill, my agent has me on an allowance," Pete told me, "and I use this cash for my gambling and women."

It wasn't that Pete was trying to cheat his agent out of money; Katz was paid on an hourly basis, not by a percentage of income like most of the agents. Apparently, Reuven Katz understood Pete's addiction to gambling and was attempting to keep him financially sound by putting him on an allowance and saving or investing his money for him.

I was not surprised when the Feds got Rose for tax evasion. He spent time in prison and, in one of the most infamous and controversial cases to ever come before a commissioner, he was banned from baseball for betting on the games. All of this occurred when he was managing the Cincinnati Reds.

Many people in baseball, including my father, believe that the worst sin for a player, coach, or manager is to bet on baseball games. Ever since the Black Sox scandal of 1919 and the subsequent banning of the "eight men out" by baseball's first commissioner, Judge Landis, betting on games has been viewed that way. There is a big placard placed in every major league clubhouse warning players that they will be suspended if they bet on baseball. Pete broke that cardinal rule.

The special investigator, John Dowd, turned up very damning evidence that Pete bet on Reds games—though his bets were always for the Reds to win. There is no evidence that he ever bet against the Reds or attempted to fix games in the way that the Black Sox did. However, the problem with Pete betting on his own team was that it could, in theory, have undue influence on the game. For example, he could overuse his best pitchers when he had placed a bet on the Reds. I've been told that the bookies figured this out and would bet against the Reds when Pete did not bet on his own team, knowing that the Reds were not fielding their best team on that day. If that's true, then even though he was betting on the Reds to win, Rose's betting was still manipulating the outcome of games.

Pete called me for advice during the early stages of his potential banishment from baseball, and I always said the same thing—"Stand up in front of the world and tell the whole truth no matter how bad it is. Say that you are sorry and ask forgiveness. The public will be forgiving."

But Pete is a very stubborn guy. He wouldn't do it.

I have met a few players who believe they are above the law. Pete Rose is one. It is a shame because he could have been a hero forever. Pete was not blessed with great God-given talent. He didn't run really fast, he did not have a great arm, and he did not have great power. He did it all through hard work and sheer determination—just like the single he stretched into a double to open up the 1976 NLCS. His nickname of "Charlie Hustle" was well deserved.

A year before my father's death, he was asked who was the greatest player he had ever seen. Warren Giles said without hesitation, "Pete Rose."

Like all the other fans of the Phillies who know what Pete did to bring the team its only world championship, I will try to remember him for what he did on the field of play.

The Team That Wouldn't Die

"I never want to go through another year like this one."
—Dallas Green, after winning the 1980 World Series

It Ain't Over Till It's Over

So there we are, three runs up and only two outs away from the first championship in the 97-year history of the Philadelphia Phillies. Given the franchise's ability through the years to snatch defeat from the jaws of victory, no one in the stadium—fans, employees, family members, players on either team, or me—considers this game to be over. Baseball has no clock, and the words of the great philosopher Yogi Berra loom over every pressure-packed late-inning moment: "It ain't over till it's over."

It's Game 6 of the 1980 World Series. The Phillies are up three games to two in the Series and lead the Kansas City Royals 4–1. We have been in total control of the game since Mike Schmidt's two-run single in the third. The great Steve Carlton has pitched us into the eighth inning, holding the Royals to four hits before giving way to our wonderfully eccentric closer, Tug McGraw.

With the field encircled by police horses and dogs to control the crowd, McGraw gets Amos Otis on strikes to start the ninth.

The 65,838 fans at the Vet are in a state of euphoria. The scoreboard reads: "Lord, This Is Heaven."

But when McGraw walks Willie Mays Aikens, doubt inevitably begins to creep in. The doubt turns to dread, and the dread to fear as Tug gives up singles to John Wathan and ex-Phillie Jose Cardenal to load the bases.

Suddenly, the game—and the whole Series, for that matter—is in jeopardy.

McGraw gets Frank White to hit a routine pop foul near the Phillies dugout along the first-base line. Catcher Bob Boone makes the call. The fans hold their collective breath, willing the ball to find its way into Boone's glove for the second out.

Which it does, only to pop back out again.

New Sheriff in the Dugout

When I reflect back on the 1980 season, it is absolutely shocking to be reminded how tumultuous and difficult it was to get to that moment in the ninth inning of Game 6.

Signing Pete Rose prior to the 1979 season was supposed to get the Phillies to the Promised Land because the excellent nucleus of the team—Carlton, Schmidt, Bowa, Luzinski, Boone, Maddox, McGraw, McBride—were still in their prime. Overshadowed by the Rose signing, we had also added second baseman Manny Trillo in a shrewd trade with the Cubs.

Then we went out and finished fourth, 14 games off the pace. We won 84 games, but frankly we were lucky to even win that many. We were outscored for the first time since 1974. Although a lot of the 1979 problems were due to injuries, our manager, Danny Ozark, seemed to have "lost the players." They were running the clubhouse instead of the manager running it—a number of them spending more time in clubhouse card games than in getting ready to play baseball.

I was the one who had recommended hiring Ozark in the first place back in 1973. By 1976 he had the Phillies in the playoffs. No other Phillies manager had ever finished first more than once, and he did it three seasons in a row.

Ozark was a nice, patient man of very high character. Patience is essential for any manager, but especially for one who has a roster of young players. I give a lot of credit to Ozark—and his patience—for helping Mike Schmidt become one of the best players in baseball. In 1973 the Phillies weren't going anywhere, and Schmidt was really struggling, batting .196 for the season and striking out about as often as he hit the ball. Ozark kept writing his name on the lineup card anyway.

"The kid's gonna be a hell of a player," Ozark said. "Anyone can see that he's got a bright future."

Not exactly "anyone." Owens and Ozark both believed in him, but there were plenty who didn't. Danny's patience paid off as Schmidt took off in 1974 and never looked back. From that point on, there was no stopping him, and he ended up in the Hall of Fame.

Unfortunately, our greatest strengths are often our greatest weaknesses. It is not uncommon to see a manager who is adept with young players but only able to take them so far—or to see a manager who is great with veterans but cannot instill confidence in young players. In part because Ozark was so kind and patient, he was not a great disciplinarian. The young players he had nurtured into veteran stars were now asserting greater control over the clubhouse. When they got out of line, took a few at-bats "off," or sleepwalked through a series, Ozark was not the best at confronting them about it. The loyalty to his players that had helped him when they were younger was now working against him.

"I just can't control these guys," Danny would say. "They're making 10 times more money than me."

With the 1979 team sloshing along below .500, in fifth place, under a manager who had seemingly lost control, I suggested in late August to Ruly Carpenter and Paul Owens that we needed a "tough guy" in the dugout. I believed that farm director Dallas Green was the right man. He was tall, blunt, and had a voice like a foghorn.

There were 30 games left in the season when Owens sent Green to the dugout to be interim manager. We had just gone 1–8 on a homestand and were in the middle of a five-game losing streak. Green, who did not really want to manage, did a great job the final month of the season. The team went 19–11, climbing past the Cubs and into fourth place. Owens kept him on in 1980.

If we thought that our strong September under Dallas meant that we were in for a smooth ride in 1980, we could not have been more mistaken. Green felt that the only thing standing between this group of players and a championship was an "attitude adjustment." You could classify the attitudes he was trying to adjust into different types: coolness and selfishness. Green loved fiery, expressive players like Tug McGraw and Pete Rose and (like our fans) got irritated by the players who did not show emotion—what he called "that macho cool crap." As for the selfishness and jealousy that had taken hold in some corners of the clubhouse, Green sent a message right away by hanging a "We Not I" sign in the Clearwater locker room during spring training. While some of the players made snide comments about such a sign being more appropriate for a high school, it was a message that would not be going away anytime soon.

If that didn't get their attention, the new club rules did: curfew and dress code, as well as curbs on drinking, card playing, and whatever Green deemed "unprofessional behavior." All this was done with the full support of Paul Owens and the front office. The only reason the team hadn't been broken up already was that we still believed they were good enough to win a championship. We were just going to do things differently in an attempt to make them less comfortable and more likely to reach their potential. Green told them in no uncertain terms that this was going to be their last chance to "live up to their talent."

Spring training didn't get any easier when, on April 1, the player reps voted to go on strike on May 22 and cancel the remaining eight spring-training games in order to put pressure on the owners to negotiate a new collective bargaining agreement.

When Owens heard the news he called Dallas Green and ordered him to continue on to Cocoa Beach, Florida, where the Phillies were to play an exhibition game. He told Dallas to have the team spend the night in Cocoa Beach and return the next day. Players were not supposed to set foot in their spring training sites, so most of the players on other teams packed their bags and left camp. Not so for the Phillies, as many of them stayed together and worked out at a high school field at their own expense—though Ruly did sneak them some equipment.

Pete Rose, never having been much of a union guy, was a key element of those "illicit" workouts. This didn't go over too well with our player rep, Larry Bowa, or with Bob Boone, who was the National League head of the Players Association. This would not be the first or the last case of players on the 1980 Phillies not seeing eye to eye. Then again, a number of our players had issues with just about everyone— not just each other, but also their manager, the press, and the fans.

Though the threat of a strike still remained, the season started on time and the owners and players finally reached an agreement on May 22 on all but one issue—compensation to teams that lose free agents. In order to allow the play on the field to continue, the owners and players decided to set up a joint committee to study the issue.

When we broke camp and headed north, there were a lot of new faces. As farm director, Dallas knew our minor leaguers very well and pushed hard to keep them on the roster and clean out some of the understated, card-playing veterans who weren't as likely to buy into his system. The unity and commitment that some of the Phillies players showed in spring training—and the infusion of emotion that the kids brought to the bench—didn't seem to help that much when the regular season began. We were very inconsistent, struggling in April, dominating in May, and playing .500 ball in June. At the All-Star Break, we were in second place with a 41–35 record—a half game behind the Expos and a half game ahead of the Pirates.

It was during the All-Star Break—three days that were supposed to be for resting, relaxing, and recharging—that we got another dose of distraction and controversy. The *Trenton Times* across the river in New Jersey reported that a number of Phillies, including Mike Schmidt, Greg Luzinski, Larry Bowa, and Pete Rose, were acquiring illegal amphetamines from a doctor in Reading, Pennsylvania. It created a media circus for a week or so, but no penalties resulted from the story and it eventually blew over.

Our inconsistent play, however, stuck around. We came out of the break by winning three, dropping three, winning three, and dropping six. We were 47–44 and suddenly found ourselves four games behind our nemesis, the Pittsburgh Pirates. Many of our veteran players were chafing under Dallas Green's in-your-face style of leadership.

Unlike Danny, Dallas certainly did not pull any punches. When the players complained about the way he treated them compared to the easygoing Ozark, Green let them have it. "Hell, it's your fault I'm here," Green bellowed. "You're the ones who got Danny fired. You're out of shape. You're playing like crap. Look in the mirror and take some responsibility."

Dallas didn't like the cliques and factions that had formed on the team. To combat that, he had the lockers of his star players moved. The veterans no longer had lockers next to their long-time buddies, but alongside rookies who were pushing them for playing time.

Greg Luzinski had developed leg problems in 1979, so Green got on him about it. While Luzinski came into camp in 1980 in good shape, he didn't stay in shape. So Green stayed on him for his training habits, or lack thereof, and eventually started giving more of Luzinski's playing time to a rookie, Lonnie Smith.

Green also got into it good with pitcher Ron Reed in Pittsburgh in the second game of a doubleheader in August. After the Phillies had dropped the opener, Dallas had gone off on the ballclub between games in such a loud and profane fashion that reporters lingering outside the clubhouse heard every word as they listened in awed silence. There wasn't much love in the air during the nightcap, when Reed showed Green up by stomping around the mound after being ordered to issue a walk. He followed that up by giving up a run-scoring double. When he got back to the bench, words were exchanged, and these two very large men almost came to blows in what would have certainly been one of the great dugout brawls in baseball history. Unlike when Billy Martin went after Reggie Jackson, Green did not need a stool to go nose-to-nose with his player.

Larry Bowa, on the other hand, who gave away about seven inches and 60 pounds to Green—and was frequently yapping at him—could have used it. Bowa had big problems with Green. Though there are many theories for the rift—Green getting on Bowa for caring too much about his fielding percentage, Bowa feeling that Green took management's side in his contract squabble—it probably boiled down to the simplest explanation of all: the two were too much alike.

"I'll say this about Bo, though," Green will tell you today. "For all the problems Larry had with me, he never took them out on the field with him. He never pouted."

Luzinski, Reed, and Bowa were by no means the only players who had issues with Green. Bake McBride—whom we'd been able to acquire from the St. Louis Cardinals because their manager, Vern Rapp, didn't like his hairstyle—certainly wasn't the president of the Dallas Green Fan Club either.

One of the few things that the residents of Green's doghouse could agree on was that they didn't like the way their manager was using the press to chew them out by name. While some managers might have one too many in the hotel bar and let something slip about his feelings for a particular player, Dallas knew what he was doing when he told a reporter exactly what he thought about one of his veteran players. It was intentional, irritating, and effective.

One of those players who Dallas conducted a running feud with in the press was Garry Maddox, who had been one of Ozark's favorites. Though it ended well, 1980 certainly wasn't the most fun Garry ever had playing baseball. The impact of free agency on salaries wasn't limited to owners' wallets, but to players' psyches as they pegged their value to Ted Turner's latest big signing and got frustrated when their team didn't see things the same way. Maddox was a prime example of that. He spent a fair bit of emotional energy in 1980 on an in-season contract dispute—one that Green was not shy about taking management's side on—and we could all see, even after it was resolved, that it was affecting Maddox's level of motivation at times. When Maddox asked out of a game without going to Green directly, he violated one of the new guy's fundamental rules.

"Maddox begged out of a game and didn't go through me," Green said. "So I let him sit for four or five. I ran Del Unser out there instead."

Maddox acknowledges now that he better understands what Green was trying to do. But in the heat of what was shaping up to be another long, underachieving season, mutual understanding was in short supply.

Clubhouse Chemistry

There were plenty of testy exchanges on that team, and not all of them involved the manager. The pitchers didn't like some of the hitters, and the hitters didn't like some of the pitchers. The veterans resented some of the rookies. Quieter players like Carlton—a real loner—didn't care too much for the banter in what was a very noisy clubhouse. Players brought in from the outside—guys who had not been "spoiled" by spending most of their playing careers under an easygoing manager like Danny Ozark and who "got" what Green was trying to do— would get frustrated with some of the homegrown veterans.

"We got guys who think they're toughin' it out if they play with a headache," Rose observed.

With Green refusing to stop preaching "We not I," and many of the players resisting both the message and its delivery, we bottomed out in early August in Pittsburgh. We scored only eight runs in the series, losing all four games, including the doubleheader sweep where Green and Reed nearly went at it. The Phillies had now faded to third place, six games behind the Pirates, and only two and a half in front of the lowly Mets.

Staring at another eight road games over the next seven days, the team could have given up and mailed it in. Instead, they snapped out of it. It was like a switch got thrown. A day after Green's tirade in Pittsburgh, the players held their own meeting in Chicago. Whatever was said, the focus, at last, was beginning to shift toward winning. The players might not have been ready to sit around a campfire holding hands and singing "Kum-ba-yah," but they were more prepared to play up to their potential as a team whether they liked each other or not. Not that it was a carefree waltz to the pennant from that point forward—far from it. In fact, they hadn't even endured their last screamfest. They got one courtesy of GM Paul Owens in San Francisco on September 1. The Pope was so angry at their play in San Diego the day before that he actually challenged the entire team to a fight.

As for what finally happened to turn the season around, Dallas is not one for convoluted explanations. "The talking stopped," Green said, "and the doing started."

You will often hear the topic of "team chemistry" being discussed and how important it is to a team's success. Green, Bowa, or just about any other member of that 1980 team will tell you that's backward.

"Chemistry doesn't create wins," Bowa says. "Wins create chemistry."

"Losing is no fun," Green says. "Winning solves all the problems. It's not all that complicated."

"Winning Solves All the Problems"

There are many great baseball teams that won despite a lack of chemistry. The early-'70s A's and the late-'70s Yankees come to mind, and you can certainly add the 1980 Phillies to that list. Members of that team had an enormous amount of talent all in the primes of their careers—the all-time hits leader, the greatest third baseman to ever play the game, a left-hander who would rack up four Cy Young Awards, and a bushelful of All-Stars and Gold Glovers—and it finally started to show down the home stretch.

"We came together as a team," Green said. "I didn't have to do much managing from that point forward."

Tug McGraw came off the disabled list on July 17 and pitched 52 innings in his final 33 appearances. He gave up only three earned runs, racking up half of his 26 saves during the last two months of the season.

Dick Ruthven, who had come out of the gate slowly, ended up with a career-high 17 wins.

At the age of 35, Steve Carlton had his greatest season since his amazing 27-win performance in 1972, going 24–9 with a 2.34 ERA to win his third Cy Young Award.

"Shake and Bake" McBride hit .309 and knocked in 87 runs.

The "Secretary of Defense," Garry Maddox, played an outstanding center field—even if he did forget to use his sunglasses on occasion. His range had become legendary, prompting Mets announcer Ralph Kiner to observe, "Two-thirds of the world is covered with water, and the other third by Garry Maddox."

Spurred on by Pete Rose, Mike Schmidt hit 48 home runs to set a major league record for third basemen. He added a league-leading 121 RBIs and a league-leading .624 slugging average on his way to being the unanimous choice as National League MVP.

Rookies like Lonnie Smith (.339), Keith Moreland (.314), and Bob "Whirly Bird" Walk (11 wins) made key contributions. None more so than Marty Bystrom, who was called up on September 1 to replace the injured Nino Espinosa in the starting rotation and went 5–0 with a 1.50 ERA.

And even with all those performances, the race still came down to the wire—not with the hated Pirates, but with the up-and-coming Montreal Expos. Philadelphia went 19–8 to close out the season, with Montreal nearly matching us win for win.

We headed into the final weekend of the season in Montreal tied with the Expos for first place. We had gone through an emotionally draining homestand—one in which emotions were raw in the clubhouse, press box, and grandstand, where Dallas had sat Boone, Luzinski, and Maddox in critical games, where we had let the Expos off the ropes by dropping two of three to them, and where Bowa had flashed the home crowd "half of a peace sign" after a 15-inning victory over the Cubs. Thanks primarily to the heroics of Mike Schmidt, who played the final games with the flu, the Phillies won both Friday and Saturday on Schmidt's late-inning, game-winning home runs. It was our fourth division title in five years, but none came tougher.

Although Espinosa was healthy by the end of the season, Paul Owens convinced Nino to claim otherwise so that we could activate

Bystrom for the postseason. Major league rules state that only players on the 25-man roster on August 31 are eligible for postseason
play *unless* a player is on the disabled list at the conclusion of the
season. If so, a member of your farm system may be added to the
25-man roster to replace him. All we ended up doing with Bystrom
was start the kid in Game 5 against Nolan Ryan to close out the
most gut-wrenching series I ever watched.

The Greatest Postseason Series Ever Played

The Astros were making their first appearance in postseason play as
veteran free agents Joe Morgan and Nolan Ryan helped put them
over the top. Their pitching was outstanding, even after having lost
the dominating J.R. Richard to a career-ending stroke at midseason.
They were also one of the weakest-hitting teams of the modern era
to ever reach the postseason. Even the 1965 Dodgers—the gold standard for weak-hitting pennant winners, a championship team whose
best hitter (literally) was pitcher Don Drysdale—managed to hit
more than the 75 home runs the Astros accumulated that season.

They couldn't hit home runs, and they couldn't run out 6'8" James
Rodney Richard in Games 1 and 5, but they were still very much a
threat. What the Astros could do was play "small ball": steal, bunt,
hit, and run—anything to scratch out a run. They had six players with
more than 20 stolen bases on the season: Joe Morgan, Enos Cabell,
their entire outfield (Terry Puhl, Cesar Cedeno, Jose Cruz), and their
backup second baseman (Rafael Landestoy). In addition, they had the
home-field advantage in the series and—now that they were filling the
Astrodome again—played in the loudest ballpark in baseball.

The first two games of the series were in our place, which wasn't
the easiest place to play either. Game 1 pretty much resulted as
expected—right down to the opening ceremonies, in which Bowa
and Maddox wouldn't shake Dallas Green's hand during the
pregame introductions. Between the lines, Steve Carlton pitched
well, Tug McGraw got a save, and Greg Luzinski hit a two-run
home run. The Phillies prevailed 3–1, which was as close as this

series would get to a blowout. The next four games were all extra-inning games with many twists and turns.

In the ninth inning of Game 2 in Philadelphia, with the score tied at 3–3, McBride and Schmidt singled, and Lonnie Smith hit a soft line drive to right field that dropped in front of Terry Puhl. McBride was held up at third by third-base coach Lee Elia to the surprise of 65,476 fans and Houston pitcher Frank LaCorte.

"When he hit the ball, I figured the game was over," said LaCorte. "I was already starting off the mound."

There was LaCorte, head down, dejectedly heading toward the visiting dugout thinking his team was down 0–2 for the series, when he spotted McBride still on third.

"As soon as the ball was hit, I took off because I didn't think Puhl would catch it," said McBride. "I got a step from third and Lee told me to stop. I stopped and he said, 'Go!' You know, by the time he says go, it's too late. It's just one of those things."

"It was no fault of Bake's that he didn't score," Elia admitted. "My hands went up as if to say 'stop,' and at the same time, I said, 'No, come on.' He saw my hands go up and stopped."

Houston scored four in the top of the tenth to even the series at 1–1, and then won Game 3 in Houston 1–0 in 11 innings. We brought Tug McGraw into Game 3 in the eighth inning, and he was gassed by the time Joe Morgan touched him for a leadoff triple in the eleventh.

In Game 4, facing the possibility of going home for the winter a few weeks early yet again, the Phillies trailed the Astros 2–0 in the eighth inning. The Astros were six outs away. Our ace, Steve Carlton, was already out of the game. We hadn't scored in 18 innings, stranding 16 base runners. In a series filled with moments when fans all over the Philadelphia area thought, "Here we go again," this may have been the low point. Things were not looking good for us at all.

I was already emotionally spent, having gone nuts in the fourth inning. With men on first and second, Garry Maddox hit a soft line drive back to Houston pitcher Vern Ruhle. The Phillies entourage was sitting by the third-base dugout, and we could all see Ruhle had trapped the ball. But when he threw to Craig Reynolds covering second, who then threw on to first, Doug Harvey ruled a triple play.

Are you kidding me?

Pope was so mad that Ruly had to keep him from charging down onto the field. But Carpenter could only restrain one of us, so I ran through the stands from our box by third base to a first-base box where National League president Chub Feeney was sitting.

"Goddammit, Chub!" I yelled at the top of my lungs. "Ruhle trapped that ball. That's no triple play."

So was it a triple play, a double play, or just one out? The umpires conferred with Chub Feeney for what felt like hours before ultimately arriving at what seemed more like a compromise than a definitive ruling. The call was changed from a triple play to a double play, but we failed to score anyway.

I didn't have much of a voice left when, in the top of the eighth, pinch-hitter Greg Gross sparked a rally with a leadoff single. We strung together some singles, knocked out Astros starter Vern Ruhle, and went ahead 3–2. With Warren Brusstar trying to close the game out, the Astros played the "small ball" they'd specialized in all season—leadoff walk, bunt, run-scoring single—to tie the game at 3–3. It was their first hit since the fifth inning—and it would prove to be their last hit of the game—but it certainly came at the right time for them.

In the tenth inning, Pete Rose did his thing. Rose singled, and Luzinski hit a pinch double down the left-field line. Rose never broke stride and gave Astros catcher Bruce Bochy a forearm to the face to score the go-ahead run. The Phillies won 5–3 to even the series 2–2, with a winner-take-all Game 5 on Sunday.

After the game Philadelphia Eagles coach Dick Vermeil said, "Rose could play linebacker for me tomorrow."

As wild as Game 4 was, Game 5 was the most emotional game I have ever witnessed. The game lasted three hours and 38 minutes—which, back then, was a marathon—with 80 percent of the TV households in the Philadelphia area watching. And, just like Game 4, we were deep in a hole in the late innings.

Now if you wonder what the front office does during games like this, it wasn't much different than most hardcore fans—we ate hot dogs, drank a beer or a soda, and acted like nervous wrecks. The Phillies entourage that sat with me was Ruly Carpenter, Paul Owens, Hugh Alexander, George Harrison, and our wives. During the most nerve-wracking moments there was very little discussion—we were studying every pitch, worried to death, knees shaking, knuckles white, afraid to say much of anything. We also had our superstitions. If we had won the game before, we sat in the same seat and wore the same clothes.

The Phillies actually led 2–1 as late as the sixth inning, going up in the second inning on a two-out, two-run single by Bob Boone. Houston tied it in the bottom of the sixth on an unearned run, then plated three in the bottom of the seventh. With pinch runner Dave Bergman on third after an Art Howe triple, Ron Reed bore down to get Alan Ashby and kept the Phillies within three runs. Even three runs seemed like a nearly insurmountable lead, with Nolan Ryan on the mound for Houston. His record with a late-inning lead was nearly perfect.

Larry Bowa got us started with a leadoff single, and we loaded the bases without getting a ball out of the infield. Boone scratched out an infield single, and Greg Gross, acting on his own, laid down and beat out a bunt. Ryan, rattled—if that was even possible—walked Pete Rose to force in a run. With a 5–3 lead now, Astros manager Bill Virdon called on left-hander Joe Sambito to face Bake McBride, while Green responded by pinch hitting Keith Moreland. Moreland grounded into a force play that scored Boone to make the score 5–4. Virdon then called on Ken Forsch—the Game 1 starter—to face Mike Schmidt with a man on third. A fly ball would tie the game, but Forsch got Schmidt looking, and the spirits in the Phillies box began to sag. It looked like the Astros were going to wriggle out of this one.

Del Unser pinch hit for the pitcher, Ron Reed, and singled to right to tie the game. Then Manny Trillo followed that up with a triple to left to score two more runs. Down 5–2 against Ryan, we had put five runs across to take a 7–5 lead. The Phillies that Green had felt were too calm and cool were spilling out of the dugout, pumped and delirious. The Astros couldn't possibly bounce back this time, right?

Wrong.

The Astros strung together enough singles in the eighth against McGraw to tie the game at 7–7. In the top of the tenth, Del Unser came up big again. He hit a one-out double off LaCorte and scored on a two-out double by Garry Maddox. Dick Ruthven—the Game 2 starter—retired all six batters he faced to be the winning pitcher in one of the greatest games ever played. The Phillies were heading to the World Series to play the Kansas City Royals.

And the World Series Wasn't Too Bad, Either

The tug of war and dramatics of that electric Houston series created the greatest anticipation for a World Series in baseball history, resulting in the highest World Series TV ratings ever.

Kansas City was an outstanding team, winning their division by 14 games and sweeping the Yankees team that had beaten them in the ALCS the three previous times they faced each other. But it was the Phillies that had captured the imagination of fans throughout the world. Royals third baseman George Brett was about the only marquee player on the Kansas City team, as he flirted with .400 most of the season—ending up with a .390 batting average with 24 home runs and 118 RBIs. Brett was also getting a lot of media attention because he was playing the entire postseason with a bad case of hemorrhoids.

If the Phillies were either tight or exhausted, you couldn't tell it from our closer, Tug McGraw. He was showing up in our sales office before Games 1 and 2, with glove and in full uniform, to help answer the phones. The biggest problem for Game 1 at the Vet was not our mental condition, but the physical state of our starting pitchers. The Phillies' top pitchers had all been "spent" in the LCS. Who would pitch Game 1?

Manager Dallas Green went with rookie Bob Walk, the first rookie in 28 years to start a Series opener. Not having pitched since the regular season, Walk was understandably rusty, allowing four runs in the first three innings. But, as the Phillies had been doing for the last six weeks, they roared back from a 4–0 deficit to take the lead. It all started with a decidedly unconventional move made by a player acting on his own. Larry Bowa singled and took off for second on the third pitch, sliding in safely with a stolen base.

"I knew if I was out," Bowa said, "I might as well keep running."

It was a crazy thing to do, and it lit a fire under a team that was still emotionally hung over from the Houston series. We ended up putting five across in the third on Royals ace Dennis Leonard, capped by a three-run home run by Bake McBride. We took a 7–4 lead, then hung on for a 7–6 victory as Tug McGraw shut the Royals down in the last two innings.

Game 2 was another come-from-behind victory for the Phils. Steve Carlton was not at his best, and the Royals held a 4–2 lead going into the eighth inning. The Phillies scored four in the bottom of the eighth off Royals closer Dan Quisenberry, thanks to yet another key pinch-hit by Del Unser followed by big hits from Bake McBride and Mike Schmidt.

It was great to see Schmidt plate the go-ahead run in front of the home crowd. They had gotten on him a lot in '76, '77, and '78 as he struggled at the plate in the NLCS. Prior to the Houston series, his postseason batting average was below .200, and he was homerless with only four RBIs in 11 games. Even in the Houston series, he had managed to hit only .208 with one RBI. As Schmidt himself put it, "It was Rose who led us in the playoffs. I was just a spectator."

We were off to Kansas City on our team charter. As was the case all season, and even more so in the postseason, we had an enormous amount of quality food and wine and beer. For those who liked hard liquor, it was a custom for them to have it hidden in their briefcases. For the Kansas City trip, we invited all of our scouts, front-office employees, player personnel instructors, and key sponsors to come along. We had a blast. We had parties before and after each game, winning many points with our sponsors and our staff in the process.

Before Game 3, the biggest question was whether Royals star George Brett would be able to play. He'd been forced to leave Game 2 because of his hemorrhoid problem, but he did play. He hit a home run in the first inning and made an outstanding defensive play at third base. After the game, Brett declared, "My problems are behind me."

Despite a valiant effort by Dick Ruthven and the first postseason home run of Schmidt's career, the Royals won 4–3 in 10 innings on a big hit by Willie Mays Aikens off Tug McGraw.

Game 4 might have been the best loss in Phillies history, even though the Royals had pulled even in the Series—all because of one pitch thrown by reliever Dickie Noles. Larry Christenson had been knocked out of the box in the first and the Phillies trailed 5–1 in the fourth inning. With an 0–2 count on Brett, Noles threw a 95 mph fastball at Brett's head, knocking him right on his butt with dirt flying.

Kansas City manager Jim Frey came storming out of the dugout, yelling for the umpires to throw Noles out, while Pete Rose charged in from first base to confront Frey. Although the Royals held on for a 5–3 win, that pitch seemed to change the momentum of the Series. Brett had been 6-for-11 before getting flipped, 3-for-3 afterward.

Game 5, with the Series tied even at two games apiece, was huge. Green gave Carlton an extra couple of days' rest by gambling on rookie Marty Bystrom. Bystrom, as he'd done since we called him up late in the year, came through again. It was a real nail-biter, as the Phillies trailed 3–2 going into the ninth inning. Our guys got to Quisenberry again, with Schmidt, Unser, and Trillo delivering key hits—all on playable balls—to put us up 4–3 going into the bottom of the ninth.

We were counting on Tug McGraw, in his third inning of relief, to yet again close out the game. And McGraw, as always, made sure to keep things interesting. He walked two batters—while striking out George Brett in between—and then faced the very underrated and very dangerous Hal McRae with the game on the line. McRae hit a bomb out of the park, but it was just foul. My heart—and all of Philadelphia's—was pounding at 100 mph. McGraw, always loose, pounded his left hand on his chest to let us know we weren't the only ones whose hearts were racing. "The Tugger" ended up getting McRae out, walked Amos Otis to load the bases, then faced Jose Cardenal with the game on the line. If that wasn't interesting enough on its own, McGraw added even more drama when the bat slipped out of Cardenal's hand and rolled out toward the mound. McGraw grabbed the bat and, in the process of handing it back to him, stuck him in the gut with it. McGraw was jamming Cardenal with everything else during that plate appearance, so why not the bat? Tugger struck him out to end the game.

"Everybody knows McGraw is crazy," Cardenal said later. "Jab me in the stomach with my own bat."

The overworked McGraw had a different explanation. "I'm mentally exhausted. It's a good thing I don't pitch with my brain or I'd have to soak my head in a bucket of ice."

We certainly earned our nickname—the Team That Wouldn't Die— in Game 5. It was our 14th consecutive game decided by one or two runs. Flying home to Philadelphia, I was feeling confident that the Phils would win their first World Series in history with Carlton on the mound, momentum on our side, and more than 65,000 people cheering us on. The players were confident, too.

"Tug, Lefty's going tonight, and I know we are going to win," Schmidt told McGraw as they were driving to the stadium for Game 6. "And I know you will be in there at the end. So I have a favor to ask of you."

"What is it?" McGraw asked.

"Every time I see a picture of a championship on the cover of *Sports Illustrated*, there is always a picture of the winning pitcher jumping into the arms of the catcher. When you get that final out, I want you to jump into my arms."

The mood before and during Game 6 was a combustible compound of fear and anticipation. Even during batting practice you could feel the energy in the stands and in the Phillies clubhouse. It even managed to look easy for a while, with Carlton dominating and the Phillies up 4–0 going into the eighth inning.

It was then that Wilson Goode, the managing director of the city of Philadelphia and future mayor, walked into my box. "We are going to bring the horses and dogs onto the field now," Goode explained.

To which I responded, "The horses are okay, but please don't bring the dogs on the field. It will make Philadelphia look like some sort of police state."

"I have to protect city property," Goode replied. "I'm bringing the dogs."

And he did.

It was really surreal to see the police, all with helmets on, surrounding the perimeter of the field on horses or with German shepherds. A few of the horses were relieving themselves right on the warning track in the middle of the game. A new ground rule was needed—animals were in play.

Even Carlton—who pitched with earplugs and whose concentration was legendary—might have been disturbed by this bizarre scene. The first two Royals reached base in the top of the eighth, and he was replaced by McGraw. Frank "Tug," "the Tugger" McGraw had already earned a new nickname—"Tylenol Tug"—when he revealed during the Series that he was taking six painkillers every morning to help the pain in his arm due to his almost daily pitching in postseason games.

Tug got out of the eighth allowing just one run, but the ninth inning was very, very, very interesting. With one out, a walk and two singles loaded the bases. It brought Frank White to the plate and manager Green to the mound.

"Hey, Tug," Green told him, "let's not make this son of a bitch overly exciting."

Trying to heed his manager's advice, McGraw got White to hit a pop-up toward the Phillies dugout, right in front of one of the police department's German shepherds. Catcher Bob Boone and first baseman Pete Rose converged on the ball. The ball popped out of Boone's glove, but the alert Rose caught the ball. It became one of the signature plays in Rose's career and certainly the most famous play he ever made with a glove.

"You know, everyone gives Rose all the credit," Boone said a few years later, "but it was really his play in the first place."

McGraw only had Willie Wilson standing between him and the 27th out of Game 6, but Tug was running on fumes. No reliever before or since, not even the great Mariano Rivera, had been asked to play as much a role over as many innings in as many close post-season games as McGraw. If he could get past Wilson, he would have saved four of the Phillies' seven postseason wins—to go along with his win in Game 5 of the World Series. As Tug acknowledged later, he was planning to call Dallas out to get him if he didn't retire Wilson. With a 1–2 count on the speedy left fielder—who had been flailing away futilely at Philadelphia pitching all Series—McGraw reached back and threw one final high fastball past him for the final out of the first world championship in Phillies history. And, true to his word, McGraw waited for Schmidt to get to the mound and into the picture.

The entire Philadelphia region, including my family and me, celebrated into the wee hours after the Phillies' finest victory in history. The *Philadelphia Inquirer* front-page headline captured the scene in six simple words that had been a century in coming: "Phils Win Series, City Goes Wild."

The Parade

What happened the next day was as overwhelming as the end of Game 6. Phillies players, staff, and all employees boarded flat-top trucks behind the Philadelphia Museum of Art to begin one of the most emotional and heart-warming rides of my life. As we all traveled down the parkway to Broad Street, all you could see were beaming faces. Delirious people in Phillies jerseys and hats. People hanging off of any structure that would carry their weight and afford them a better view. People throwing flowers. People getting out of wheelchairs to get near the players or to touch the trucks that were carrying them. We had never seen so many people in our lives. Or seen such unabashed joy.

When we rounded the corner and pulled into JFK Stadium (which is where the Wachovia Center now stands), we saw another 60,000–70,000 people. The absentee rate of school kids throughout the Delaware Valley must have been off the charts. The celebration reached its crescendo as Harry Kalas introduced the entire team. Ruly Carpenter, Paul Owens, Dallas Green, Mike Schmidt, Bob Boone, and Larry Bowa all spoke, but the most memorable moment was Tug McGraw's final message as he held up the *Philadelphia Daily News*, which had a two-word headline on its front page: "We Win."

"New York," McGraw exclaimed, "You can take this championship and stick it!"

A Valley between the Peaks

Claudell Washington's Role in Phillies History

The 1980 championship was the high point of the golden decade of Phillies. The team won more games between 1974 and '83 than any other team in baseball and played 36 postseason games. For the rest of their history, they've played 21.

Thirteen years passed between center fielder Willie Wilson's swing and a miss to end the 1980 World Series and center fielder Lenny Dykstra's walk to open the 1993 classic. Those two seasons are the most exciting in Phillies history, but a fair bit happened in the years between. On March 7, 1981, fewer than five months after winning the World Series, Ruly Carpenter shocked the baseball world and Phillies Land by announcing that the team was for sale. The Carpenter family bought the franchise for $400,000 in 1943 and was one of the longest-standing baseball families left in the big leagues. The Carpenters were growing fearful of skyrocketing salaries, and they weren't alone.

The Cincinnati Reds and Oakland A's—winners of each World Series played from 1972 to 1976—had let their stars walk away via free agency rather than pay them the increased salaries that free agency was creating. The Griffith family, whose ties to the Minnesota Twins extended back 60 years to the Washington Senators, wouldn't pay those salaries either and found it increasingly difficult to field a competitive team. Philip Wrigley dismantled the Cubs in the late

1970s before selling the team, unloading what stars they had rather than pay the going rates.

"No ballplayer is worth more than $100,000, and I'm not sure they're worth that much," Wrigley said. "The time is approaching when big-league clubs will have to be subsidized by local subscription in the manner of opera companies and symphony orchestras."

Those comments may seem silly now in the context of today's baseball reality. But in the late '70s, player salaries were exploding while the enormous growth in television revenue—a growth that would eventually lead to some star players making $100,000 *per game*—was just not on many people's radar screens. Simply put, it was a very disconcerting time to be an owner.

The final straw came for the Carpenters when Atlanta owner Ted Turner gave reserve outfielder Claudell Washington a $700,000 contract after the 1980 season. It was a seemingly outrageous amount a quarter century ago. Washington had played seven mediocre seasons in the big leagues, accumulating all of 57 home runs, and was being rewarded with an annual salary in excess of what the Yankees were paying Reggie Jackson.

"I just don't think you can continue to operate this business paying players this kind of money," Ruly said. "I can't fault players and agents for taking this kind of money, but I can fault my peers for giving it—including myself."

The very next day I asked Ruly if he and his family would sell the Phillies to me if I could raise the money. He told me they would definitely like to sell to a "baseball guy" like myself. So I flew back to Philadelphia to pursue my dream of running a major league baseball team, refusing to let the minor detail of my net worth being $50,000 stand in my way.

How to Buy a Major League Team for $50,000

A few years before, I'd been having cocktails with a couple of sports lawyers and lamenting my woes about not being able to run the entire operation of a major league team. They explained to me that a guy with my reputation in the baseball community could buy a team without putting up any significant money of his own. They said I could get 10 percent ownership and run the club by raising money from rich folks who wanted to be involved in owning a sports team.

That really got me thinking. Since I did not believe the Carpenter family would ever sell the Phillies, I had first focused my attention elsewhere. When a rumor went around that Phil Wrigley was going to sell the Chicago Cubs, I thought very seriously about taking a run at them. I always thought the Cubs were a sleeping giant. They didn't even try to sell season tickets and did no marketing. But by the time I got up the courage to pursue the purchase of the Cubs, the Tribune Company bought the team.

So when the Phillies actually did end up on the market, I wasted no time in going after them. I formed a team of three: Phillies lawyer Bill Webb, my right-hand man Dave Montgomery, and me. Dave and I worked on an income statement for the Phillies, projected out 10 years, to present to prospective partners. It was amazing how accurate our projections turned out to be, except for two line items in particular—player salaries and television revenues. Both numbers grew to be much, much larger in a few years than what we had anticipated. I believe the technical term that financial analysts use is "humongous."

Bill Webb worked on an outline of a Pennsylvania partnership agreement, with me as the general partner owning 10 percent of the club and all other investors being limited partners owning the other 90 percent of the team—a common arrangement. I would have complete autonomy in running the team for a minimum of seven years. The limited partners would receive:

free tickets in the owner's suite to all Phillies games (with dinner included, and we weren't talking a dog and a beer)

a free trip to spring training

two VIP parking spaces

the fun of owning a piece of a major league baseball team (without the headaches of being the general partner!)

With the help of my accountant, some friends in the banking business, and the law firm of Ballard Spahr, we made a list of 200 wealthy people in the Philadelphia area. I actually knew only about 10 of them and had heard of about 40 more. We also studied our season-ticket-holder list for people or companies who might be candidates.

When I asked Ruly how much the family wanted for the team, his response was, "What anybody will pay." I estimated that price would be in the neighborhood of $30 million, for two primary reasons. First, the New York Mets had sold for $21 million a year before. Second, Mike Megna of the American Appraisal Associates said that a major league franchise in a one-team market the size of Philadelphia was worth more than a team like the Mets in a two-team market—especially when the other team in the market was the New York Yankees.

Having established a target price, Bill Webb and I started to make calls to the list of 200 prospects. Sometimes we would make individual presentations, and often we would have five or six prospects for dinner in a private dining room at the Union League to tell them our story. We asked for a minimum investment of $1 million with no maximum.

It was fairly easy to get people interested at the million-dollar level, but I soon discovered that I could not have more than five partners. This was because of the Pennsylvania Securities Act, which states that if you had more than five purchasers of partnership interests then you had to go public with all financial statements of the selling party. The Carpenter family did not want the public to know how much the Phillies had made or lost over the years or what their net worth was.

This made the task much more difficult because I had to raise the minimum investment to $5 million. People like Roger Penske (now the famous race-car guru and multimillionaire), Harold Yoh, and Herb Middleton were interested in only a $1 million investment, so they dropped out. Fitz Dixon, former owner of the Philadelphia 76ers basketball team and part owner of the Philadelphia Eagles, and Bob Levy, an entrepreneur and an owner of racehorses and race-tracks, were in for a million, but they got together and said they would form their own entity and put in $3.5 million if we needed it. Brothers Jim Buck, Bill Buck, and Alexander Buck had a family partnership in which they did a lot of venture capital investments. They were season-ticket holders and big baseball fans. They were the first to commit to the $5 million investment.

So I now had $8.5 million committed, but I was struggling to find more investors willing and able to come up with the funds I needed. The fact that all signs were pointing toward a players' strike that could wipe out most of the 1981 season certainly wasn't helping any.

Bob Hedberg represented Jack Betz, who owned Betz Laboratories, a water-purifying company. Bill Webb and I went to Hedberg's office in Paoli, Pennsylvania, and presented our case to him for Mr. Betz to consider. While we were there, he called Mr. Betz at his home.

"Jack, I have some clown by the name of Bill Giles in my office who wants you to invest $5 million in the Phillies."

"Bob, you know I am more of an Eagles fan than a baseball fan," Betz replied.

It might have been another "0-fer" for Webb and me if not for Jack's wife, Claire. Claire overheard the conversation and said, "Jack, I love Tug McGraw and the Phillie Phanatic, we need a better parking pass for the Eagles, and we've invested $5 million in dumber things."

It wasn't easy for Jack to argue with that kind of logic.

Sold!

So now I had $13.5 million committed but continued to really struggle to get the rest. Most of the people I reached out to would not even talk to me.

With my contact list running out and three other groups trying to buy the team—one led by real estate developer Herb Barness, another led by paper company owner Ben Alexander, and the third led by Chuck Barris, a TV personality who owned and hosted *The Gong Show*—things were looking bleak. Barness approached me to join with them, but I knew that if I did so my control of the team would be diminished, so I declined.

In mid-May I tried a new tack. I would ask for a $10 million to $15 million commitment from CBS Radio or the two independent TV stations in Philadelphia. In exchange for their investment, the Phillies would sell them radio or TV rights for 11 years.

Bill Webb and I negotiated an 11-year radio rights deal with CBS. The payment would be made annually, or they would pay us $19 million up front. Our thinking was that we would use the up-front money to buy the team and would relinquish the annual payments if we could not find investors.

It turned out that we did not have to use that option.

The Provident Publishing Company (owners of Channel 17) and the Taft Broadcasting Company (owners of Channel 29) both had interest in our proposal. On June 15, 1981, I received the most important phone call of my financial, and perhaps my baseball, life. It was from Dudley Taft, the president of Taft, which was head-quartered in my hometown of Cincinnati, Ohio.

"Bill, the Taft board met last night and decided to invest anything you want up to $30 million to help you buy the team."

Hallelujah!

My dream of running a baseball team was now much closer to becoming a reality.

We met with the Buck brothers, Betz, Dixon, and Levy to explain the Taft call. They did not want any entity to own more than 50 percent of the partnership, so we settled on accepting $15 million from Taft, giving me $28.5 million in equity. We accelerated $3 million in payments from the CBS radio deal and used half of that for working capital and the other half to make a $30 million offer to the Carpenter family—the highest price for any major league team up to that time.

It took some time to negotiate the TV deal with Taft, but by August we made our offer and on October 28, 1981, it was announced that the Bill Giles Group was the new owner of the Phillies.

Boy, was I on cloud nine!

An Unhappy Bowa

At the press conference I announced that one of my goals was to have the Phillies be the Team of the Decade for the 1980s. It seemed like an achievable goal at the time. We had won the World Series in 1980 and made the playoffs in 1981—taking the Expos to five games, until Gary Carter's bat and Steve Rogers's right arm proved too much for us.

Achieving that goal would require some difficult and, at times, flat-out unpleasant decisions. My introduction to the not-so-fun part of being a general partner was the fallout from a promise Ruly Carpenter had made to Larry Bowa.

"Ruly promised me a four-year extension," Bowa told me, "at $400,000 a year."

I asked Ruly about it.

"I told Bowa I would give him the extension," Ruly replied, "if I still owned the team."

Though Bowa had been a key member of the Phillies since 1970, he was about to turn 36 and his skills were going backward. I did not believe a four-year extension made sense, and I told him so.

Larry didn't care for that answer.

He went to the news media and called me a liar and a few other unpleasantries. Having a star shortstop who is a very unhappy camper and calling you a liar in public did not seem like the best way to start a new regime, so I looked around for a team that could use a shortstop. It didn't take long to find the right place for Bowa.

Dallas Green had taken over as president of the Cubs just a month before. Even though he and Bowa had butted heads a bit when Green was managing the team, Dallas was trying to change the atmosphere in Chicago and felt that bringing in a proven winner like Bowa would help his efforts. We agreed that a straight-up swap of Ivan DeJesus for Bowa wasn't fair because DeJesus was seven years younger. Green wanted us to throw in a prospect, and he said he would take any one of five young players, including a kid named Ryne Sandberg.

Our own people were not that high on Sandberg, who had been a 20th-round pick in the 1978 draft. The consensus scouting report on Sandberg from our baseball people was that he couldn't hit well enough to play third and couldn't field well enough to play second. History shows that we were all wrong on Ryne Sandberg. Even the Cubs had some of the same concerns that we did, toying with the idea of converting him to a center fielder.

This move was not very popular in town, not so much because of that "throw-in" named Sandberg but because Bowa was a fan favorite in Philadelphia. It just got even worse as time went on and Sandberg became a great player and a Hall of Famer. The play of DeJesus, a fellow who turned out to be wrapped a bit too tight for a place like Philadelphia, seemed to get worse in lock step with Sandberg's remarkable ascent. With Sandberg establishing himself as the best player in baseball by 1984, Ivan's error total climbed higher and higher. In what I guess could be considered an act of mercy, we traded him to St. Louis at the beginning of the 1985 season.

The Wheeze Kids

In 1982 we came very close to being back in the postseason for the sixth time in seven years. Though we got off to a terrible start in April and fell way behind the Cardinals early, we battled back and eventually took over the lead in the division. When we were winning—like in May and July—we were an "experienced" team. When we struggled, we were an "old" team. Our bullpen "committee" featured Ron Reed (age 39), Tug McGraw (age 37), and Sparky Lyle (age 37). Carlton was 37 years old and still dominant, winning 20 games for the final time. Rose was holding down first at age 41, but there wasn't much left in his tank. What pop we generated at the plate came from three sources—Mike Schmidt, Bo Diaz, and Gary Matthews—who combined to hit two-thirds of our home runs.

Even so, we were in first place as late as August 11, until the Expos knocked us out with a doubleheader sweep the next day. Still, the team didn't give up. We fell behind the Cardinals by as many as three and a half games, only to fight back and take over first place again in early September. When we beat the Pirates on

September 10 while the Mets were holding off St. Louis 2–1, we were back in front with three weeks to go. St. Louis took the lead back, then we beat them at the Vet on September 13 to go in front again. They took the final two games of that series, and the see-sawing at the top of the NL East stopped. They pulled away and didn't look back.

The 1982 Cardinals were a younger, faster, and more balanced team than we were, with future Hall of Famers Ozzie Smith at short-stop and the unhittable Bruce Sutter in the bullpen, former batting champion Keith Hernandez at first, and old friend Lonnie Smith blossoming into a star in left field. They would go on to win the World Series in seven games. If the press thought we were too old in 1982, they hadn't seen anything yet.

The design of the 1983 team really started in September 1982 when I was on vacation with my wife and friends in Williamsburg, Virginia. I spent just about the entire vacation on the phone with my former boss, Gabe Paul, trying to trade for right-handed pitcher John Denny of the Cleveland Indians. Phillies fans were happy—but my wife was not.

To that point, John Denny's career had been fairly ordinary, and he'd been downright lousy in 1982. But my top scouts, Hughie Alexander and Ray Shore, were very high on him. Denny bounced back from a poor 1982 season to win the Cy Young Award in 1983. He was the main reason the Phillies won the pennant that year, winning 19 games and losing only six. And I didn't have to give up that much to get him: a guy named Wil Culmer, who ended up going 2-for-19 in his big-league career, and two pitchers, Jerry Reed and Roy Smith, who would combine to win 10 games for the Indians.

I made a blockbuster, six-player trade on December 9, 1982. Unlike most six-player trades the Phillies have been involved in through the years, five of the six players were heading out of town and only one was heading in. Again, it was with Cleveland and my old boss, Gabe Paul.

Here's what I thought Gabe was getting: a solid but past-his-prime second baseman (Manny Trillo), a reserve outfielder (George

Vukovich), a minor league pitcher we weren't real high on (Jay Baller), a minor league catcher we weren't real high on (Jerry Willard), and a 24-year-old shortstop we suspected was older than that and who had a very awkward batting stance that we didn't think would allow him to hit major league pitching (Julio Franco). While the first four players didn't end up amounting to much, Franco is still playing as this is written—at the age of (at least) 47, with more than 2,500 hits, and he is the proud holder of the records for oldest man to hit a home run and oldest man to steal a base.

In return we got a young, sweet-swinging outfielder–first baseman who was only 24 and was being heralded as the next Ted Williams. I thought I had made the trade of the century. As it turned out, Von Hayes had a few good years but was certainly no Ted Williams. Hayes was referred to by the media and the fans, derisively, as "Five for One."

Gabe Paul kept telling me how his wife, Mary—who helped raise me—loved Hayes and that he might have to get a divorce over this trade. I think he told me this so he would get more in return.

You see teams making a lot of trades with one another not just because there is a fit in terms of players but because there is a fit between the general managers. If you're dealing with a GM who has wildly different assessments of players or who you don't feel is being honest with you, you're going to have a hard time doing any business. I always enjoyed dealing with Gabe because he was tough, reasonable, and ethical, but by no means a pushover.

For the same reasons, I really enjoyed dealing with Bobby Cox when he was the general manager of the Braves in the late 1980s. He would always be very honest and open when making a deal. If he felt a player had issues or limitations, he'd tell you. His open-and-honest approach certainly didn't keep him from making the Braves better; his acquisition of John Smoltz for Doyle Alexander is one of the greatest trades ever made. I have enormous respect for Bobby Cox, not just as a GM but also as a manager. He is a great baseball man.

Rather than let the team continue its downward trend, I orchestrated still more player moves to overhaul the Phillies. Pitchers Mike

Krukow and Mark Davis and outfielder C.J. Penigar went to San Franciso for my old friend Joe Morgan and closer Al Holland. I signed free agents Bill Robinson, who was 40, and Tony Perez, who was 41.

During that season we made three other important trades. On May 22 we traded relief pitcher Sid Monge to the San Diego Padres for outfielder Joe Lefebvre. The same day, we traded pitchers Dick Ruthven and Bill Johnson to the Cubs for reliever Willie Hernandez, and on August 31 we traded pitchers Ed Wojna, Marty Decker, Darren Burroughs, and Lance McCullers to San Diego for outfielder Sixto Lezcano and pitcher Steve Fireovid.

All of these player moves proved to be very important in the success of the 1983 team. When we went out and made the playoffs for the sixth time in eight years, our unexpected success earned the team a very memorable nickname. In a tribute of sorts to the young, pennant-winning Phillies team of 1950 ("the Whiz Kids"), the 1983 squad of aging veterans came to be known as "the Wheeze Kids."

Like many baseball seasons, what was expected to go right went wrong, and what was expected to go wrong went right. Von Hayes and Pete Rose were mediocre, Mike Schmidt hit only .255 (though he did lead the league in home runs with 40 and drove in 109 runs), Steve Carlton lost more games than he won for the first time in 10 years, Gary Matthews hit weakly, and the team batting average was an anemic .249. Joe Lefebvre gave us a bit of a lift, hitting .310 after coming over from San Diego and getting a chance to play.

We did it with pitching—the team's ERA was 3.34 and Denny, Hernandez, Reed, and Holland all pitched brilliantly and far better than we expected.

And if all that wasn't topsy-turvy enough, I fired our manager while the team was in first place. I believe I am the only team president to ever do that. When I took over the reins of the Phillies, I wanted to keep Dallas Green as manager, but he moved on to the Chicago Cubs to run their baseball operation. As he departed, he recommended that I hire coach Pat Corrales as the Phillies new manager. I did that, and Corrales got a lot out of the team in his first season. But by 1983, Corrales had become very distant from his players.

"I hate most of these guys," Corrales would tell me.

I did not like the idea that the manager hated most of his players, so I fired him in mid-July despite the fact that the Phillies were in first place. Though we were in a good spot, it wasn't like we were hitting on all eight cylinders. We were tied with the Cardinals, the Pirates and Expos were right on our heels, and we were only one game over .500.

I asked general manager Paul Owens to take over the team, and the team responded magnificently. A team this old was supposed to falter in the dog days of late summer, but the opposite happened. The Phillies won 11 in a row and 14 of their last 16 games in September to win the National League East by six games.

The road to the World Series was not going to be easy since the Phillies had to face their nemesis, the Los Angeles Dodgers, who had won 11 of the teams' 12 meetings during the 1983 season and had kept Philadelphia out of the World Series in 1977 and 1978.

It was redemption time, particularly for Pete Rose—who was playing his final season in a Phillies uniform—and for Gary Matthews, who had a less-than-mediocre regular season. "Sarge" Matthews was absolutely awesome and carried the team in the Series. He hit .429 with three home runs and a record-tying eight RBIs. He was named the MVP of the Series as the Phillies won three out of four games, scoring seven runs in each of the last two games at the Vet. Carlton—another player coming off a disappointing regular season—won two games, allowing only one run in $13^2/_3$ innings. Schmidt and Rose chimed in with key hits, Holland pitched great in relief, and the Pope headed to the World Series as a manager for his first time.

"Nobody gave up," Owens said. "Even after all the baloney we went through, everybody kept at it. To me, this is a season I will never forget."

The energy in the crowd for the fourth and final game at the Vet was unbelievable and reminded me of the night when the Phillies won the World Series in 1980. The standing ovation that Matthews received when he hit a three-run home run in the first inning was the loudest I have ever heard.

More so than the three World Series the Phillies played in at the Vet, it was the three League Championship Series—1980 against Houston, 1983 against Los Angeles, and 1993 against Atlanta—that were the most exciting and entertaining baseball games I have witnessed in my 70 years of baseball. And I must admit I celebrated a bit much after the final game and asked my wife to drive me home.

Unfortunately, the World Series against the Baltimore Orioles was not nearly as much fun. There was not the excitement in the stands like the NLCS, and I still don't know why. The Phillies won the first game when John Denny out-dueled Scott McGregor, winning 2–1 as Joe Morgan homered in the sixth inning and Garry Maddox hit a game winner in the eighth. We lost Game 2 but still felt pretty good going home to Philadelphia with the Series tied at 1–1 and Steve Carlton, who had pitched superb baseball in the LCS, on the mound.

Game 3 will be embedded in my mind forever for two things that occurred. The first one was Pete Rose's agent, Reuven Katz, frantically coming into our pregame party to tell me that Pete was not in the starting lineup and that he was going ballistic in the clubhouse. Owens was going with Tony Perez instead of Rose to face Orioles left-handed pitcher Mike Flanagan because Rose had not been swinging the bat well from the right side.

"You've got to call Owens and tell him to put Rose in the starting lineup," Katz insisted.

"I don't make out the lineup cards," I replied, "and I won't interfere."

The other incident involved the field tarp, and I still believe that a hole in it could have cost us the entire Series. The score was 2–2 in the seventh inning, and the Orioles had a man on second with two outs when Dan Ford hit a routine ground ball to shortstop. Just as the ball got to Ivan DeJesus, it hit a puddle in front of him and skidded through his legs as the winning run scored. It had rained before the game and the tarp was covering the field, but there was a big hole at the shortstop position that caused the error.

The final two games of the Series were anticlimactic as the Orioles won 5–4 and 5–0. The Orioles batted only .213 in the Series, but the

Phillies batted a measly .195. Schmidt, in particular, really struggled in what would be the final postseason series of his career—going 1-for-20 with zero RBIs and six strikeouts. The only highlight of those final games was that Game 5 drew the largest baseball crowd in Philadelphia baseball history—67,064.

It was not the greatest year of my baseball life, but I have to say that the way we beat up on the Dodgers in the NLCS—after they knocked us out in 1977 and 1978—definitely goes on my list of the top 10 thrills of my career.

MY TOP 10 BASEBALL MOMENTS

10. Watching the great Karl Wallenda tightrope walk at the Vet
9. The love between the fans and both Mike Schmidt and Richie Ashburn when they were inducted into the Hall of Fame in Cooperstown in the same year
8. Accepting the plaque for my father when he was inducted into the Hall of Fame
7. Opening the Astrodome in 1965
6. Opening Citizens Bank Park in 2004
5. Winning the 1983 NLCS against the Los Angeles Dodgers
4. Signing Pete Rose
3. Buying the Phillies in 1981
2. Winning the 1993 NLCS against the Atlanta Braves
1. Winning the 1980 World Series and riding in the parade through Philadelphia

The End of an Era

This Series, in many ways, represented the end of an era in Philadelphia. We wouldn't be back in the playoffs for another 10 years. I released Pete Rose three days after the World Series ended. His Big Red Machine teammates, Morgan and Perez, were both gone soon after. By 1984, Schmidt was the only member of our starting lineup who played for the

1980 team. By the end of the season, Carlton and McGraw were the only members of the pitching staff who dated back to 1980—and McGraw had thrown his last pitch in the big leagues. We ended up in fourth place at 81–81, collapsing in September.

It was time to try to rebuild.

Hughie Alexander was my key talent evaluator in the early '80s when Paul Owens was managing and Dallas Green had left for Chicago. Hughie was right more often than he was wrong, but when he was wrong he could be *way* wrong. We had a young left-hand-hitting outfielder named Steve DeAngelis who was hitting .370 with a lot of home runs in the minors, so I sent Hughie to scout him for a few days. When Hughie returned to give me his report, he walked into my office shaking his stub hand at me like he always did when he was excited.

"Bill, that kid DeAngelis can hit," Hughie said. "He is going to be the next Mel Ott."

Turns out he wasn't even the next Ed Ott.

We went into spring training with very high hopes for him, and he did not do well at all. We sent him down to AA Reading, where he put up some pretty ordinary numbers, and we ended up releasing him the next year. I should have known that he wasn't going to be much of a hitter when I was paired with him in my annual team golf tournament and he couldn't hit the ball more than 10 feet.

Another young player we thought we could build our team around for the rest of the decade was outfielder Jeff Stone. He was one of the sweetest and most humble players I have met. He had been brought up in a very small house in Missouri with 15 people living with him and no indoor plumbing. "Stoney" arrived in the big leagues in 1983 after showing fantastic potential in the minor leagues, stealing 123 bases one year and 93 the next year. In only nine games with the Phillies he stole four bases and hit .750.

Stone's naiveté showed up frequently and immediately. I was sitting with Stoney and Pete Rose in 1983 on a bus at the Montreal airport that took passengers from the terminal to the plane.

Stoney said to Pete, "Pete, this plane has no wings."

I took him to dinner in Chicago in 1983, and the waiter asked him if he'd like a shrimp cocktail.

Stoney replied, "I don't drink!"

That same time in Chicago, the team bus drove by Lake Michigan. Stoney asked me, "Mr. Giles, is that the Atlantic or the Pacific Ocean?" While playing winter ball in Venezuela he asked, "Is that moon the same as the one in Missouri?"

He had a television set in Venezuela but left it there.

"Why didn't you take the TV set home with you?" he was asked.

"They only talk Spanish on it," he replied.

Everyone saw Stoney's potential, and everyone really liked him. And, because of that, everyone tried to help him become a better player. The more advice he received, the more confusing the game became for him. Paul Owens recognized how confused Stoney had become.

"Stoney, stop listening to everything people are telling you," Owens said. "Just go up to the plate, see the ball, and swing."

That worked for a while, and in 1984 he hit .362 and stole 27 bases in only 51 games. Local papers were referring to this as the beginning of the "Stone Age." It wasn't to be.

What a sweetheart he was. Everyone wanted to see him succeed because he was such a good guy. However, mental mistakes really made him a detriment to the ballclub. As a result, Jeff Stone lasted with us only through 1987 and was out of the big leagues before he turned 30. I believe he is now a policeman in Missouri.

Stone wasn't the only one who kept things interesting. We acquired a pitcher from the White Sox before the 1987 season who some folks in the organization thought could blossom into a star in Philadelphia. He'd been 21–8 over two seasons with the Yankees before the White Sox got him. Unfortunately, the longer Joe Cowley stayed in the big leagues, the harder it was for him to find the plate. By the time he got to Philadelphia, he was an absolute train wreck.

In fewer than 12 innings, he gave up 21 hits and 17 walks. His ERA was 15.43. We weren't ready to give up on him, so we sent him to a psychologist out in Arizona. It was the same guy who handled Steve Sax when the Dodgers' second baseman couldn't throw the ball to first base. After a few days, I called the doctor to check in.

"So how's Joe doing?" I asked.

"Well, Mr. Giles, I don't really know."

"You don't know?"

"I can't find him," the doctor explained. "He took my Cadillac and is shacked up in Vegas with my secretary."

Needless to say, Cowley, Stone, and DeAngelis were not exactly the second comings of Carlton, Schmidt, and Luzinski.

A Dust Bowl in the Farm System

The success the Phillies enjoyed in the golden decade—with the Carltons, Schmidts, and Luzinskis—can be attributed to two things: the solid core of young players our organization drafted and developed and the willingness of Hughie Alexander and Paul Owens to trade prospects for one key guy when we had a chance to win the pennant.

The struggles the Phillies endured from 1984 through 1992 were because of our inability to restock that depleted farm system. Winning consistently resulted in lower draft picks—draft picks that we were not converting into big-league regulars. While professional basketball and football drafts have produced a number of first-round flops and legendary blunders (Sam Bowie drafted ahead of Michael Jordan comes to mind), compared to baseball drafts, they are an absolute certainty. For example, if you can convert only three of 10 first-round picks into big-league regulars, you're doing great. Kind of like hitting—which is appropriate, given that they say that baseball is about successfully dealing with failure.

Unfortunately, we were well below the Mendoza Line (a phrase coined by George Brett for batting .200, a level that shortstop Mario Mendoza often failed to reach) with our first-round picks. Since snagging Lonnie Smith in 1974, we'd selected the following players in the first round: Sam Welborn, Jeff Kraus, Scott Munninghoff, Rip Rollins, Lebo Powell, Johnny Abrego, John Russell, Ricky Jordan, Pete Smith, Trey McCall, Brad Brink, Pat Combs, and Jeff Jackson. There are some names in there that even the most devoted of Phillies fans won't recognize. It wasn't until 1990, when we got Mike Lieberthal, that we broke out of our slump and turned a first-round pick into a big-league regular.

We weren't doing much better in the lower rounds of the draft, either. Since signing Juan Samuel as an amateur free agent and drafting Darren Daulton in 1980, the only regular our organization was able to develop in the 1980s was Mickey Morandini. There is only so much you can do with free agency and trades, and it began to show up in our win-loss records. By 1988 and 1989, we were a 90-plus loss team, and we were running through managers fairly frequently.

Our fans certainly weren't shy about voicing their displeasure. It's not much fun being the owner when the team is doing badly. You don't even want to go out. When the team is doing badly and I'm out and about, I'll hear "What's wrong with *your* Phillies?" But when the team is going well, I'll hear, "Boy, *our* Phillies are doing great."

At the ballpark, our passionate supporters were taking out their frustration on players such as Von Hayes, who cared more than his laidback approach suggested, free-agent disappointment Lance Parrish, or shortstop Steve Jeltz and his lifetime .210 batting average.

Perhaps the guy who had it roughest was a shortstop who came after Jeltz, Juan Bell. Bell joined the team in 1992 and wasn't all that bad. But in 1993, it was a nightmare. He was our Opening Day shortstop but made a lot of errors the first week of the season. The local sports radio station, WIP—which is not exactly known for its calm and rational discussion of the events of the day—hammered him mercilessly. This just made the fans boo him even more—so much that he couldn't handle it and we had to send him out of the league. Juan left town with the kind of fielding percentage that hasn't been seen much since the dead-ball era—.909.

The Makings of a Modern-Day Gas House Gang

However, just like in the early '70s, there were signs of good things to come in the late 1980s and early 1990s—if you knew where to look. June 1989 would be a good place to start. We went 9–17 on the field—which was actually an improvement over our May effort, if you can believe that—but we won big in the front office.

I was traveling with the team on a western road trip, which I typically did about once a year. A player caught my eye in San Diego. He was splitting time with the Padres between first base, right field, and left field. In batting practice he would hit line drives everywhere. During one game I was watching, he was playing right field, and he caught a fly ball by diving into the bullpen in the right-field corner. I said to myself that this fellow was a real "gamer," and I would like to have him on the Phillies.

On June 2, new GM Lee Thomas, whom we had hired away from the Cardinals, brought him to Philadelphia. Though John Kruk was only hitting .184 at the time and not playing regularly, Lee Thomas acquired him, along with Randy Ready, for Chris James.

"Bill Giles, president of the Phillies," I said when I was first introduced to him.

"John Kruk, ballplayer," he replied.

Kruk became a fan favorite right away as we stuck him in the lineup and he hit .331. Sixteen days later, we traded Juan Samuel—a player I loved—to the Mets for center fielder Lenny Dykstra and reliever Roger McDowell. Unable to decide who would be their regular center fielder—Dykstra or Mookie Wilson—the Mets ended up trading them both and going with Samuel. Juan had been great for us from 1984 to 1987, but his career faded fast right when he should have been heading into his prime—as the league figured out that you didn't need to throw him a strike.

The same day, we traded reliever and former Cy Young Award winner Steve Bedrosian to the Giants for Terry Mulholland, Dennis Cook, and Charlie Hayes.

In December 1989, we raided the Padres again—this time for an infielder languishing in their farm system. This took place during what is called the Rule V Draft—named for a rule that was put in place to keep teams from "sitting on" minor leaguers. After a certain number of years, players who had not been added to the team's 40-man roster were exposed in the Rule V Draft. An opposing team could draft away a Rule V player—but could keep him only if they left him on their 25-man big-league roster all season. Dave Hollins only hit .184 for us in 1990 after we drafted him, but he was a productive regular by 1992.

In 1990 we traded pitcher Jeff Parrett to the Braves for Dale Murphy—one of the nicest guys to ever play the game and who, during his time in Philadelphia, prompted Kruk to describe the Phillies as "24 morons and a Mormon." Murphy was once one of the league's best players, but when his bat speed went, so did both his batting average and his power. It was a player to be named later in that trade who made the most impact for us—a pitcher and former first-round pick of the Braves, Tommy Greene, who would throw a no-hitter for the Phillies and win some big games for us in 1993.

Lee Thomas spent most of 1992 acquiring much of the rest of our 1993 staff—all in minor deals. In April, we sent Jason Grimsley to the Astros for a talented young pitcher from Alaska who "could not put it together"—Curt Schilling. In May, Thomas traded Donnie Elliott to the Braves for Ben Rivera. In November, it was Joel Adamson and Matt Whisenant to the newly formed Marlins for veteran left-hander Danny Jackson. And in December, it was Mike Hartley to the Twins for David West.

The pitchers we traded away won four games in 1993.

The pitchers we traded *for* won 47.

Add to the mix some under-the-radar players we'd picked up along the way—Mariano Duncan, Pete Incaviglia, Jim Eisenreich, Mitch Williams—and we had the makings of one of the most popular teams in Philadelphia sports history.

A modern-day Gas House Gang.

Last to First

Colorful Renegades, Throwbacks, and Macho Row

I always liked players who were colorful and fun to watch. I was never particularly fond of players like Eddie Murray, John Olerud, and Todd Zeile. They were good, consistent players, but they lacked that extra flair that some guys have. What do I mean by flair? Think of Willie Mays chasing a fly ball, hat flying off. Think of John Kruk's at-bat against Randy Johnson in the All-Star Game. Think of Pete Rose diving headfirst into third base. Think of Mitch Williams "pitching like his hair is on fire."

By 1992 Lee Thomas was able to assemble a group of players with flair, but we finished dead last because many key players got hurt. In 1993 these colorful renegades stayed healthy, won 27 more games than they had in 1992, and took the pennant. Only three other teams in baseball history had gone from last place to the World Series the very next year. What a ride we had in 1993.

Lenny Dykstra, John Kruk, Darren Daulton, David West, Larry Andersen, Mitch Williams, Dave Hollins, Danny Jackson, Pete Incaviglia, Jim Eisenreich, Mariano Duncan, Curt Schilling—the list goes on and on—gave the team a special persona that the fans and I just loved. They were brash and exciting and we won a lot of games, sometimes in miraculous fashion. And we drew more than 3 million fans. The '93 Phillies attendance averaged more than 39,000 at home games, attracted more than 50,000 fans 16 times,

181

and had eight sellout crowds in cavernous Veterans Stadium. We were getting day-of-the-game walk-up sales of 15,000.

The city was in love with this team. There was someone for everyone. The ladies loved Daulton—and the men wanted to be him. The burly slo-pitch softball players could see two of their own in Incaviglia and Kruk. For anyone who ever had to overcome a serious obstacle in life, Jim Eisenreich—who battled Tourette's syndrome— was an inspiration. If you were a bit crazy, you might find yourself drawn to Mitch—though, as you'll see, he wasn't even the second biggest nutcase in that clubhouse.

That team had many nicknames, including the "Broad Street Bellies." When we ended up in the playoffs against the Braves— self-proclaimed "America's Team"—we were dubbed "America's Most Wanted Team." We were also known variously as "Blue-Collar," "Crazies," "The Nuthouse," "Gypsies, Tramps, and Thieves," and "Throwbacks."

"We're throwbacks, all right," John Kruk said. "Thrown back by other organizations."

Outside the organization, hopes were not that high for the Phillies in 1993 after having missed the postseason every year from 1984 on. The 1992 season had started with high hopes, new uniforms, and a huge Opening Day crowd—only to have Lenny Dykstra end up on the disabled list after being hit with the second pitch. It was pretty much all downhill from there. After the 1992 season, we went after David Cone and Joe Carter, with the perception that we ended up having to "settle" for Danny Jackson and Pete Incaviglia. With no big-name signing made over the winter, we were being written off by many before spring training even started. Fortunately, our players didn't put much stock in what was written in the papers.

None of the pundits could foresee the way this team would come together with one goal—play today, win today. The team's special camaraderie started in spring training. After home games at Jack Russell Stadium, 10–15 of the veteran players would go out for a beer and some conversation. After away games, the regulars who hadn't made the trip waited around for those who had—something that pretty much *never* happens. They talked about what had to be done to win games, and they also talked about their personal lives. They became a truly close-knit gang of veteran leaders known as "Macho Row." Though these players were close, they were not a clique; younger players like Mickey Morandini and, later, Kevin Stocker, were brought in, not excluded. It was a team of diverse personalities, but those differences were respected—provided you played hard and put the team first. You can find plenty of examples of teams that get along well but don't produce on the field, but this team's togetherness really seemed to help them be successful.

They got on each other—players and coaches alike—with just about everyone getting a chance to laugh at themselves at some point. Mariano Duncan got on his teammates about how they dressed and how badly they tried to dance. Mitch was especially good at taking a joke, whether it was a coach telling him during a drill on intentional walks to just be himself or John Kruk (frequently) threatening to kill him for making things too interesting in the ninth inning.

Nicknames—Or Are They Insults?

Just about every player and coach on the team had a nickname, and few were flattering. Along with Dutch, Nails/Dude, Krukker, Schil, and Wild Thing, there was also Grandpa, Load, Beaker, Tankhead, Big Bird, and Tomato Face. We even had not one but two players named after serial killers: Jim Eisenreich, a perfect gentleman whose teammates just happened to think looked like noted cannibal Jeffrey Dahmer, and Danny Jackson, who was nicknamed Jason because he would occasionally transform into a creature out of the *Friday the 13th* movie series. Tearing his shirt to shreds and flexing his muscles until his neck looked like it would explode or attacking a bus luggage rack with his head—those were just a few of Jackson's finer moments. And it wasn't Jackson—or Dykstra, Kruk, or Mitch—who was considered the most psychotic force in the clubhouse.

That honor belonged to Dave Hollins. He'd told the pitchers the season before that he didn't want to get suspended again for charging the mound—so if any of them failed to retaliate for a hitter being thrown at, he'd charge them in the clubhouse instead. Given his frightening intensity, they all fell into line. No one wanted to mess with Hollins.

Jokes, nicknames, and threats of bodily harm aside, when things got heated on the field those guys had each other's backs. We even had bench-clearing brawls in spring training—*three of them.* You see, the pitchers were taking Hollins very much at his word.

When I see these players now, they all have many fond memories of that season and their teammates. You'll even find that players like Danny Jackson—who pitched for many teams, winning championships in Kansas City and Cincinnati, and spent relatively little time in Philadelphia—still thinks of himself as a Phillie because of that year and that ballclub.

The Dutchman

On a team of great players and memorable characters, catcher Darren Daulton was one of my favorites. Daulton, who was a skinny 165-pound kid from Kansas when we signed him, became one of the toughest players I ever knew. He had to come back from seven knee operations, but he became one of the top catchers in the game and extremely popular with the fans—particularly those of the female persuasion.

"Dutch" had become the leader of the team, and I could sense something special was happening that spring. He was going to be a free agent at the end of the season, so I sat down with him in my office at Jack Russell Stadium in late March and gave him a three-year extension at $5 million a year. The negotiation was *mano a mano* with no agent directly involved. After I extended his contract, he called me Uncle Bill. From then on, the entire team all referred to me as Uncle Bill.

"A Joy to Be Around"

When we played the better teams that spring, there was an unusual effort to win the games, and the winning feeling we created carried over to the start of the season. We opened the season by sweeping the Astros in a three-game series in Houston. By the end of May, our record was 34–15.

You could really feel the extra determination and effort of that 1993 team. The clubhouse was usually filled with loud music blaring from a boom box atop Curt Schilling's locker. After most night games, you would find half the team in the trainer's room with a keg of beer and buckets of fried chicken, talking baseball until the wee hours. On a couple of occasions, Uncle Bill joined in the fun. Most owners, me included, treat the clubhouse as the players' office and try not to intrude. I found myself spending more time in the clubhouse that year than any other season. I genuinely liked those guys.

Others who were around them a lot felt the same way. Harry Kalas and Richie Ashburn loved that group of players. Ashburn regularly set up blackjack games at the back of the plane, where you could find Dykstra, Andersen, Daulton, Kruk, and Williams. If you got blackjack, it was your turn to deal, and whenever Richie dealt, no matter what cards he turned up, it was "Nothing there, nothing there, nothing there, read 'em and weep, boys."

Unlike another wild bunch from that era—the '86 Mets—the '93 Phils truly were, in Harry's words, "a joy to be around." That team could be raucous, arrogant, funny, feisty, and nasty, but they could also play the game of baseball about as well as any team to put on Phillies uniforms.

Because the Phillies were so focused on winning, manager Jim Fregosi was able to run a loose clubhouse. It is a characteristic of many successful teams that they are self-policing, and Dutch certainly took the lead in that. It is also true of many successful teams that the manager will allow the team's leaders to instill order in the clubhouse, something Fregosi encouraged. Daulton let the guys have their fun—and they certainly had a lot of it—but he made sure they were ready to play. In a team without many rules, that was Fregosi's only one: be ready to play. And if you weren't—or if you were popping off in the press or anything else that took the focus off the team's objective—he'd let you know about it. If a player tried to take advantage of the lack of rules, he'd have Dutch and the other veterans in his face. As a result, the off-field antics of that team—unlike, say, the Mets post-1986—didn't end up taking any games out of the win column.

Home Away from Home

It probably helped that most of the team's off-field antics took place in the clubhouse. Those guys made it their home away from home. Kruk even made it a habit to spend his Saturday nights there rather than go home and turn right around for a day game on Sunday. It was here that the team staged its belching contests (where Larry Andersen was truly Olympian), planned its pie fights (no one was off limits, not the GM and not me), and ate like fiends (David West's ability to put away ridiculous quantities of food had him likened by a teammate to a wood chipper). It was here that the team gathered after most games—usually in the trainer's room where Daulton would sit icing his knees—to talk baseball, drink beer by the pitcher, and smoke. Choir boys they weren't. They stayed so long after games that the clubhouse staff—who would have to stick around to lock up after them—eventually had a second exit punched through the wall—one with a door that locked by itself.

Not surprisingly, that quirky bunch was very superstitious. Dykstra would discard batting gloves and chewing tobacco after every out. He might even change his entire uniform in midgame. He limited his at-bats in spring training out of fear of "using up his hits" before the regular season started. Fregosi kept wearing his warmup jacket for games, even throughout the summer. Players weren't allowed to get haircuts or shave. When Larry Andersen was presented with Harry Kalas's alcohol-permeated tie in the clubhouse after we clinched the pennant, he kept it in his locker—hung just so, home or away, and smelling quite pungent—for the rest of the season. Even the execs got in on it. The front office and I would watch the games from the executive box, flipping our ties over our shoulders in the late innings when we needed some runs.

"People think we have a bunch of loose cannons," said Fregosi. "That's simply not true. If crazy is running out ground balls, playing hard, and getting the uniform dirty, then, yeah, we're crazy."

TRYING TO PUT IT INTO WORDS

The 1993 team certainly gave the press a lot of material to work with. Many tried to capture what it was like to be around that group of players:

"They're sloppy, grubby, and always stuffing their faces with something."
—Mike Downey, *Los Angeles Times*

"If John Kruk, Lenny Dykstra, Darren Daulton, and Pete Incaviglia were in the same grade-school class, they would not be allowed to sit together."
—George King, *Trenton Times*

"Whatever the Phillies sink their teeth into—beer can, sandwich, or the other team's throat—they stay with it and shake and chew and swallow until it is all gone. Then they burp and ask for seconds."
—Bill Lyon, *The Philadelphia Inquirer*

"They have stubble on their chins and tattoos on their arms and look a little like a slo-pitch softball team in town for a state championship tournament."
—Neil Hohlfeld, *Houston Chronicle*

"The Phillies, all hairy and lumpy, look like the supporting cast in a biker movie about the softball team from a slaughterhouse. They scratch a lot and adjust their underwear on TV."
—Ron Green, *Charlotte Observer*

"Oh, they be bad. They be bold. They be ballsy. But most of all, they be comely as a baboon's butt."

—Rosie DiManno, *Toronto Star*

John Kruk's rebuttal:
   "I'm not a model. I don't get paid to look good. You go to a rock concert and a lot of people look like that, but they can't play ball."

First Pitch: 1:26 AM

And there were many crazy moments.

On April 26, the Giants had us 8–0 when their pitcher woke the team up by spiking the ball after snagging the third out of the fifth inning. We came back to win 9–8 in 10 innings, despite 14 walks issued by our pitchers.

On April 29, Milt Thompson robbed the Padres of a grand slam in the eighth inning in San Diego to preserve a 5–3 lead. Some players called it the greatest catch they'd ever been on hand to see.

The next evening in Los Angeles, Mitch came in to try to nail down a 7–5 victory. He wasted little time in loading the bases with no one out, only to be bailed out by a different defensive hero as Mickey Morandini dove for a line drive up the middle and turned it into an unassisted double play.

On Mother's Day, the Vet erupted when Mariano Duncan hit a grand slam off elite closer Lee Smith in the eighth inning to erase a 5–2 deficit against our division-rival Cardinals.

On June 20, we ran our Sunday record to 11–0—a performance Fregosi attributed with a straight face to "clean living."

Of all the strange moments that season, nothing will top the evening of July 2—and morning of July 3. We were coming back from a rough road trip that was capped off by two routs at the hands of the Cardinals. It was so bad, Daulton had to call out his team in the press for the first time all year. With half of our lead frittered away in a month, the papers and airwaves were filled with talk of 1964. The players aired things out before the first game of the July 2 doubleheader, fingers pointed at themselves and not each other.

If they were eager to take their frustrations out on the Padres on the playing field, Mother Nature had other ideas. Rain fell relentlessly all day. There were three rain delays, totaling more than five hours, and the first game did not end till 1:00 AM, with San Diego winning 5–2. The second game started at 1:26 AM, and almost all of the 54,617 fans had left the park. But once word spread that history was in the making, hundreds of fans flocked back to the stadium. Last call in the local watering holes probably had something to do with it, too. The game ended at 4:41 AM, the latest finish in big-league history, with the Phillies winning, 6–5, on an improbable tenth-inning single by relief pitcher Mitch Williams—off future Hall of Famer Trevor Hoffman, no less.

Major League Baseball instilled a rule the next year that stated that no game could begin after midnight. Incredibly, just four days later (July 7), the Phillies won another marathon, beating the Los Angeles Dodgers 7–6 in 20 innings on Dykstra's two-run double. I was still listening at about 3:00 AM Philadelphia time. Fresh from the minors, pitcher Mike Williams threw six innings, allowing one run, and got carried to the clubhouse for coming up so big.

On August 1, we had Nostalgia Day at the Vet as we tried to bring back the 1930s with baggy uniforms, FDR, and vintage jazz music. Unlike most days in the 1930s, the Phillies won—beating the Pirates. Another day, another hero—this time it was backup catcher Todd Pratt who hit two home runs.

In early September, we broke the National League record of 150 consecutive games without being shut out. It was a season in which the Phils led the division for all but one day, and for the first time in club history held down first place on May 1, June 1, July 1, August 1, and September 1. The Phillies' 97 wins were the third-highest total in franchise history. We were considered a "Cinderella" team because the Phillies had finished last in 1992, but this was not a team that won with smoke and mirrors. They had a single-minded focus on winning at the expense of everything else, including personal statistics. *Especially* personal statistics. And whenever any players started to get hung up a bit on personal accomplishments, Daulton was there to set them straight—like the time at midseason when he felt two of our better young pitchers were letting a preoccupation with making the All-Star Team affect their performance. After jacking one of them up in the clubhouse after a game and telling the other one on the team charter how badly he wanted to kick his ass, Dutch had them back in line.

The 1993 team was not just fun and cohesive, they were physically talented and mentally tough. The '93 Phillies led the league in runs, hits, total bases, and grand slams. They scored more runs than any National League team since the 1962 San Francisco Giants. In pitching, the club was first in complete games and strikeouts.

Five players each reached double figures in wins, the first time since 1932 that the Phillies achieved such a feat: Curt Schilling (16), Tommy Greene (16), Ben Rivera (13), Terry Mulholland (12), and Danny Jackson (12).

Lenny Dykstra led the league in runs (143), hits (194), and at-bats (637).

Darren Daulton knocked in 105 runs.

John Kruk (.316), Lenny Dykstra (.305), Jim Eisenreich (.318), and rookie shortstop Kevin Stocker (.324) all topped .300.

All impressive, but how exactly do you quantify the selflessness that propelled this team to the postseason? Perhaps the most revealing stats on a team that didn't care about stats were bases on balls and the production we got out of second base, left field, and right field.

Lenny Dykstra, Darren Daulton, and John Kruk all drew more than 100 walks. They worked pitchers relentlessly, driving many starters out of the game in the middle innings, and the rest of the team took their lead from them. If the team's biggest hitting stars could take pitches for the good of the team, then the rest of them figured they could do the little things it takes to win, too.

As for the production out of our second basemen, left fielders, and right fielders, it wasn't the numbers but the fact that we got those numbers from three platoons. The 1993 Phillies only had four players with more than 500 at-bats. In the baseball world of free agency and multimillion-dollar contracts, how often do you see a manager keep that many platoons going without any sulking or pouting?

Mitchy-Poo

No review of the statistics of that ballclub would be complete without Mitch Williams and his club-record 43 saves—as he made few, if any, look easy. He went the month of August and most of September without recording a 1-2-3 inning. Manager Jim Fregosi was once asked why he smoked cigarettes. Before he could answer, John Kruk said, "You'd smoke, too, if Mitch Williams was your closer."

Most of Wild Thing's saves were heart-stopping. It seemed like every time he came in to save a game he would walk two or three but would somehow wiggle out of the jam and not allow a run to score. Kruk resigned himself to the fact that the leadoff man was getting on: "I just hoped that the guy who led off the inning was a nice guy to talk to." Daulton would wait for a couple of runners to get on before he paid Mitch a visit: "Are you done now? You gonna get serious?"

Many fans, including myself, would close their eyes or turn off the TV when "Mitchy-Poo," complete with red glove, long, straggly hair, and bad beard, was called into the game. One of the memorable images of that season was Curt Schilling sitting in the dugout with a towel over his head, too anxious to look at what Williams was doing on the mound.

Even though we ended up going wire to wire, the season was not without its tense moments. First came the late June, early July swoon against the Cardinals that we snapped out of with Mitch's game-winning hit an hour or so before sunrise. The Cardinals fell out of the race, only to be replaced by the Expos who went 20–3 from August 20 to September 16 to pull within five games. We headed up to Montreal for a three-game series where the Expos drew more than 135,000 fans. In later years, that would be a good month for them. Mitch ended up taking the loss in the first game in extra innings and blowing the lead for another loss in the third game. We were victim-ized by a bad call in the ninth inning on a ground ball to Kruk with Mitch covering the base. Kruk would say later that the call didn't shock him as much as the sight of Mitch actually covering first. Our lead was down to four games, and the talk outside the clubhouse was turning yet again to 1964 as we came back to Philadelphia.

Leave it to Larry Andersen to keep everyone loose. Expecting a rough reception for the Wild Thing, Andersen put his acknowledged fear of possible snipers to the side and switched warm-up jerseys with Williams before the game. Curt Schilling did the rest, defining "stopper" with a complete-game victory.

On September 28 in Pittsburgh we finally clinched the pennant behind yet another Mariano Duncan grand slam, our club-record eighth for the season. John Kruk's pants were ripped down the back, but he kept them on throughout the game because, as he later explained, Williams was pitching so well.

If you wonder how many bottles of champagne are needed for a clubhouse celebration, I can tell you that our club went through—appropriately enough—a gross. Twelve dozen. And 15 cases of beer. Boys will be boys.

"It won't sink in till tomorrow morning when I wake up and feel like hell," Kruk observed. "Then I'll know that something happened here."

Harry Kalas was a bit more succinct, telling the team, "Gentle-men, thank you for giving me the best year of my life."

The team's record-setting streak of 174 games without being shut out was snapped shortly after we clinched, as the players rested up for the NLCS and blew off any remaining steam. The streak was snapped by knuckleballer Tim Wakefield after we clinched the pen-nant. Hitting a knuckleball is hard enough. Now try to imagine doing it with two hours of sleep and a hangover.

Umpire Eric Gregg told a funny story of Lenny Dykstra arguing a call early in one of the last games of the year. Gregg knew he had the call right—and so did Lenny, for that matter—but the Dude was trying to get the rest of the day off by getting tossed. Gregg told him he knew what he was up to and wouldn't eject him, which made Dykstra so mad he wouldn't talk to him until well into the following season. Only a member of the 1993 Phillies would harbor a grudge for not getting run.

That was Nails. He wasn't at his best unless the games really meant something, as the nation was about to find out. Jim Fregosi had a term for guys like that: "red-light players."

"When they see that red television light go on," Fregosi explained, "they're able to go up to a level that other players can't reach."

The Unbeatable Braves

After a regular season of great performances, wild and wacky moments, and tremendous excitement, the Phils had to go up against the NL West champion Atlanta Braves in the National League Championship Series. This was going to be no easy task. On paper they looked like the better team, having been to the World Series in both 1991 and 1992. The Braves' starting rotation of Greg Maddux, Tom Glavine, John Smoltz, and Steve Avery was one of the greatest ever assembled. Many thought they were unbeatable. As a result, they were huge favorites to win the series and the pennant.

After all, they had been playing "lights out" for the past 100 games or so—going 72–29 after a sluggish 32–29 start, coming back from a 10-game deficit to catch Barry Bonds and the San Francisco Giants on the last day of the season to take the division. This was the last full season before the wild-card was introduced—so the Giants ended up winning 103 games and going home.

Thanks to cable television and the TBS superstation, the Braves had become perhaps the most-watched sports team in America. You either loved or hated them. Their colorful owner Ted Turner and his actress wife, Jane Fonda, sitting in the front row, would give their "tomahawk chop" cheer that two-sport star Deion Sanders had brought in from his days at Florida State.

With postseason baseball returning to Philadelphia for the first time in 10 years, we decided that we needed to do something special for the occasion. What we ended up doing was actually a suggestion from the wife of Mayor Rendell: a red Phillies cap on top of the statue of William Penn that tops City Hall. Since that statue is as tall as Fenway Park's green monster, any old hat would not do. We found a guy who was able to construct and install a 140-cubic-foot Phillies hat. In one day.

In Game 1 at the Vet, seldom-used utility infielder Kim Batiste went from goat to hero in the incredibly short span of one inning in a tight, high-tension game. Batiste had entered the game in the ninth inning as a defensive replacement for Dave Hollins at third base and proceeded to throw a potential double-play ball into right field, which allowed the Braves to score the tying run. But in the tenth inning, Batiste's double scored John Kruk, who had doubled, for a 4–3 Phillies win. Curt Schilling had pitched superbly, striking out 10 Braves but having to take a no-decision.

The Braves bounced back in Game 2, hammering starter Tommy Greene and others for a 14–3 Braves victory. Atlanta's midseason acquisition, Fred McGriff, became one of a very small and select group to reach the Vet's upper deck with a home run.

As the series moved to Atlanta for Game 3, Atlanta newspapers were filled with headlines like, "Keep the Wife and Kids Off the Streets—the Phillies Are Coming," and "Hide the Women and Children."

In Game 3, Terry Mulholland, who had pitched just five innings after September 1, was masterful through five innings but ran out of gas. The Braves erupted with five runs in the sixth and added four more in the seventh for a 9–4 victory that gave them a total of 23 runs in successive games, a new LCS record. The next day, the headline in the Philadelphia Inquirer read: "Phillies Appear Dead in the Water."

Ye of little faith.

Danny Jackson—that guy they said we had to "settle" for in the off-season—pitched brilliantly, and Milt Thompson made a game-saving catch in the eighth inning as the Phillies won Game 4 2–1, evening up the series at two games apiece. Mitch tiptoed through the minefield yet again in the ninth inning after he misplayed one bunt and nearly threw another one away, but he somehow managed to extricate himself with no runs scoring.

The following afternoon, strong pitching, sparkling defense, and timely hitting put the Phillies one game from the World Series. The Phillies took a 3–0 lead and a four-hitter by Schilling into the bottom of ninth, only to watch the Braves storm back with three runs to send the game into extra innings. Schilling left the game in the ninth after giving up a lead-off walk to Jeff Blauser and a made-to-order double-play grounder that Batiste booted. Shaky relief by Williams cost Schilling a well-deserved win. Again.

Mitch's extra-inning dramatics were even more stomach-twisting in the postseason than they'd been all season—because the games meant so much more and because his performances were erratic even by Wild Thing's standards. This series is when Curt Schilling first took to putting a towel over his head in the dugout, something even Mitch himself found humor in: "(Schilling)'s probably the only one who has the nerve to put a towel over his head. The rest of them watch. But they'd rather be under the towel with Schil. They ought to get a blanket. Then they could cover up the whole team. You'll see them in the ninth inning—all of them down under the tarp."

In the top of the tenth with one out, Dykstra demonstrated he was not just a red-light player but also an incredibly astute hitter. Astute, you say? Lenny Dykstra? Nails never got the credit he deserved for what a great student of the game he was. Curt Schilling learned a lot about hitters from listening to Dykstra talk about his approach during games. Here's what Lenny said to Schilling in the dugout before his at-bat in the tenth inning: "If [Mark] Wohlers goes to a full count, he's gonna try to bust me inside, and I'm gonna turn on it and take him deep."

Which is exactly what happened.

Dykstra hit a towering home run to right center that might have been the most important home run in Phillies history, giving the Phillies another 4–3 victory. Larry Andersen got the Braves 1-2-3 in the bottom of the tenth, striking out Ron Gant to end the game with a forkball—which would not be worth noting except that Andersen did not have a forkball. Andersen, never a big fan of the expected, decided it was as good a time as any to try throwing one.

Game 6 was one of the most exciting games I ever attended. The Phanatic set the tone by poking fun at Jane Fonda, the wife of the Braves owner, who was sitting down front in VIP seating. Since Fonda was well known for her fitness tapes, we put some clips of those on the scoreboard while the Phanatic did a few push-ups at home plate and attempted a few scissor kicks, all while wearing a garish sweatsuit. Jane was not pleased, but she had to realize that this was Philadelphia and the Phanatic takes no prisoners. He may be fat, green, and lovable, but he's also tough.

Greene, bouncing back from a brutal Game 2, pitched brilliantly against Greg Maddux. Maddux was off his game, having been nailed in the leg by a Mickey Morandini line drive in the first inning. It would prove to be his worst start in more than two years. Clutch hitting by Daulton and Hollins—and clutch hitting and fielding by Morandini—propelled us to a 6–3 victory as Williams struck out two of the three batters he faced in the ninth. That's right—three batters. Wild Thing had just his second 1-2-3 inning since July.

"Of all the improbable endings to this season," Tim McCarver said in the broadcast booth, "the most improbable is Mitch having a 1-2-3 inning."

Hoisting the Warren Giles Trophy at the Vet

As Williams was striking out the last batter and leaping into the air and then into Daulton's arms, pandemonium broke loose in the entire Philadelphia area. Most of the 62,502 fans stayed for more than an hour cheering the National League champs as I jumped into a convertible with general manager Lee Thomas and manager Jim Fregosi. We circled the field holding up the Warren Giles Trophy, which goes to the National League pennant winner. Phillies players kept running onto the field with champagne, pouring the bubbly on most everything and everybody. Pitcher Danny Jackson concluded the celebration by tearing off his own shirt while standing atop home plate while he flexed his muscles and beat his hands on his chest like a gorilla.

In a bizarre series in which the Phillies were both outpitched and outhit—statistically, anyway—Curt Schilling was named MVP even though he didn't earn a victory in either one of his starts.

"I never had a feeling like that on a baseball field," said Daulton after the game. "I went crazy out there. I just never had that kind of emotion before. I saw the house rocking. To know that something has happened that means so much to 3 or 4 million, it was just an unbelievable feeling."

For me it was more than unbelievable. The Phillies, the team that I thought would be the team of the 1980s, had endured some very rough years. Those lean years helped make our victory extra special. To make 4 million people happy and for them to think you are a pretty smart guy—for a while, anyway—is something you never forget.

One of my most memorable phone calls—and I believe the only phone call I ever received from George Steinbrenner—came the day after we beat the Braves.

"Bill," George said, "I want to congratulate you on having one of the most exciting and colorful teams I have ever seen in baseball."

The Cold and Efficient Blue Jays

Baseball's 90th World Series was a battle of the prince and the pauper.

When the Phillies arrived north of the border we got a quick picture of how Canadians felt about the Blue Jays' opponents. The newspapers in Toronto characterized the Phillies as "a motley crew of hairy, beer-soused brutes," "long-haired, slack-jawed," "butt ugly," "pot-bellied and snarly lipped," and "phat Phil."

"Honest, we're not bad people," Kruk explained. "But you wouldn't want us in your home."

There were some great guys on our team, many of whom were misunderstood. The fans in Philadelphia loved them, even if they weren't the neatest or cleanest group of athletes ever assembled. Philadelphia has never much cared for neat, clean ballplayers anyway—they think those types aren't trying hard enough.

Toronto, on the other hand, was a colorless, cold, efficient band of professionals and high-priced free agents. After winning the 1992 World Series, they added 11 new faces to the 1993 team—including future Hall of Famer Dave Winfield. At the time, it was an unprecedented roster turnover for a defending champion—a team that had put together 11 straight winning seasons and been in the playoffs four of the past five seasons.

GM Pat Gillick would go on to add Dave Stewart and future Hall of Famers Paul Molitor and Rickey Henderson to the squad during the season. Not surprisingly, the Blue Jays were considered the best team in baseball. They posted the best record in the American League, 95–67, ending up with the top three batting averages in the AL—courtesy of John Olerud, Paul Molitor, and Roberto Alomar—a trifecta that hadn't been achieved in either league in the 20th century. They finished seven games ahead of the Yankees in the AL East and then beat the Chicago White Sox in six games to reach the World Series for the second straight year.

The Phillies had no such résumé. We were that gang of misfits and miscreants from the boo-bird capital of the world. But with Atlanta out of the way, we were America's Team for the duration.

The Phillies might not have been getting much respect in the Toronto papers, but the Blue Jays certainly knew what they were getting into. Pat Gillick will tell you, "We had a tremendous amount of respect for that team. They'd been down in the NLCS and came back. They had a good mix of older and younger players. And Darren Daulton was an exceptional player. From across the field, we could tell that Daulton had that team under control."

Game 1 went to the Blue Jays 8–5 despite three hits each by Mariano Duncan and John Kruk as Curt Schilling was uncharacteristically rocked for seven runs. The Phillies bounced back in Game 2 by collecting 12 hits, three RBIs by Jim Eisenreich, and good pitching by Terry Mulholland.

We returned to Philadelphia for Game 3, which was a bummer as a huge rainstorm delayed the start of the game by 72 minutes and the Blue Jays jumped on starter Danny Jackson for three runs in the first inning to win the game 10–3.

Two of the Worst Losses I Have Ever Witnessed

Though the first three games were rather routine, the next three were anything but. The three most crushing defeats during my tenure with the Phillies were the 6–5 loss to the Dodgers in Game 3 of the 1977 NLCS and Games 4 and 6 of the 1993 World Series.

"This will go down in the annals as one of the all-time great World Series games," manager Jim Fregosi said after Game 4. He wasn't smiling when he said it.

It was an eerie night. The game was played in fog and drizzle, reminding me of a scene from a Frankenstein movie. I didn't have many fond memories of rainy postseason games at the Vet, and Game 4 wouldn't be any different.

It was a game filled with bizarre twists and an unbelievable outcome. With a chance to even the Series, the Phillies took a 4–3 lead after one inning as they worked starter Todd Stottlemyre mercilessly—taking 25 of the first 27 pitches he threw. In a game in which both starters were knocked out early, we took a 14–9 lead into the eighth inning and blew it, losing 15–14 and leaving a teary clubhouse deflated and bewildered. It was the highest-scoring game in history for World Series play, surpassing the record of 22 in 1936 between the Yankees and New York Giants. The two teams combined for 32 hits, 13 of them for extra bases. Dykstra hit two home runs and Daulton hit one, while Dykstra, Duncan, Milt Thompson, Devon White, Joe Carter, and Tony Fernandez each had three hits.

"It's a terrible loss," sighed Thompson, who in the final innings of the third game and early innings of the fourth had hit for the cycle. "But it was for real. We all saw what happened."

The line score will show that the pitchers on both teams pitched poorly, but the field was wet, the ball was hard to grip, and the outfielders were having trouble seeing fly balls because of the fog and drizzle. In fact, the winning triple by Devon White in the eighth inning was a very routine short fly ball to center field that Dykstra could not see. Though Dykstra had a huge night in which he scored four runs and drove in four, many people only remember his troubles in the field in the eighth inning.

We were leading 14–9 in the top of the eighth when all hell broke loose against Andersen and Williams as Toronto scored six times for a 15–14 lead with four of the runs coming with two out. The deflated Phillies went meekly in the eighth and ninth with four of six batters striking out. It was an ugly ending to a weird game that saw a little bit of everything, including a breakdown in the Blue Jays' telephone to the bullpen resulting in the wrong pitcher warming up, and the right one—Tony Castillo—getting extra time to warm up when summoned to the mound. The four-hour, 14-minute skirmish was the longest nine-inning game in World Series history.

A lot of teams would have folded after that crushing defeat, but this group was determined not to let the season end on a sour note like Game 4. Thanks primarily to a gritty 148-pitch effort from Schilling, they won a pulsating Game 5 by the score of 2–0. Schilling, who was already making his name as one of baseball's great big-game pitchers, tossed the Phillies' first complete game in a World Series since Robin Roberts did it in Game 2 in 1950 against the Yankees.

"We had no choice," said Kruk. "We had to win, and we had to get nine innings from our starter."

Schilling needed no prodding from anybody. The big right-hander stood up in the clubhouse before the game and told his teammates that he was going to give it everything he had.

"It would have been very easy to have been down," added Hollins. "But we weren't going to do that, and the fans weren't going to let us do that. They kept us up. They were just great."

So we headed back to Toronto for the conclusion of the Series. In Game 6, the Phillies were trailing 5–1 going into the seventh inning. With the end of their season looming, Philadelphia rallied for five runs, mainly on the heroics of Dykstra, who hit a three-run home run to put us up 6–5 with nine more outs to get to force a Game 7.

At this point, I said to everyone seated with me in our suite, "Hey guys, I believe we are going to win the whole thing. Ol' 'mo' is now on our side."

Pitcher Larry Anderson wiggled out of a bases-loaded situation in the eighth. In came Williams to get the final three outs, and, for the umpteenth time that year, "Mitchy Poo" walked the lead-off batter, Rickey Henderson. White flew out, Molitor singled, and Joe Carter worked the count to 2–2.

At this point, time stood still.

Almost in slow motion, I can recall Carter hammering a low fastball over the left-field fence.

Blue Jays win 8–6.

Series over.

It was only the second time in history that a home run ended the World Series.

"It was a weird feeling, watching that ball go out," Dykstra said. "Helpless. I can't really describe it. I didn't want to watch it. I really thought this was meant to be our year. We battled and battled and battled. But we had two heartbreaking losses. We were the second-best team in baseball this year, and that's nothing to be ashamed of. Now, its over. That's it. Uncle."

"We Almost Won It for You, Uncle Bill"

After the game, I went to congratulate the Toronto owners and then to our clubhouse to thank our players. Daulton was in the trainer's room; I went over to hug him and thank him. He hugged me back and said, "We almost won it for you, Uncle Bill."

And let it be known that, despite the 1993 team's reputation for being a bunch of maniacs, Pat Gillick assures me that we left the SkyDome's visitors clubhouse in one piece.

Mayor Ed Rendell wanted to have a parade for the team, but I felt parades should be only for world champs. Looking back on it, I wish we had done the parade. Even though the 1993 Phils came up short in the World Series, this was a special team that galvanized a city.

On our flight back to Philadelphia, I grabbed the plane microphone and congratulated the team for the most exciting baseball season Philadelphia had ever witnessed and then, overcome by all that had happened, I broke down in tears.

Though we weren't coming home with the trophy, we were greeted at the airport in the wee hours of the morning by a large gathering of the greatest fans in the world.

Field of Dreams

Letting the Wild Thing Walk

There are a lot of great things about running a big-league baseball team and a lot of not-so-great things. There is little better than helping put together a ballclub that goes out and does well. And there is little worse than helping put together a ballclub that falls flat on its face. Having to make tough business decisions about players you care for and respect isn't easy either. Perhaps toughest of all is doing all that while the public perception is that you and your ownership group care more about making money than winning games. This is simply not true. Our goal was and is to win as many games and championships as possible without going broke.

Making money is good for winning. You won't find many teams with their finances in a mess and their win-loss record a success. The 1997 world champion Marlins are one notable exception—and they had to begin dismantling that team before the champagne had even been mopped up in the clubhouse.

When you're running a big-league club with the twin objectives of making money and winning games there really is no off-season. Following the 1993 season, I was immediately presented with two tough decisions: whether to re-sign Mitch Williams and whether to extend Lenny Dykstra's contract.

GM Lee Thomas convinced me we should let Williams go. This was tough for me to approve, as I really liked him as a person. He was great fun to play golf with, particularly when John Kruk was in the foursome. There were always lots of jokes and insults being bandied about, but few that are printable. A common observation made by Kruk, whenever Mitch hit one out of bounds—which was frequent—was, "You golf like you pitch."

Mitch was really colorful and despite the Wild Thing's propensity to make things exciting, it was fun to watch him pitch. My son, Mike, was heartbroken when we let him go. It turned out to be the right baseball decision; after 1993, Mitch's ball had nothing on it except his fingers.

Wild Thing returned to the Vet for the last time as a major league player in late May 1994, shortly before he was released by the Astros. He was greeted with more cheers than boos and an insistent chant of "We want Mitch!" A good sport to the end, Mitch walked out to the bullpen between innings in the middle of the game with the Phillie Phanatic right behind him, a water gun pointed at his back. With Mitch, what you see is what you get.

He had stood up and answered every question after the Game 6 loss in Toronto until Fregosi came out and got him. Several years later, at a Phillies fantasy camp in spring training, he grabbed the microphone from the emcee as he was being introduced and said, "It was a low, inside fastball. I suck, and I'm sorry."

Mitch got the blame for the 1993 World Series loss, but the fact is that the entire bullpen was pretty much gassed by then. Wild Thing just happened to be the last one out there chucking and ducking when the end came.

Nailing Down Nails

As for Lenny Dykstra, he was going to be a free agent at the end of the 1994 season. Nails had been sensational during both the season and postseason, and he was a fan favorite. I met with Lenny and his two agents a couple of times during the off-season, with Lenny doing most of the talking.

"Look at these stats," he'd say, pointing to what he'd done in 1993. "League leader in runs scored, hits, and walks. Second in doubles. Third in on-base percentage. Fourth in total bases. Tenth in stolen bases. Runner up in the MVP voting to Barry Bonds."

"Who else puts up these kinds of numbers?" he'd say. "I'm the seventh-best player in baseball."

"Look at these salaries," he'd say. "Look at what the top 10 players in baseball are making. I'm underpaid at $3 million."

"Look at how many fannies I put in the seats," he'd say. "People pay to come see me play."

We finally agreed to a four-year extension worth $27.5 million, which put his pay in the top echelon of all major league players. For the 1994 season, I believe that only Barry Bonds, Jeff Bagwell, and Greg Maddux made more than Dykstra.

In the spring of 1994, I went to my favorite breakfast place in Clearwater, Florida—The Apple Cobbler. When I went in the restaurant, Dykstra was sitting in the back finishing his breakfast.

I took a table next to him.

When I went to pay my check, the owner said to me, "Do you know who you were sitting next to?"

Playing dumb, I said, "No, who was it?"

"That was Lenny Dykstra, the center fielder for the Phillies," he said. "I read in the paper the other day that some stupid jerk is paying him over $7 million a year."

I was looking forward to seeing Nails, dirt on his uniform and an enormous wad of tobacco in his cheek, in a Phillies uniform for years to come—patrolling a stretch of chaw-stained turf at the Vet that Pittsburgh Pirate Andy Van Slyke had likened to a "toxic waste dump."

As it turned out, the contract was not a good investment for the Phillies. Injuries limited Dykstra to fewer and fewer at-bats in each of the next three seasons, and his bad back eventually forced him to retire after the 1996 season at the age of 33.

At the same time that Dykstra's career was winding down, Lee Thomas and Jim Fregosi were getting into a public debate about who was to blame for the demise of the Phillies. The relationship got so difficult that one of them had to go. It was a close call, but I decided to fire Fregosi. It really didn't help Jim's cause when he went public with comments to the effect that no manager could win with the players he'd been given to work with.

After the news broke, I got a call from Dykstra at home requesting a meeting at my house on a Sunday night. When he arrived, the conversation went something like this.

"Uncle Bill, I want to be your next manager," Dykstra said. "My back is killing me. Kruk is hurting, and he will be my hitting coach. Daulton is hurting, and he will be my bench coach. We'll turn this whole thing around."

"I don't think that's in the cards," I replied. "But I'll think about it."

I did talk to Thomas about it, but we both agreed it was not a good idea. I told Dykstra so the next day. These days Dykstra runs a series of very successful car washes in Southern California, but to me he will always be the Dude who helped ignite that very special 1993 ballclub.

"I Cannot Make This Work"

Any work stoppage that ends up canceling the World Series is, by definition, poorly timed. Few franchises, however, suffered more than the Phillies from the 1994 players' strike, a fiasco that wiped out the fall classic and carried over into spring training the following season.

The Phillies were as popular as they ever were coming off the amazing 1993 season, with attendance in 1994 on its way to eclipsing the record 3.1 million we had drawn—even though the Expos had left us in the dust, more than 20 games back by August. We would never top 3 million at the Vet again, and we wouldn't exceed our 1993 attendance levels until we opened Citizens Bank Park in 2004.

The cancellation of the postseason, compounded by the use of replacement players during the spring of 1995, really took an emotional toll on me. Moreover, there was a severe financial toll as well. The strike cost the Phillies more than $30 million. The franchise had never lost money since my group had purchased the Phillies.

On the field—as Dykstra had laid out in his "sales pitch" to me—our star players were indeed getting hurt and getting old. Our farm system was weak, which it would remain until Mike Arbuckle came in and turned things around in the late 1990s. Much to my chagrin, I saw no way that we could win games without losing money, and I would often sit in my office after losing a game, talking to our longtime PR director, Larry Shenk.

"Larry," I would say, "I cannot make this work."

I was emotionally drained from the losses and my inability to make the economics of the franchise work. I had just been through the most difficult negotiation of my career—the Curt Schilling contract. It wasn't just that it was a lot of money, it was the fact that he'd gone public with it, talking about it with sportswriters and on the radio. Steve Carlton got a lot of criticism for not talking to the press, but I sure appreciated that when it came time to negotiating a contract. Carlton also despised agents, so I was able to deal directly with him late in his career. He still ended up with a deal that made him the highest-paid pitcher in the game without having to pay any agent commissions.

DAVE THOMAS AND BILL GILES: SEPARATED AT BIRTH

In the middle of a very difficult stretch in the mid-'90s, I did get to have a few laughs when I entered the "Dave Thomas Look-Alike Contest" being sponsored by the Wendy's chain of fast-food restaurants. Dave Thomas was the corporation's owner and the plain-speaking spokesman featured in their advertisements.

I was at a Boy Scouts banquet to honor Richie Ashburn, and I was sitting next to Don Cannon, a popular Philadelphia DJ.

"You really do look like Dave Thomas," he said, telling me about the contest. "You really should enter."

So I did. I had a picture taken in a tie and white short-sleeved shirt—and I found myself picked to be a finalist. I was invited to a Wendy's in Manhattan, where I dressed up like Dave again, holding a tray and saying, "Service is our policy."

I didn't end up winning it all, though the final judge—Dave's daughter, Wendy—did say I looked the most like her father. They just didn't want another CEO winning their CEO's look-alike contest, so they announced that I was runner-up. I did get $100 worth of hamburgers and a glass "Oscar" statue of Dave Thomas.

My favorite part of the whole experience, however, came the day before the final judging. I was driving up to my place in the Poconos and stopped at a Wendy's in Wind Gap, Pennsylvania. I decided it would be a good time to campaign for election, so I asked the woman taking my money at the drive-through, "Do you think I look like Dave Thomas, the owner of Wendy's?"

"No," she replied, "but you look exactly like Bill Giles, the owner of the Phillies."

Building a Ballpark (Not a Stadium)

I was asked in the spring of 1997 by my fellow owners to retire so that my chief operating officer, Dave Montgomery, could take over as CEO. It was the right decision for the club and for me. Besides, I had another dream now—the dream to build a new, baseball-only ballpark in Philadelphia. Moving from the role of CEO to that of chairman would allow me more time to make my new dream a reality.

Since I was raised in a ballpark, I have always had a real affinity and special appreciation for them. I am fortunate to have spent my early life in baseball in the classic neighborhood ballparks like Ebbets Field, Sportsman's Park, Connie Mack Stadium, Wrigley Field, and, of course, Cincinnati's Crosley Field. Each major league park back then had its own special peculiarities, whether it was the terrace in Crosley's outfield, the ivy at Wrigley, or even the weird shape of the Polo Grounds, where it was about 250 feet down the lines and 480 feet to dead center. Having experienced life in baseball parks, building them was a lot of fun.

After so many fun years in Houston, it was time to move on, and I entered into a wonderful marriage with the Philadelphia Phillies that is still going strong today.

My Veterans Stadium promotions became the stuff of legend, especially when things didn't exactly go off as planned. In the top photo, Cannon Man prepares to launch, and below, the Great Wallenda pulls off one of the most amazing stunts of all time.

Kiteman III (top) prepares for a landing while the Phillie Phanatic tries to get out of the way. Benny the Bomb pauses for a moment before detonation (bottom).

President Gerald Ford was on hand to witness the celebration that was the 1976 All-Star Game at Veterans Stadium.

Two popular innovations that arrived at Veterans Stadium in the late 1970s, which are still are going strong today: the Phanatic (above), and the use of ballgirls (right).

One of the proudest moments of my entire life: accepting my dad's plaque from Commissioner Kuhn at Cooperstown in August 1979.

I've loved every minute we've spent in Philadelphia. Some fans sent me a warm greeting in the top photo, and below I'm posing with then-manager Terry Francona before a game in 1999. *Top photo courtesy of Paul H. Roedig.*

I've had a wonderful career in this great game, and I don't think I'd change a single thing.

When these parks were closed or torn down, they were replaced with multipurpose stadiums. Nowadays, most people decry the era of the multipurpose stadium. With the opening of the new ballpark in St. Louis in 2006, all of them are gone from the National League. But for me, and for many Philadelphians who fondly remember the great years the Phillies had there, the Vet was a very special place. Hard as it might be to imagine now, Veterans Stadium had actually opened in 1971 to rave reviews. "It's beautiful," blared *Sports Illustrated*. "No more bad jokes about Philadelphia," proclaimed the *New York Post*.

I got goose bumps every time I arrived at the Vet during my 33 years working there. Unlike others who were glad to see the Vet go, at 7:00 AM on March 21, 2004, when the Vet was imploded in 58 seconds, I cried. I watched the dust blow over to cover the new Citizens Bank Park and thought it fitting that the ashes of the Vet were being spread on our new home.

It was sad how much the Vet was maligned during the last 10 years of its existence. Comments by Mike Schmidt didn't help. He talked about the cats, rats, and stench. Once he said those things, it really snowballed into a "Dump the Vet" campaign by the press and many fans. Of course, there were real problems with the facility, and the Vet was not maintained the way it should have been by our landlord, the city. When a railing collapsed during an Army-Navy game, causing several cadets to fall out of the stands and get hurt, the complaints and criticism only multiplied.

But for me personally, the prime of my baseball life was spent at Veterans Stadium, starting with its opening in 1971 all the way through the 2003 season. Despite these fond memories, I decided in 1992 that to be competitive the Phillies needed to build a park just for baseball.

The Baltimore Orioles, since moving from St. Louis in the early 1950s, had played their games in Memorial Stadium, located in a residential section on the city's north side, which they shared with the Colts until the Colts skipped town in the mid-1980s. Like most neighborhood facilities, parking was a problem, but so was a design that accommodated both football and baseball. Some insightful people had an idea to re-create the ambience of the old classic ball-parks, and in 1992, Oriole Park at Camden Yards was opened. The park was the crown jewel of the project to renovate and revitalize the Baltimore waterfront on the Inner Harbor. Like many baseball fans, I wanted to experience Camden Yards.

When I attended an Orioles game in their new ballpark, it proved to be a life-changing experience. Camden Yards manages to capture the feel and tradition of the old neighborhood parks while providing wonderful modern amenities—lots of parking, access by public transportation, huge concourses with lots of restrooms and plenty of food stands, comfortable seats with great sightlines, the quirkiness of angles and an asymmetric shape of the field, and more. Having experienced it, I was reminded of my first baseball home—Crosley Field in Cincinnati.

"This is a real baseball park," I said to myself. "We've got to make this happen in Philadelphia."

I had to make it happen for competitive reasons as much as aesthetic reasons. Camden Yards became a magnet for Orioles fans and for baseball fans all over the northeast. Attendance skyrocketed. In fact, the Orioles essentially sold out the entire first season, and attendance stayed very strong throughout the 1990s. As a result, Baltimore's revenue increased $60 million a year when they moved into Camden Yards. Phillies attendance, meanwhile, had fallen from 3.1 million in 1993 to 1.5 million only four years later.

New ballparks were under construction in many other major league cities, too. I knew the Phillies would not be able to compete financially if we did not build a baseball-only park to attract fans, build (or rebuild) attendance, and create additional revenue. Not only did the Vet have the typical problems of multipurpose stadiums, we were operating under a very difficult lease with the city. Our revenue was constrained by this lease, under which the Phillies received a relatively small portion of revenues from auxiliary enterprises such as concessions, parking, and suite rental.

With a sense of urgency, I went to work to make my new dream a reality. It would only take 12 years.

Building a new ballpark is a huge project, and I had to take many steps to initiate the project. First, I met with architects at the Ewing Cole firm to draw up a design. Obviously, you don't finalize a design right away, and the plans for what became Citizens Bank Park evolved over time.

New ballparks represent a huge investment, so I met with financial people to draw up projected-income statements. As in virtually every project of this type, there was a need to partner with state and local government. So, on February 4, 1997, I met with Philadelphia mayor Ed Rendell, who fortunately is a huge baseball fan—not to mention a huge football and basketball fan. Even as the current governor of Pennsylvania, he not only attends Eagles games, but he is also a commentator on the local sports network's postgame show.

Since the state would have to "step up to the plate" as well, I met with Pennsylvania governor Tom Ridge. I then created a basic concept to finance the new ballpark. The estimated cost of $320 million would be paid one-third by the state, one-third by the city, and one-third by the Phillies.

Rendell first suggested that we build a new baseball park for the Phillies and keep the Eagles in a renovated Vet. The Eagles, of course, would have none of that.

The already difficult task of selling the idea to state officials, city council, and the business leaders was looking even tougher. With their leases at Three Rivers Stadium coming to an end, there was talk that one or both of the Pittsburgh Pirates and Pittsburgh Steelers might leave the state to a new location. Now the original idea of just building one park for the Phillies mushroomed into building four new facilities at a total cost of about $1.5 billion. Securing the approval of the state legislature and Philadelphia City Council was not going to be easy, as both the city and state had many financial challenges.

"Why give money to rich sports owners when we don't have enough money to keep our schools running right?" was the argument by many people.

I believed we could prove that building new stadiums was an economic gain for the cities and the state. Economists, politicians, team executives, and citizens have long discussed the issue of public funding for sports arenas and stadiums. While there is some disagreement about how much benefit arises to localities from public funding of new facilities, there are benefits and they are significant. In our case, the Wharton School of the University of Pennsylvania created a report that projected the additional tax dollars that the cities and state would collect by building four new stadiums.

Governor Ridge formed a "stadium task force" committee headed by Paul Tufano, Ridge's chief of staff, to study the feasibility of building the stadiums. While this was going on, I was going everywhere selling the idea of new stadiums—particularly a new Phillies park. My selling tools included pretty pictures of a new park, schematic drawings, and financial reports showing how the city and state would benefit financially.

My biggest selling point was that for Philadelphia to be considered a truly world-class city, its sports teams should be playing in first-class venues. Hockey and basketball had just gotten their great facility—a beautiful arena initially called the CoreStates Center, and, after a couple of bank mergers, now called the Wachovia Center. By stark comparison, the Eagles and Phillies were playing in a much-maligned stadium, and the negative comments constantly broadcast on national television were painting a very poor image of the entire region.

I also felt that the project would be an easier sell if the Phillies ballpark was built downtown. There would be lots of ancillary benefits to the city. Fans would spend more time spending money before and after the game in existing restaurants, parking lots, bars, and hotels. Tax revenue would be greater for everyone. Plus, downtown parks such as St. Louis's had more consistent attendance, which would be good for the Phillies as well as the city.

I found a site at 16th Street and Spring Garden Street, just a few blocks from City Hall, the true center of Philadelphia, which would have been a perfect location for a ballpark. We did an extensive study of parking and traffic to ascertain for ourselves and others that the site would really work.

The Philadelphia Inquirer and GlaxoSmithKline owned the property and were willing to sell it to us at a very reasonable price. In fact, the cost would have been quite a bit less than the site next to the Vet in the South Philadelphia sports complex. However, there was opposition to the downtown site from a number of directions. Some of the Phillies partners did not like a downtown site. Mayor Ed Rendell was not really enthused. State Senator Vince Fumo was very opposed because he had a home just six blocks from the site and supported his neighbors who feared more traffic in their neighborhood. All this opposition put great pressure on city councilman Darrell Clark. There is an unwritten rule that there could not be any public structure built in a district unless the councilman of the district introduced the bill. Clark was not anxious to have the park built in his district.

The site issue got stickier when John Street replaced Ed Rendell as mayor of Philadelphia. I had worked so hard on selling Street on the downtown ballpark site that he offered a couple of alternative proposals, one in Chinatown, just a few blocks east of City Hall, and one at 12th and Market Streets, knowing that my idea of the Spring Garden site was dead. But there was opposition to the Chinatown site and to any other downtown site that was mentioned. Ultimately, the downtown ballpark idea was dead. I still wish we had built it there, and I feel that Philadelphia missed a golden opportunity to really show off the city in a way that Pittsburgh can at PNC Park, which is directly across the river from the Golden Triangle.

Nevertheless, I continued to go to almost every state and city political fund-raiser or gathering, schmoozing politicos until we finally got the vote from the state legislators in February 1999 to provide $85 million for the Phillies' new ballpark, as well as a similar amount for the Eagles, Steelers, and Pirates. For me, this was a big day, right up there with getting to the World Series three times. I knew that if we got the commitment from the state, the city would come through. And it did.

There were still important issues ahead. We had to negotiate a lease with the city, complete a complicated financial package with a number of entities, and select a site. I had done my job of getting the financing from the state and the city, but now it was up to Dave Montgomery, Bill Webb, Jerry Clothier (Phillies CFO), and others to finalize the very complicated deals. The ownership group ended up putting in $235 million of its own money to build the ballpark because we wanted the fans to enjoy the best possible environment to watch a Phillies game.

After a year of debate and delay on the site and the financing plan, the result is what we have today—Citizens Bank Park for the Phillies and Lincoln Financial Field for the Eagles—both a few feet from where the Vet used to stand. Philadelphia is the only city in the entire world that has four major sports teams within 500 yards of each other in world-class facilities. And there are some significant benefits for fans in terms of access to the facilities by local highways and bridges, plus ample parking, making the location quite convenient.

"Field of Realized Dreams"

Now that we had the funding, the next step was to make the Phillies new park the best ballpark ever built. This was the fun part. I focused on the big picture and the theme of the park, while others worked out all the details. Our goal was to build a park that was intimate, fan-friendly, fun, and open—to make it a "ballpark," not a "stadium." In fact, we instituted a new rule in the Phillies organization: if anyone referred to the new facility as a stadium, he or she was fined one dollar.

My requests were to have a lot of brick like my favorite park— Wrigley Field. I didn't want much cement or aluminum showing, and I wanted the fans to feel in touch with the game when they were going for food or to the restroom. It was important to me to have a fun-and-games area and to have very attractive signage throughout the park.

The architectural firms of Ewing Cole of Philadelphia and HOK Sport of Kansas City joined forces to design the park. John Stranix was hired as the Phillies owners' rep to oversee the entire project.

The contractor was a joint venture between Philadelphia-based L.F. Driscoll Co. and the Hunt Construction Group of Indianapolis. Everyone in the Phillies organization chipped in to develop the program for the park, and then Dave Montgomery, Richard Deats, and my son Joe worked tirelessly with Stranix and the architects to complete the project. They met every Tuesday morning, got input from everyone—from baseball people on the design of the clubhouse to sales people on the sightlines—and were blessed to have a project manager who had no problem telling the big shots that it was time for them to make a decision or a decision would be made for them.

Our team of design people, including myself, visited every new park built in the last 10 years. This proved to be invaluable, as we were inspired by many of the features we liked and avoided the few mistakes that we observed. In order to make our new ballpark as fan-friendly and appealing as possible, we wanted to talk to a lot of people about what they wanted in a ballpark. We obtained ideas for the design not only from every Phillies employee, but from fans as well. We had focus groups and asked questions such as:

"What does Philadelphia mean to you?"

"What kinds of foods say Philadelphia?"

"What would you most like to see in a new ballpark?"

We also received a ton of emails and letters from fans suggesting ideas. Some ideas were good, some were strange, many were not possible, but we didn't dismiss any of them. We threw all of the ideas on the table and then smaller committees got together to write the program—a summary of all the things we wanted to see in the ballpark, such as wide concourses, great concessions, no exposed aluminum, etc. The architects would use this to create an initial design of the park. Our concept was to celebrate not just baseball but the city of Philadelphia.

According to Bob McConnell of Ewing Cole, one of the architects on the project, in a December 2005 *Contract* article, "We took a cue from the city plan established by William Penn in the early 1600s, which is an egalitarian grid of 400 by 400 blocks laid out around four public squares with a fifth in the center as the location of City Hall. We played on that idea in our design of the ballpark by creating four entry plazas, with the fifth being the ball field."

The ballpark's exterior red brick façade, open-laced trusses, and toothpick-style light towers also honor Philadelphia. "We wanted to interpret the traditional architectural elements of the city—its red brick row houses and colonial buildings, like Carpenters' Hall and Independence Hall, and the gutsy, exposed steel of its bridges, ports, and navy yards—in a modern way," said Don Jones, project designer for the new park, in the same article.

What's unique about Citizens Bank Park is the accessibility of the field to the fans from the minute they enter and throughout the entire game. Unlike most ballparks, where the field is at street level and fans are forced to climb flights of stairs before entering the seating bowl and getting a view of the field, the architects positioned the field 23 feet below grade with home plate centered in the middle of the block. As a result, a view of the field is the first thing fans see upon passing through the four main entry gates, which are located behind first and third bases and behind right and left fields. This approach not only aids in orientation, minimizes the height of the seating bowl in the city skyline, and contains the park within a single 21-acre city block, but it also maximizes sightlines for the fans, keeps spectators close to the action, and allows 75 percent of the seats to be open to the sky. The park is the only one ever built where you can stay in touch with the game from every level while you are at the concession stands or heading to a restroom—the concourses are all opened to the field, and wide, which lends to many fans parading around socializing before, during, and after the game. This is probably why it's not a coincidence that we're drawing a much younger crowd at Citizens than we did at the Vet.

Honoring Richie Ashburn was one of our main goals in the design of our park, and many fans wanted the park to be called Ashburn Field. We did the next-best thing and created a fun entertainment area called "Ashburn Alley"—a 625-foot gallery of food and games located in the outfield concourse. There are running, hitting, and throwing games, picnic tables, a barbecue restaurant named "Bull's BBQ" in honor of Greg "the Bull" Luzinski (a nod to Boog's Barbecue, located in the right-field concourse at Camden Yards, which honors Boog Powell, a member of the great Orioles teams of the late 1960s and early 1970s).

We also offer concession stands featuring Philly cheesesteaks, souvenir shops, and a double-decker restaurant named "Harry the K's" after Ashburn's broadcast partner and great friend, Harry Kalas. There is also a pictorial display of Philadelphia baseball history, including the A's, the Phils, and the Philadelphia Stars of the Negro Leagues attached to the back of the brick center-field wall. Ivy grows on the front of that wall, my personal homage to Wrigley Field.

The premium seats were very upscale—the 75 suites, the 1,200-seat Diamond Club behind home on field level, and the 2,500-seat Hall of Fame club seating midway up the park. The Diamond Club seats offer the best seats in the park, and package deals include parking and quality dining, plus a view of the indoor batting tunnels. The Hall of Fame Club offers dining and comfortable seats in a glassed-in air-conditioned area. The highlight is the "Cooperstown Gallery"—an art gallery displaying a rendering of every Phillies, A's, Negro Leagues, and Philadelphia-born player who is in the Hall of Fame.

McFadden's Restaurant and Bar on the main concourse behind home is a very popular watering hole, especially with the 20-something crowd, and it's open even when the Phillies are not playing. It serves fans coming to the Sports Complex to see the Eagles, Sixers, Flyers, and other events at the Wachovia Center or Lincoln Financial Field. A children's playground called "Phanatic Phun Zone" is located on the main concourse behind first base.

The economic realities of professional sports in the 21st century make it mandatory to find a good naming-rights partner, and we found such a partner in Citizens Bank. The name sounds good, and the bank executives have a strong commitment to the Philadelphia community. Dave Buck, the Phillies' vice president of marketing, and our lawyer, Bill Webb, put together a naming-rights deal that was one of the best in its era—$105 million for 25 years.

When Citizens Bank Park opened on April 3, 2004, I was as proud as a peacock. The fans and news media raved about everything. The headlines read: "Citizens Bank Park Stacks Up to Best in the Country," "New Park Arrives in Style," "Phils' New Ballpark Is a Beauty," and "Field of Realized Dreams."

This was one time where reality was better than my dream.

The Economic Evolution of Major League Baseball

"A few years ago Phillip K. Wrigley invented his famous aphorism, 'Baseball is too much of a sport to be a business, and too much of a business to be a sport.' As a sport it speaks for itself—to millions every summer day. But as a business it is curiously mute. As the devil fears holy water, so does the baseball owner or general manager flinch at a request to see a balance sheet or a profit-and-loss statement. What, as the season opens, becomes the national game and requires the presence of the president to pitch the symbolic first ball becomes, at the end of the season, a very private bookkeeping matter."

—*Sports Illustrated*

Sport or Business?

As timely as that sounds, it was actually written 50 years ago.

In 1956, as a senior at Denison University in Granville, Ohio, I cited that article in a senior thesis I wrote for my economics seminar titled "A Study of Some Economic Aspects of Organized Baseball." While that passage is still relevant today, the economic data I presented are a virtual time capsule. I was writing about baseball in an earlier and vastly different era, before Marvin Miller, Messersmith and McNally, the YES Network, and the many other huge changes in baseball's economic landscape. These data, which I've since updated,

219

present some pretty startling comparisons between then and now in the economics and finances of major league baseball.

Though the number of the zeroes after the dollar signs has changed dramatically over the past 50 years, what has not changed is this uneasy coexistence between sports and business. It's an issue today just as it was when *SI* wrote about it 50 years ago. It was an issue back when I first went to baseball games in the late 1930s. And it was an issue well before I was born.

The fact is that major league baseball has always been a game *and* a business, even back in the days of baggy flannel uniforms and black-and-white newsreels. And you can't tell the story of the game of baseball over the course of my lifetime without talking about the business of baseball and how much it has changed.

Let's start at the bottom—bottom line, that is.

The *P* Word

I fully understand that the word *profit* can generate wildly different emotions depending on who you're talking to and what you're talking about. Major league baseball is especially susceptible to this phenomenon, given its exalted place in our country's heritage. Because baseball has enormous symbolic importance to America and how we define ourselves, many folks choose to see it as neither sport nor business but as sacred cultural tradition. As such, they believe the athletes should play "for the love of the game" and the owners should view any profits they make as unnecessary and undeserved.

Let's look at "playing for pay" first, or the "love of the game" argument. The way this argument is typically expressed: back in the good old days, players played because they loved the game and would have gladly played for free because it was a privilege to wear the uniform; nowadays, players don't work as hard or care as much about the game because they're wealthy and spoiled.

I guess the only criticism I could offer of that argument is that it isn't based on reality. It's based on romantic but inaccurate memories of the past. Today's high salaries don't cause players to be lazy and underachieve. There have been lazy underachievers since the major leagues were first formed, and there will always be lazy under-achievers. It's human nature that some people will work harder than others, regardless of their level of compensation. The only difference now is that you're more likely to hear the phrase "not earning his money" rather than "wasting his talent." For every player who worked less hard the more financially set he became, you will probably be able to find a player who played better the less concerned he needed to be about providing for his family.

You will also find plenty of examples of very wealthy players who would exemplify professionalism in this or any other era. Aaron Rowand was under contract for $10 million over three years when he ran full-speed, face-first into a center-field railing in 2006 to make a game-saving catch. John Smoltz in 2003 and Curt Schilling in 2004—to offer just two examples—pitched through intense pain in the postseason, even though they were financially set for life. Derek Jeter is an even better player, teammate, and leader now, making $20 million a year, than he was before he "cashed in."

The owner's side of this argument—"paying for play"—is similarly flawed. The way this one is typically expressed: baseball owners who are concerned about profit and loss are greedy bastards putting dollars ahead of wins because the "sheer joy" of owning a major league baseball franchise is not enough for them.

Actually, very few owners go into major league baseball to make money. It certainly wasn't a bad investment for anyone who timed the market perfectly, buying in before the cable boom into a market that could successfully weather today's revenue disparity. But if you have enough money to buy a major league team and wealth accumulation is your sole motivation, you'll look elsewhere for less risky and less frustrating ways to make a buck.

Testifying before Congress in 1952, Commissioner Ford Frick discussed the owners of the 16 franchises then in existence and said that at least 10 of the 16 owners were "men whose fundamental business interests lie outside of organized baseball." Frick went on to say, "With them, baseball is an avocation. They are primarily in baseball because they are interested in baseball as a game. They are not dependent on it for a living, and they are well aware that the financial return from baseball does not justify it as an investment."

I believe that's still true today, even though the dollar figures we have to manage are so much larger. Most people buy baseball teams for reasons that have nothing to do with dollars: they like competing 162 games (and hopefully more) a year, they like the thrill of victory, they like the association with the players and staff, and they like the attention an owner receives. In one case I know of, Ewing Kauffman owned the Kansas City Royals strictly for civic reasons. He wanted Kansas City to be "major league," despite the fact that he personally lost a lot of his own money. That's a big reason why a cash-strapped franchise like the Royals has foregone some revenue to keep this man's name on their park.

If owning baseball teams was such a great investment, you wouldn't see large corporations like Disney and Fox bailing out as quickly as they did. If you don't love the game, it isn't worth the headaches.

In addition to the fact that the "profits before wins" argument falsely assumes that profits are the main reason why people buy baseball teams, there is also the flawed assumption that wins and profits are somehow mutually exclusive. While many believe it's one or the other, I'd argue it's both. After all, attendance correlates more strongly with on-field performance than anything else—if you don't win, you aren't going to make as much money as you would if you did. And if you don't turn a profit, you aren't going to be as successful on the field year in and year out as you would if you did.

Wild, uncontrolled spending—even by an owner who "puts wins ahead of profits"—does not necessarily produce titles. The Orioles, the Dodgers, and the Yankees have shown that in recent memory. The Yankees were much more successful in the late '90s when their focus was on ballplayers, not stars, and their payroll was in line with the top teams in the league, not in a separate area code entirely, as it is now.

When you throw money at a problem and financial losses begin to mount, it's inevitable that you will lose your long-term perspective.

Your organization becomes inherently less stable and predictable. You take your focus off areas where the returns are not immediate, like scouting and player development. With fewer young players being produced by your underfunded scouting and development organization, you are forced to acquire talent by throwing money at players—not necessarily players who fit your scheme, but free agents who happen to be on the market at the time. This typically results in even more erratic financial and playing field results, which leads to even shorter-term decision making. It's a vicious cycle.

Successful players and owners have more in common than you think, first and foremost being discipline. Successful players tend to be very disciplined in how they approach their craft, regardless of their salary, and it shows over the long haul. Successful owners tend to be very disciplined in how they run the operations of their team, and it shows over the long haul. History shows that successful teams, year in and year out, tend to have both disciplined players and disciplined owners.

Stability and predictability, after all, have always been underrated attributes in just about any field of endeavor you can name. In contrast to their recent performance, the success of the Orioles and Dodgers of the 1960s, 1970s, and early 1980s was due in no small part to the consistent manner in which these organizations went about all aspects of their business, on the field and in the front office. You could say the same thing about the Atlanta Braves of the past 15 years.

Baseball Was Never "Like It Used to Be"

Simply put, the folks who want baseball to be "like it used to be"—only about wins and losses, and never about profits and losses—are pining for a bygone era that never really existed. Like it or not, major league baseball was never "just a game." The institution has endured for more than 100 years because of, not despite, the fact that it's a business—a business where playing-field performance and income-statement performance are interrelated and interdependent.

This has remained true even as the number of zeroes required when discussing a team's profits and losses has grown significantly over time. The New York Yankees were the most profitable franchise in the first half of the 20th century, earning about $8.5 million between 1920 and 1950. During the same period, the St. Louis Cardinals, the most profitable National League franchise, earned a total of about $6 million. They were also the most successful franchises on the field over that period, winning 19 championships between them.

Those earnings look paltry today. By comparison, major league baseball is expected to generate earnings of $450 million in 2006, a 50 percent increase from the $300 million in earnings in 2005. While only five teams reported profits in 2001, there were 21 profitable teams in 2005 and, according to MLB executives, 25 of the 30 franchises should be profitable in 2006.

After many years where baseball's financial picture was much direr, this is good news for everyone involved with the game. Though much doubt was cast on owners' claims of financial hardship during previous negotiations, those claims were absolutely legitimate. Revenues have grown dramatically from the years BC (before cable), but player salaries have also grown dramatically— and not at the same rates or at the same time.

Follow the Money

Like Cal and Billy Ripken, profits and revenues are related but very different. Profits and revenues are as distinct as salary and net worth. We all know some folks who make plenty of money but still live paycheck to paycheck, buried in credit card debt. It's no different for a business. Many high-revenue companies have gone bankrupt because their expenses kept them from turning those revenues into profits.

Even so, many members of the sports media will incorrectly use the terms interchangeably. During the 1994 work stoppage, you heard major league baseball described as a $3 billion business—referring to our collective revenues. If the industry had been described as a $3 billion business running at a loss, it might have helped people better understand what we were all bickering about.

Though it hasn't always translated to profits, the growth in the amount of revenue generated by major league baseball has been staggering. Back when I first went to games, the only revenue a major league team received was from tickets, a few signs on the outfield fences, a 10¢ scorecard, hot dogs, peanuts, Cracker Jacks, beer, and soft drinks. The only marketing my father did as general manager of the Reds was to purchase a two-inch ad in the local paper and put up a sign in front of the park that read "Game tonight—8:15."

The *Supreme Court Reporter* in 1953 included data that showed that in 1929, just before the stock market crash led to the Great Depression of the 1930s, major league revenues amounted to approximately $10.5 million. That's not an average team's revenue—that's all 16 teams in aggregate.

Revenues had risen to only $12.3 million by 1939 because of the dampening effects of the Depression. By 1950, however, the great postwar economic boom helped boost revenues to $32 million. Though this was only $2 million per team, it was still enough to have *Sports Illustrated* openly worrying about its impact on the game's "amateur status."

By comparison, at the beginning of the 21st century, baseball revenues are heading past $5 billion. This phenomenal growth has been fueled by the ongoing popularity of the game itself, combined with new streams of revenue and much more aggressive and sophisticated marketing, and has taken place despite the damaging effects of periodic work stoppages.

The game's total revenues have risen steadily from $3.5 billion in 2001 to a projected $5.1 billion in 2006. Total gate receipts have grown from $1.4 billion in 2001 to a projected $2 billion in 2006. Do the math, and you'll see that non-gate revenue (luxury boxes, broadcasting rights, concessions, etc.) has grown even more rapidly over the past five years: from $2.1 to $3.1 billion.

To give you an idea on the changes in both amount and type of revenue, the following chart compares the Phillies in 1970 when I joined the organization to our situation in 2004:

Source of Revenue	1970	2004	Increase
Tickets	$4,000,000	$83,000,000	20x
Radio	$200,000	$2,000,000	10x
Over-the-air TV	$1,300,000	$10,000,000	7x
Cable TV	0	$22,000,000	
Concessions	$500,000	$17,600,000	35x
Parking	0	$5,200,000	
Advertising and publications	$120,000	$12,200,000	100x
Premium-seat rental	0	$9,400,000	
Other local revenues	$100,000	$4,100,000	40x
MLB centrally generated	$300,000	$28,250,000	95x
Total	**$6,520,000**	**$193,750,000**	**28x**

However, the Phillies' entire player payroll was $1.2 million in 1970, compared to $97 million in 2004. That's a nearly 80-fold increase in player salaries compared to the 28-fold increase in revenue.

The Gate—Real and Virtual

What is behind these huge numbers and big changes in baseball's finances? In its early days and right up to the 1950s, baseball's main source of income was "the gate." From 1929 to 1950, the percentage of revenues accounted for by gate receipts dropped from 88 percent to 74 percent, while radio and TV revenues increased from 0 percent to 10.5 percent. During the same period, revenue from concessions remained relatively constant at approximately 6–7 percent.

For the Phillies in 1970, gate receipts had dropped to 64 percent of total revenue. By 2004, tickets still accounted for more revenue than any other source—but only 45 percent of the total. Check out what we brought in from sources that were virtually nonexistent in 1950: $22 million from cable TV, $9.4 million from premium seat rentals (luxury boxes), and more than $28 million from MLB (which includes national TV and satellite radio broadcasting rights). That's nearly $60 million, or more than 30 percent from sources that generated essentially nothing 50 years ago.

Teams first began to receive revenue from radio broadcast rights in the 1940s. Over-the-air television revenue started to boost revenue even more in the 1950s, and, although the extra revenue was helpful to all teams, it was the beginning of the disparity of revenue that prevails today. Big markets like New York, Chicago, and later Southern California were growing their broadcast revenue faster than cities like Milwaukee and Kansas City.

A sampling of local TV and radio rights as reported by *Television Age* in 1956 showed that the Brooklyn Dodgers made $750,000 in TV and radio rights, while the New York Giants made $600,000, the Phillies made $300,000, and both the Chicago Cubs and the Cincinnati Reds generated $200,000 in rights fees. In the American League, the Yankees (some things never change) led with $750,000, while Cleveland sold their TV and radio rights for $350,000 and Boston made $300,000 from TV and radio.

With this in mind, I wrote in my thesis that "television will mean more to baseball in 1956 than ever before." That might seem obvious now, but at the time major league baseball's commitment to television was tenuous at best. Back then the primary concern wasn't revenue disparity, as it is now, but whether offering games on free television might reduce fans' desire to see the game in person. In a confidential report he authored as National League president in the mid-1950s, my father wrote, "I would be remiss if I did not express some alarm over the inroads television is making in our attendance. While it may be premeditated, I see a tendency in some clubs to give greater consideration to the sale of telecasting rights when considering their schedules than to the 'gate.' I recognize fully the great source of revenue which television provides—necessary revenue, too—but this must never be first in our consideration."

While acknowledging the positive effect of television, my dad went on to argue that baseball without enthusiastic fans in the stands is not baseball, and that "ticket purchasers are our life-blood."

He was right back then, and he's still right today.

Even though television generates 100 times the revenue it did 50 years ago, even though the share of revenues accounted for by the gate has dropped below 50 percent, even though local and national cable television broadcast rights now total $750 million, even though gate receipts are not growing as fast as other revenue sources, the gate remains the most important player in baseball's financial lineup.

The large and growing popularity of the NFL and NASCAR have led many to conclude that major league baseball is in trouble, is no longer the national pastime, is too slow-moving, is beset with controversy, and on and on. Those folks are not letting facts get in the way of a good argument.

Reports of baseball's demise, to paraphrase Mark Twain, have been greatly exaggerated. Attendance surpassed 76 million in 2006, which translates to more than 30,000 people per game. By comparison, in the 1950s, drawing 1 million people in a year was considered an impressive achievement for a major league franchise.

Major league baseball did not top 50 million in attendance until 1987 (24,500 per game) and did not top 30 million until 1973 (15,500 per game). It wasn't until 1962 that the 20 million level was reached, the year that baseball expanded to 20 teams and lengthened the season to 162 games. The per-game attendance was less than 14,000. Going all the way back to 1956, total major league attendance was 16.5 million, or about 13,000 per game.

Those trends, illustrated in these graphs, certainly do not support the argument that major league baseball is past its prime.

Gate receipts are a function not just of attendance, of course, but of ticket price. While attendance has gone up nearly fivefold in the past 50 years, ticket prices have gone up tenfold. The average ticket price was less than $2 in the 1950s and has risen to more than $22 in 2006, with some franchises, such as the Red Sox and the Yankees, charging close to $100 for premium tickets. A box seat for the Phillies, which was $4.25 in 1971 in the first year at the Vet, is $40 today. The

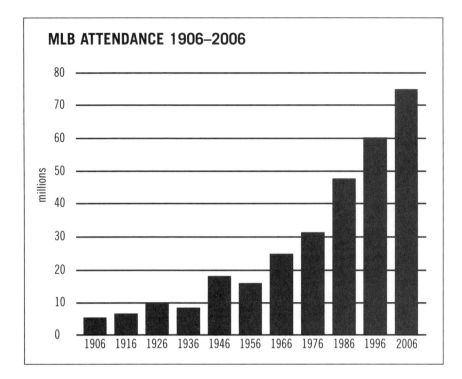

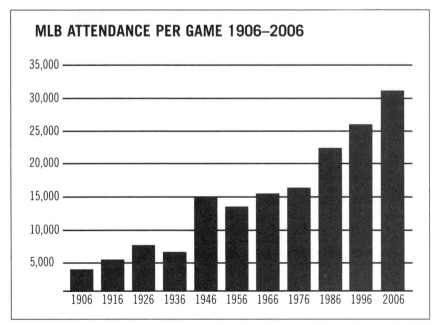

best seats (the Diamond Club) are $90, which includes a $30 allowance for food and beverages. The Dodgers and Cubs have both recently installed a few rows of superpremium seating right next to the field that attract the high rollers. On average, it costs a family of four about $170 to attend a major league baseball game, a figure that includes the cost of tickets, hot dogs, soda, and a scorecard.

For many years, ticket prices remained fairly stable, but since the 1990s, the increase has far exceeded the rate of inflation. And yet, attendance now is at an all-time high, so it's clear that people are willing to pay these prices.

In most industries, when price goes up the quantity purchased goes down. So what's happening? One way that demand and price can both go up is when the quality of the product or service goes up, which has certainly been the case for the big-league ballpark experience.

Since Camden Yards ushered in the "back to the future" era of retro ballparks with all the modern conveniences, it's been rare that a year has gone by when a team has not relocated to a new "old" park.

1992—Oriole Park at Camden Yards
1994—Jacobs Field, Ballpark in Arlington/Ameriquest Field
1995—Coors Field
1997—Turner Field
1998—Safeco Field
2000—Comerica Park, Enron Field/Astros Field/Minute Maid Park, Pacific Bell Park/SBC Park/AT&T Park
2001—Miller Park, PNC Park
2003—Great American Ball Park
2004—Citizens Bank Park, Petco Park
2006—Busch Stadium

With more on the way.

2008—Washington Ballpark
2009—Yankee Stadium II, Mets Ballpark
2010—Twins Ballpark

And the Marlins and the A's are looking to join the club, too.

By 2010, it could well be that the list of oldest ballparks will include not just the ancient Wrigley Field and Fenway Park, but the didn't-we-used-to-be-new Rogers Centre (SkyDome), Kauffman Stadium, Angel Stadium, and Dodger Stadium.

Teams have raised ticket prices an average of almost 50 percent when they opened a new ballpark. Fans are willing to pay these higher ticket prices because their experience in these new ballparks is so much better than in the old stadiums they have typically replaced. While the Vet was a great place for the Phillies for more than 30 years and fans that grew up going to the Vet have many fond memories, there is no comparison between our former home and Citizens Bank Park.

The obstructed views of the first generation of ballparks and the long distances from the field of the second generation of ballparks are (mostly) gone. (You can still find examples of both in Chicago.) Also rapidly disappearing from the scene is ticket pricing based solely on the proximity of a seat to the field.

Though major league baseball is still a long way from the complexity of airline ticket pricing—which has evolved into something just short of rocket science—the principle remains the same: higher demand for a product or service means a higher price can be charged. Most teams now use some type of variable ticket pricing, so that higher prices can be charged for premium dates—typically weekends, interleague games, and rivalries, such as when the Cardinals visit Chicago. This type of ticket pricing policy is no different than other service businesses. Value dates with lower ticket prices help attract one group of fans, while another group is willing to pay more for attractions such as the Yankees.

The final source of revenue for major league baseball now centers around the Internet, satellites, telephones, and electronic and wireless devices of all kinds.

Baseball, which historically had lived in the past, finally became very forward-thinking by creating a subsidiary named BAM, which stands for Baseball Advanced Media. MLBAM is a wholly owned subsidiary of MLB and generates revenue through the Internet by selling tickets and merchandise online while also offering both audio and video play-by-play, highlights, subscription fantasy games, scores, and updates to fans on their computers—and now other digital devices such as cell phones and PDAs. A virtual gate, if you will. MLBAM is growing rapidly and will continue to do so, generating more than $300 million in revenue in 2006, up from only $5 million in 2000.

Another source of technology-related growth is satellite radio. MLB signed an exclusive deal with XM Radio starting in 2005, which generates about $60 million a year. Gone are the days of fans trying to catch a St. Louis night game through the static of their AM car radio. Now you can get all home-game broadcasts beamed down, crystal clear, from a satellite—which is as close to baseball heaven as you can get. Though XM offers more than 200 channels of programming, many subscribers pay the $150 per year for the baseball alone. Another development could be baseball's own cable TV channel, which has been a topic of discussion for several years among the owners and the commissioner's office.

Another significant source of revenue is MLB Enterprises, Inc., which includes merchandising, sponsorship, licensing, and international operations. MLB centralized these efforts several years ago and added a good deal of marketing muscle so that more than $200 million will be generated from these operations in 2006.

These revenues are shared equally by all 30 teams, so the disparity between teams will not be affected by continued growth in these areas—which is a good thing when you look at how drastic that disparity has gotten.

Haves and Have-Nots

I guess if all we owners cared about was money, George Steinbrenner would be the most popular man in the game. But we don't, and he's not. Even though he gives up more than $100 million to other teams through revenue sharing and luxury tax and pays a fortune to field a perennial contender in New York that draws more fans to other parks who pay more money for tickets, the resources

George has at his disposal make it very difficult to compete with him and some resentment does result.

From 1980 to 1986—after the birth of free agency and before the days of extreme revenue disparity—20 of baseball's 26 teams made it to a League Championship Series. From 1995 through 2001, only 11 of baseball's 30 teams made it to a League Championship Series. No team outside the top 25 percent in team payroll won a single World Series game in the years from 1995 to 2001.

Historically, teams in larger markets have always had an advantage. It's pretty simple: when there are more people in your market, you will generally sell more tickets and have more people watching your games on TV and buying merchandise. In addition, large markets mean more businesses and more corporate support through season tickets and sponsorships. The Yankees and later the Dodgers were consistently the big-money clubs, but the difference in revenues from top to bottom in baseball wasn't all that huge.

The gap between the haves and the have-nots was much smaller back in the 1950s because revenues were still almost entirely attendance-driven. For the decade, the Yankees drew 16 million fans. Washington—first in war, first in peace, last in the American League—drew 5.6 million fans. A small-market team that fielded a winner—the Milwaukee Braves—actually outdrew the Yankees every year after relocating from Boston, where they couldn't draw flies.

The disparity in team revenues didn't start to get very serious until the late 1980s, when a variable other than gate receipts was introduced—a variable where the gap between have and have-not was far wider than the gap between 7,000 fans per game at Griffith Stadium to watch Mickey Vernon compared to 21,000 fans per game at Yankee Stadium to watch Mickey Mantle.

Ted Turner and his TBS Superstation started the cable ball rolling, and it continues to grow in popularity as a delivery service for sports of all kinds. The fact that the Atlanta Braves baseball games could be seen on TBS prompted cable operators all over the country to pay a few cents a month to Turner in order to get more cable subscribers and therefore more revenue. I wonder if cable television would be where it is today had Ted Turner not televised his Braves games on TBS.

"You know, Bill," Turner told me in the early 1990s, "there never would have been a CNN had the Braves not been on the TBS Superstation."

WGN in Chicago copied this model and began to broadcast Cubs games all over the country. Harry Caray broadcast baseball for almost 60 years, but he never became a cult figure until the 1980s when Cubs telecasts were available all over the country. Remember Walter O'Malley's argument that televised baseball games would actually help attendance? Well, no team has seen their attendance increase more since the pre-Superstation days of the early '80s than the Cubs. In 1982 they drew fewer than 15,000 per game. Now, even with their games available on TV just about everywhere, they don't play to very many empty seats at Wrigley Field. They drew 38,000 per game in 2005 to watch a 79-win team. People who watch the Cubs on television see a one-of-a-kind ballpark that they want to experience for themselves.

George Steinbrenner saw the value of cable television and created the YES Network, which carries Yankees games and related programming, and an income stream that allows him to have payrolls in the $200 million range. Thanks to Steinbrenner's YES Network, the Yankees took in $62 million in cable TV revenue in 2005 alone.

So what happens when you combine large markets with broad television exposure? You increase the value of your sponsorships. This is another area where the rich get richer. For example, the Yankees generated $49 million in sponsorship income in 2005 and topped $50 million in 2006, while the Oakland A's get only about $8 million from sponsors.

The growth in cable TV revenue—and, in turn, its impact on sponsorship revenue—has led to an ever-widening gap between the haves and the have-nots in major league baseball. The difference in total revenue between the highest- and lowest-grossing franchises, which was a few million in the 1950s, grew to $30 million in 1989, topped $160 million in 2002, and was up to $260 million by 2005.

Instead of just being outdrawn by a factor three-to-one at the gate, the Washington Senators of the modern era—the Tampa Bay Devil Rays—are being trounced even more severely at the cable box, too.

By now you've seen a lot of numbers, but if you're looking for just one to sum up the current disparity between rich and poor in major league baseball, take a look at the analysis done by *Forbes* magazine in 2006. The Yankees are estimated to be worth $1 billion, five times more than the Devil Rays, who are at the bottom of the list at $200 million.

Sharing the Wealth—Somewhat

Hence the push for "sharing the pie" more equally, as the NFL has done for years. Easier said than done, I assure you.

There's a joke that goes something like this:

A man finds a bottle in an abandoned corner of a large library. When he opens it, a genie appears.

"To thank you for rescuing me," the genie says. "I will grant you one wish."

The man thinks for a moment, then says, "I would like peace in the Middle East."

The genie asks to see a map. After studying it for several minutes, he finally says, "It can't be done. Make another wish."

The man says, "I'm a Pittsburgh Pirates fan. I would like to see all owners agree on a way to share their revenues fairly to ensure competitive balance in the major leagues."

To which the genie responds, "Let me see that map again."

Getting 30 major league owners to agree on anything is hard enough—but getting us red-blooded capitalists to agree on how to share each other's money is brutally difficult. That's the main reason why the labor negotiations of the 1990s were so protracted. They weren't a test of wills between two groups (players and owners), but among three (players, small-market owners, and large-market owners). The small-market owners wanted to solve their financial problems through revenue sharing. The large-market owners wanted none of that and wanted something that would benefit all teams—a salary cap. The players didn't want a salary cap and changed the subject to revenue sharing. And around the circle it went.

Nevertheless, Major League Baseball has made some progress in addressing the issues of competitive imbalance—for which I give Bud Selig a lot of credit. He was able to garner enough support from enough owners to push through both a revenue-sharing system and a luxury-tax system. Under this system in 2005, baseball transferred $312 million from 13 high-revenue teams to the other 17 teams. Of that amount, the Yankees, with revenues of $354 million, kicked in $77 million, while the Boston Red Sox chipped in $51 million. George Steinbrenner's Yankees also paid a payroll luxury tax of $34 million on his 2005 payroll of $223 million.

From a competitive balance perspective, revenue sharing appears to be working. During the past six years, 19 different teams have reached the postseason. And there has been a different World Series winner each of the past seven years, including the Red Sox in 2004 and the White Sox in 2005, ending two of the longest droughts (Red Sox since 1918 and White Sox since 1917) in baseball. Cubs fans (last championship in 1908) are, unfortunately, still waiting for the "If Brothers"—the oft-injured Kerry Wood and Mark Prior—to lead them there.

Baseball's revenue-sharing systems are far from perfect. The smallest-market teams will still argue that they have no legitimate shot at contending unless the stars completely align. The larger-market teams will complain that there is no requirement that the teams receiving revenue will spend that money on improving the team, either in terms of higher team payroll or investment in the minor league system. For example, it has been reported that the Florida Marlins received revenue-sharing income of more than $30 million in 2006 but cut their payroll to only $15 million this season.

As recently as 1990, the gap from highest to lowest player payroll was more than $12 million. In 2006 the gap between the Yankees and the Marlins is almost $188 million. The increasing disparity of team payrolls, of course, matches the increasing disparity in team revenues.

I believe that there should be a minimum team payroll so that teams cannot let their revenue-sharing income simply drop to the bottom line. The whole point of revenue sharing is to address the competitive imbalance created by the disparity of team revenues, but the point is missed if the receiving teams don't use the money to invest in building their ballclubs.

Hurricane Marvin, Arbitration, Free Agency, and the End of the World as We Knew It

Back in the late 1970s, small-market teams used free agency to do just that—build their ballclubs—and they didn't need other teams' money to do it because free agents were more "affordable" back then. For example, in the first free-agent class of 1976, there were two future Hall of Famers. One went to the Yankees (Reggie Jackson), but the other went to the fifth-place San Diego Padres (Rollie Fingers). While the big-market Angels were very active, snagging Don Baylor, Bobby Grich, and Joe Rudi, so too were the Brewers (Sal Bando), the Expos (Dave Cash), the Rangers (Bert Campaneris), and the then-small-market Braves (Gary Matthews).

Put another way, there was competitive balance in the acquisition of free agents. And this contributed, in part, to greater competitive balance on the field.

But not for long. The most dramatic (and some would say traumatic) impact of the elimination of the reserve clause and the institution of a free-agent system has been on the expense side of baseball's income statement, which has priced many teams out of the market for premium free agents.

To fully understand why the elimination of the reserve clause was so dramatic/traumatic, it helps to understand where we came from. The reserve clause was in effect from the earliest days of organized professional baseball. Owners first agreed to "reserve" five players in 1879. This effectively bound those players to the teams for which they played. Gradually, the reserve clause was expanded to cover all of the players on the major league roster because it kept owners from raiding each other's teams and driving up salaries.

Here's how Commissioner Ford Frick described the reserve clause in *Organized Baseball*:

> The reserve clause is not merely a provision of the contract, but also incorporates a reticulated system of rules and regulations which enable, indeed require, the entire baseball organization to respect and enforce each club's exclusive and continuous right to the services of its players. The club is given the right to renew the contract on the same terms for the following year.... The renewed clause obviously gives the club a perpetual option on the player's services. This rule deprives every baseball player, once he has signed his first contract and until he is given a release, of any right to elect or even bargain about what club he shall play for.

From its beginnings through the 1975 season, Major League Baseball adhered to this reserve system, which gave the owners 100 percent of the power in bargaining with players. As a result, salaries in that bygone era look remarkably low today. Richie Ashburn told me that Phillies owner Bob Carpenter gave him only a $1,000 raise the year after he led the National League in batting in 1955. Superstars such as Joe DiMaggio, and later Mickey Mantle, were the highest-paid players in the game at $100,000 a year.

To offer some perspective on just how major league salaries have escalated with the changing economic conditions of the game, I can point to data in my thesis that came from the 1955 National League President's Report. (It was certainly convenient that my dad was NL president.) In 1951, the average salary for all National League players was $12,102, and by 1955 that figure had increased 15 percent to $13,920. By comparison, the average salary for the 25 National League All-Stars in 1955 was $24,420. Only one NL player at the time had a salary higher than $75,000. The combined salaries of all of the players in the American and National Leagues amounted to $3.3 million in 1939 and rose to $5.9 million in 1950. That's less than Steve Karsay made last year. Back then, major league players made approximately four and a half times what the average American earned.

Not a bad living by any means, if you could accept the fact that you weren't going to have any control over where you played and who you played with. For just about its entire history, Major League Baseball has been the only game in town. The most recent example of a competitive "major league"? The Federal League, in 1914 and 1915. The increased competition for talent drove up salaries, but they came right back down after the league folded. In the 1940s, some players "jumped" to Mexico for more money. When they tried to return to the major league, suspensions were handed down by the commissioner's office.

So when did it all start to change? When Marvin Miller took over as executive director of the Major League Baseball Players Association in 1966. Up to that time, the Players Association had been run by Judge Robert Cannon almost as a house union, and there had been no labor disagreements. Miller was an experienced labor economist, and he was both shrewd and very smart. He worked patiently and diligently with the players on issues such as the minimum salary, the pension fund, and a grievance procedure. I can't say he was motivated by a love of the game. I think he just wanted the players to get their fair share of revenues.

The story about the end of the reserve clause is well known. After the 1969 season, Curt Flood was traded by the Cardinals to the Phillies against his wishes. He refused to report to the Phillies and petitioned the commissioner at the time, Bowie Kuhn, that he be allowed to refuse the trade. He was told that he could not and that he either played with the Phillies in 1970 or did not play at all. Flood decided to test the reserve clause by filing a lawsuit, supported by the Major League Baseball Players Association, which went all the way to the Supreme Court. The majority opinion supported Major League Baseball and upheld the reserve clause, but its days were numbered.

In 1974 Jim "Catfish" Hunter was declared a free agent after filing a grievance based on the fact that his owner, Charles Finley, had failed to make a contractually obligated payment to an annuity. The Phillies tried hard to sign Hunter but were outbid by the Yankees, who gave him a $3.75 million guaranteed five-year contract. Both the players and owners alike saw the potential effect on salaries if the reserve clause was lifted.

Finally, two pitchers, Andy Messersmith of the Dodgers and Dave McNally of the Expos, played the 1975 season without signing contracts. They jointly filed a grievance, claiming that since they had played the season without a contract, they could no longer be held "in reserve" by their respective clubs. The case went to arbitration before Peter Seitz, MLB's designated arbitrator, who ruled that the right to automatically renew a player's contract lasted for only one year, not year after year, and declared both players free agents. The reserve clause was dead as of December 23, 1975—which for major league owners will always be a "day of infamy." A whole new era in salaries was ushered in. The rest, as they say, is history.

Even before the Seitz decision created free agency, salary arbitration was agreed to by the owners and the Players Association. Arbitration's impact on Major League Baseball's salary structure is overshadowed by free agency, but it has been very significant. In fact, you will even hear some owners speak more ill of arbitration than of free agency. Salary arbitration is granted to a player after he has played three years in the major leagues, while free agency cannot occur until after six years. If a player and team cannot agree on a contract, the player can file for arbitration. Both the player and the team submit a figure, and the arbitrator chooses one or the other. In virtually every case, even if the team's figure is chosen, the salary goes up, often dramatically. Most cases are settled before arbitration, as the team and player will often agree to a number between the two offers on the table rather than go through what is a fairly unpleasant process for everyone involved.

That's one of the worst aspects of the system. You are forced into competition with your own player. The team, in presenting its case, has to devalue the player. This can often lead to some hard feelings. As such, some agents advise their clients to not even attend.

Teams do not have to go to arbitration. Under the 2002–2006 labor agreement they can avoid it by not offering a contract to a arbitration-eligible player by December 20 of that year and trying to negotiate a better deal for the club—which occurs more frequently now than in the past. If the team can't get a deal done within a fixed window of opportunity, they can't re-sign the player until May 1 of the following year. This was the case with the Astros and Roger Clemens in 2006.

Free agency and arbitration have worked in concert to push salaries upward. A free-agent signing sets a salary standard that will affect an arbitrator's interpretation of the market value of a player. On the other hand, high arbitration awards set a standard that players strive to exceed with their free-agent contracts.

Following the advent of arbitration and free agency, the average major league salary jumped from $45,000 in 1975 to $289,000 in 1983 and continued to rise, except for a brief period in the mid-1980s—the "collusion" period you can read about in chapter 15, "The Commissioners," under Peter Ueberroth.

As rapidly as payrolls escalated in the late '70s—driving a number of long-time owners out of the game, including the Carpenters—it was a mere blip compared to the 1990s.

In 1988 the Yankees had the highest team payroll, spending just less than $19 million.

In 1990—and you can win a lot of bar bets on this one—it was the Kansas City Royals who led the way with a payroll of $23 million.

Five years later, it had more than doubled—with the Blue Jays spending just less than $50 million in 1995.

Ten years later, it had quadrupled—with the Yankees, who have had the highest payroll each year since 1999, reaching the $200 million mark in 2005.

Thirty years after the end of the reserve clause, baseball's average salary is up to almost $2.9 million. Nowadays, a utility player earns as much as all the players in the majors earned just before World War II. While players earned four and half times more than the average American in the 1950s, the major league *minimum* is now nine times the average American's salary. The major league average: 75 times the average American's salary. Alex Rodriguez is currently the highest-paid player at $25.7 million. He makes as much per at-bat as the average American makes in a year.

Four players (Rodriguez, Derek Jeter, Jason Giambi—all Yankees—and Barry Bonds) have salaries higher than $20 million. More than 400 players make at least $1 million. The minimum salary, which was $5,000 in the 1940s and $6,000 in the 1950s, and was still less than $100,000 in the late 1980s, has reached $327,000 in 2006.

Salaries have skyrocketed since 1975 not only because teams bid against each other, but because teams wind up having to give more long-term, guaranteed contracts. When the Cubs sign Kerry Wood to a large, multiyear contract—or the Phillies and Randy Wolf, or the Rangers and Chan Ho Park, or just about any team and any front-line pitcher signed to a long-term deal—and he breaks down or is ineffective, the team now needs to either attempt to replace that player with a cheap but inexperienced rookie or pay still more money for another veteran.

Disability insurance was readily available in the early years; for example, the Phillies recovered $17 million in insurance proceeds for injuries to Darren Daulton and Lenny Dykstra in the 1990s. But the insurance companies didn't have to take too many of those baths before they figured out they needed to change their pricing. Today, insurance for long-term contracts is so expensive that most clubs won't purchase it. Even when teams do have it, they can find themselves in the very awkward situation that the Astros were in with Jeff Bagwell at the start of the 2006 season—trying in vain to convince the best player the franchise has ever had to retire so they can have the insurance company be the one to pay him millions of dollars to play golf.

The combined impact of free agency and collective bargaining on salaries has been, to say the least, dramatic. But we couldn't pay these salaries if our revenues didn't support them. For a while, they didn't. A World Series got canceled over that one.

As rapidly as revenues have accelerated since the 1950s, player salaries have made them look like Cecil Fielder running into a headwind. You can see this in how much of a team's revenues go toward player salaries. This has fluctuated over time, but was typically in the 20–30 percent range for most of the pre-Seitz history of Major League Baseball. The percentage began to rise precipitously with the end of the reserve clause and passed 50 percent for the first time in 1992, reaching 54 percent in 2001. It has leveled off and is around 51 percent now.

Fiscal irresponsibility may benefit a handful of players in the short term, but it's bad for the game. Starting a few years ago, Bud Selig began making owners adhere to a debt-service provision, which means that teams can only borrow so much money before they're cut off. This is forcing teams to be more fiscally responsible—to live within their means. Since 2002 and the labor agreement, which expired after the 2006 season, the owners have tried to operate the industry more like a CEO runs a company.

Though salaries did increase 9 percent in 2006, this can be funded by the increased profits of major league franchises. Despite more responsible owner behavior in recent years, I remain concerned that uncontrolled spending could put us right back to the tight times of the late 1990s, when we exhausted new or expanding revenue sources as soon we found them.

Looking Back, Looking Ahead

I've enjoyed pulling out my old college paper to see how much has changed—and how much has stayed the same. It was also interesting to see how some of my predictions worked out. Some showed keen insight into the future—some were, well, like signing Lenny Dykstra to a $27.5 million contract right before his back gave out.

As part of my thesis, I reacted to Commissioner Frick's comments on the expansion of major league baseball, which he favored, based largely on the financial success of the three franchises that relocated in the early 1950s: the Boston Braves to Milwaukee, the St. Louis

Browns to Baltimore, and the Philadelphia Athletics to Kansas City. In fact, Frick had written in *The Sporting News* in 1957 that "I still think there will be a third Major League." He was referring to the Continental League, a brainchild of my godfather, Branch Rickey. Ultimately, of course, there was no Continental or other "third major league" but there was expansion, starting in 1961 in the AL and 1962 in the NL, which raised the number of major league franchises from 16 to 20. In the ensuing three-plus decades, the number of franchises has increased to 30.

My take on expansion in 1956: "In expanding the Major League, baseball will spread its product entirely too thin. The quality of Major League Baseball will decline, and, in the long run, the financial benefits will be less than they are today."

Well, that proved to be a poor prophecy, although each expansion did bring with it improved offensive statistics largely because of thin pitching staffs, but this result has always been short-lived. Though I still think we'd be better off with 28 teams rather than 30, I can't say that expansion has lived down to my expectations.

I took a much more accurate look into the future on the topic of expansion when I wrote: "Geographical expansion has not been limited to this country. Baseball is growing with enthusiasm on the international scene. Professional baseball leagues are already in progress in Mexico, Canada, Cuba, and Puerto Rico. Japan and European countries are growing with enthusiasm over the 'American game.' Baseball is now being played more and more in Europe and the Orient."

I don't know whether a .500 batting average for predictions is good or bad, but here's another attempt to look into the future. Instead of expansion, the topic this time is labor relations.

At the risk of jinxing it, today's high salaries and strong earnings bode well for the collective bargaining process. For years, the players felt that the owners were getting an inordinate amount of the profits. Recently, the owners have felt that the situation had reversed—even with television revenues going through the roof. Jerry Reinsdorf, owner of the Chicago White Sox, used to bemoan this state of affairs very succinctly.

"Why do we need the extra money?" Reinsdorf would say frequently after signing Albert Belle to a massive contract. "We just give it right back to the players."

It would appear to me that we may have finally reached a point where the split is perceived as equitable by both groups. When that's the case, issues tend to get resolved.

Here's hoping that, like $100,000 superstars, baseball's economic situation has evolved to a point where work stoppages are also a thing of the past.

Special Players

When I look back at my time around the big leagues, it's not the ballparks, the financial deals, or the playoff games that first come to mind. It's the players. I have known too many to count, but here are seven of the most special players I ever had the privilege to be around. They helped make my time in baseball entertaining, exhilarating, and at times maddening.

But never dull.

Mike Schmidt and the Disguise That Changed Everything

Mike Schmidt, the greatest third baseman of all time, was probably booed more by the hometown fans than any other Hall of Fame player in the history of baseball. It was hard to understand, particularly by Mike himself. The booing became particularly bad after I signed him to a $2-million-a-year contract, making him the highest-paid player in baseball in 1982.

Despite his great talent and accomplishments, Schmidt was very sensitive and possessed neither the self-confidence, nor the assertiveness, nor the expressiveness of someone like Pete Rose. To be able to perform in a high-pressure environment like Philadelphia requires some degree of cockiness—of not really caring what anyone else thinks. And when all else fails, it helps to get your uniform dirty and lose your cool—something that Schmidt didn't do enough for the fans' liking.

Schmidt may have cared too much what people thought about him—like Alex Rodriguez today, another highly paid, supremely talented third baseman playing in an intense market where it must feel like nothing he does will ever be good enough. The pressure of being the highest-paid player caused Schmidt to struggle in the beginning of the 1983 season, and the boo-birds really got to him. There was one season-ticket holder in the first row right behind third base who was merciless.

"Two million dollars, my ass!" was a constant chant.

I could tell the boos were affecting his performance, so I met with Schmidt to try to relieve his anxiety. I used a parenting metaphor.

"When your kids do something wrong, you or your wife will scold the child. But you both still love the child. It's the same principle when you come to bat. The fans really do love you, but if you strike out or pop up with the bases loaded, they are going to scold you by booing. The fans never boo a reserve infielder because they don't expect much. But they expect a lot from a player of your stature. When you disappoint them, they will let you know about it."

That last point has proven over the years to be especially true in Philadelphia.

In 1985 the entire relationship between the fans and Schmidt changed dramatically. Mike had made some negative comments about the physical condition of the Vet and had blasted the fans for being so negative. The Phillies returned home from Montreal to be greeted with a newspaper story built around Schmidt's comments. It didn't help that Schmidt was having what was, for him, an off year as he tried to learn a new position (first base) during a season where the Phillies were playing disappointing baseball. Put it all together, and it was a recipe for disaster.

Before that first game back at the Vet, Schmidt was bemoaning his situation to pitcher Larry Andersen. "I'm really going to get hammered by the fans today."

"You're right," Andersen replied. "You can't show your face out there today. We need to get you a disguise."

But Larry didn't have just any old disguise in mind. He got hold of a very large woman's wig and some dark sunglasses from Debbie Nocito in the Phillies' marketing department. Even more impressive than finding that stuff on short notice was Andersen's ability to convince Schmidt to actually wear that getup out on the field.

"The fans are just waiting to bury you right now," Andersen reasoned, "so you might as well have fun. It can't get much worse."

Schmidt ran out to first base with his wig and glasses on, demonstrating both humility and good humor. The fans laughed and gave him a standing ovation. From that point on there were only cheers for Michael Jack Schmidt.

Struggling to maintain the caliber of play he was used to, Schmidt retired suddenly and unexpectedly four years later on May 29, 1989, in San Diego. At that point, he expected me to name him general manager of the Phillies, just like the Philadelphia Flyers hockey team had done with their star Bobby Clarke.

I had met with Schmidt a number of times about his future with the Phillies. If he couldn't be general manager, he wanted to manage the big club or at least be the hitting coach. I told him no, and he was very disappointed.

"Schmittie" is a very nice man. I really like him as a person, and his wife, Donna, is exceptional—but I just did not think he would make a good manager. He had some unusual theories about playing the game, and he was basically an introverted person.

Schmidt was so naturally talented that I believed it would be difficult for him to educate the players. Most immortal players have never managed, and those who have did not achieve the same level of success in the dugout as they did out of it.

Take a look at the All-Century Team that was picked back in 1999. Of the 30 players on that team—which included Mike Schmidt as the starting third baseman—only six managed at least one full season in the big leagues: Walter Johnson, Christy Mathewson, Rogers Hornsby, Yogi Berra, Ted Williams, and Pete Rose. Only one got a team to the World Series without being able to put himself as a starter in the lineup (Yogi

Berra), and he wasn't able to win one. Of that group, the player whose personal style may have been closest to Schmidt's was Ted Williams, and his struggles with managing a team of mere mortals are legendary.

Fifteen years after his retirement as an active player, and after serving as a special spring training instructor for a number of years with the Phillies, Schmidt finally did manage the Phillies Class A Clearwater team in 2004. Unfortunately, it didn't really work out well for him or the team.

Ted Williams took up fly fishing after he retired and came to excel at it. I see professional golf as something Mike Schmidt could do. He and I have made a number of golf trips to Ireland, Scotland, and Spain together, and I'm proud to say that he has never won money from me on the golf course. Of course, he gives me a stroke a hole. He is an excellent golfer—his power translates very well from baseball to golf—and he has tried to qualify for the senior tour. Don't bet against him.

Odd as it may sound, Schmidt really did me a huge favor by retiring. One of the hardest jobs I had as CEO of the Phillies was releasing star players. While being able to watch great athletes perform at their peak is one of the most rewarding aspects of being "the boss," watching great players who are past their prime but hanging on, refusing to acknowledge the decline of their skills, is perhaps the most difficult. It's hard to watch and always made me sad. When you are the executive who has to make personnel decisions, it can be downright painful.

One such decision was more painful than just about any other.

Steve Carlton and the Wine-Tasting Lesson

I released Pete Rose right after the World Series in 1983. I released Tug McGraw on Valentine's Day. I released Larry Christenson on his birthday. The hardest cut I ever had to make, however, was releasing Steve Carlton, one of the greatest pitchers of all time, in the middle of the 1986 season.

Carlton was a dominating pitcher for 18 years, first with the Cardinals but mostly with the Phillies. He won more than 300 games and amassed more than 4,000 strikeouts. During his prime, he was virtually unhittable. But in 1985, he started to struggle and was plagued by injuries, winning only one game and losing eight. He was still ineffective in the early part of 1986. It was brutal to watch.

I went to visit Steve and his lovely wife, Bev, in their Rittenhouse Square apartment. I told them how difficult it was for me and all Phillies fans to see him struggling to get hitters out. I asked him to retire. I told him I would pay him for the remainder of the year and honor him with a Steve Carlton Night where we would retire his number, 32. I wanted him to go out on top and be remembered for his greatness, not as a "hanger-on."

"I'm not going to retire," Steve told me. "I'm going to pitch until I'm 50 years old."

Being a great pitcher interfered with his ability to see the reality of what was happening on the field. A month passed and Carlton was still not pitching well. I asked him again to retire, but the answer was still no. We were at an impasse, and I had no other choice but to release him. It was a difficult and emotional day, but under the circumstances I felt I had to do it. He did try to pitch two more seasons, having brief stints with San Francisco, Cleveland, Minnesota, and the Chicago White Sox, but never came close to the dominating presence he once had.

"He's the best pitcher in the world," Pete Rose once said, "unless the Russians have got one I haven't seen."

Steve Carlton's greatness stemmed from many characteristics. At 6'4", he was able to exert tremendous leverage in his delivery. He also possessed fantastic concentration, sometimes using earplugs to block out the crowd noise. He had immense determination. He had command of a great fastball and a virtually unhittable slider. He did not pitch to hitters, he pitched to sectors of the plate. Carlton did not get hung up on the strengths and weaknesses of the opposing batters; he knew that if he executed his pitches, it did not matter who was at the plate. And he kept himself in fantastic physical condition.

Carlton's workouts with the Phillies' strength and conditioning coach, Gus Hoefling, were legendary. Carlton would do 1,100 sit-ups at a time with 15-pound weights on both his wrists and ankles. Why sit-ups? Stomach muscles—which you'll hear described as "the core"—are essential to the torso rotation that generates a pitcher's power. As part of his workout regimen, he would also spend an hour walking and exercising his arms in a four-foot-deep, 30-foot-long "rice pit." If you think that sounds easy, try making a fist and forcing it down into a bucket of dry rice sometime. With that kind of commitment to arm strength and flexibility, you can see why he was able to pitch for as long as he did and be as relatively injury free as he was.

Despite all his conditioning efforts, you wouldn't be able to find Carlton running on the field with the other pitchers before games. Why? Because he thought he looked awkward. Steve was a very proud man.

Carlton was also a very private man. He felt invaded when *Philadelphia Daily News* baseball writer Bill Conlin wrote an article about Carlton's father being an alcoholic. From that point on, Steve would no longer talk to the press. It was called the "Big Silence." He ultimately became known as "the Sphinx" because of this combination of strength and silence.

Steve, as well as a lot of the other players, did not like writers traveling on the Phillies' charter flights. I talked to team president Ruly Carpenter about it and convinced him to prohibit writers from our charters. For the writers who had grown accustomed to being part of these trips, it proved to be a very unpopular decision. In fact, I can't recall Bill Conlin writing one positive comment about me since.

Carlton wasn't too crazy about photographers, either. He and I had a little game I called "Find Steve on Camera Night." Every year we had a promotion called Camera Night, where fans were permitted on the playing field before a game. All the players, coaches, announcers, and manager would slowly parade around the field as the fans took pictures of their favorites. Carlton refused to participate. I would send a couple of my assistants to find him and get him on the field, but Steve always found a hiding place. After he retired, he finally told me where he would hide—concession stands, restrooms, broom closets, city offices, you name it.

"It's not that I don't respect the fans," Carlton explained. "I just feel silly parading around out there."

Carlton actually had an enormous respect for the fans of Philadelphia and a wonderfully understated manner of recognizing it when he was standing on the mound or walking toward the dugout. When the fans cheered him for one of his many great efforts, he would nod his head and tip his left hand to the bill of his cap. It was a simple and sincere way of saying thanks.

I love it when players give some signal to the fans to show that they appreciate them being there. Tug McGraw slapping his glove on his thigh after getting out of a tough jam. Pete Rose tipping his cap when he got a standing ovation. Classy gestures like these show that the players understand the fans are an integral part of the game.

Steve Carlton was a first-class man and somewhat misunderstood, but he certainly did have an unusual personality. When he was playing, he was difficult to communicate with for most people—except Gus Hoefling, his favorite catcher Tim McCarver, and a few others. McCarver joked that when they died they'd be buried 60'6" apart. Harry Kalas will tell you that one on one—provided there was no tape recorder present—Lefty would talk his ear off. Unlike Gus, Tim, and Harry, I had a real hard time talking with him.

Steve kept to himself for the most part and didn't much care for all the banter in the clubhouse, especially on the days he was pitching. At his request, we built him a soundproof "mood room" in the clubhouse, where he could relax in a lounge chair surrounded by soothing pictures of waves and clouds and listen to calming music. He read Eastern philosophy and would practice tai chi in the clubhouse before games. Scoff if you want, but, as with most things that have to do with Lefty, the results on the field speak for themselves.

Carlton was also a fanatical nutritionist and a wine connoisseur. In fact, it was his passion for wine that allowed me to see the Sphinx one time in a very un-Sphinx-like state. After the Phillies won the World

Series in 1980, we were invited to go to Honolulu to participate in the Super Teams competition. It was one of those made-for-TV competitions, consisting of the two NFL teams from the last Super Bowl game and the baseball teams participating in the last World Series. The Phillies, Kansas City Royals, Oakland Raiders, and Philadelphia Eagles were the participants. They competed in swimming, volleyball, rowing, track and field, and tug-of-war. I will never forget what great swimmers Greg Luzinski and Dick Ruthven were.

On the final evening of our trip, I held a party at the Third Floor restaurant in Honolulu for the Phillies' group of 40 people, including wives. I was afraid that if I did not order the wine in advance, Carlton would wind up buying $1,000 bottles of wine for everyone. But I didn't want to seem cheap, so I bought about a dozen bottles of $120 wine, half chardonnay and half merlot, and had them distributed on the tables before anyone arrived. I watched Carlton arrive, and he immediately looked at the wine. He then looked at me and gave me a thumbs-up, showing that he was pleased with my choice.

He was not happy, however, with the way I was drinking my wine. He was sitting at the far end of a rectangular table from my seat on a red leather bench. After a few minutes, he headed toward my wife and me with a glass of red wine in his hand.

"Bill, that was a great choice of wine, but you and Nancy are not drinking it properly," he said, taking a seat next to me on the bench. "You do not sip wine. You take a big swig of wine and let it rest in your mouth for a few seconds and swirl it around to give your taste buds a chance to savor it. Then you swallow."

Of course, as he was explaining how to drink, he was downing his merlot.

After about 15 minutes of demonstrating, his rear end started to slip off the bench we were both sitting on. He excused himself to the men's room. Forty-five minutes lapsed and Carlton did not return. I went hunting for him, to no avail. I called the Honolulu police to be on the lookout for a 6'4", dark-haired man who might be staggering around Waikiki Beach. His wife, Bev, Nancy, and I went back to our hotel and up to Carlton's room. There he was, passed out on the couch.

I still *sip* wine.

Steve's personality changed after he was inducted into baseball's Hall of Fame. He became very outgoing, personable, and he loved to talk to people. I still remember how he handled himself at Steve Carlton Night at Veterans Stadium. You never know how professional athletes will do in front of a microphone, out of their element. We especially wondered about Carlton, given how little he spoke to anyone.

His remarks that night were as magnificent as his pitching.

The Many Things to Admire about Joe Morgan

Hall of Fame second baseman Joe Morgan and I started our baseball careers together when he was one of the Houston Colt .45s and I was the team's publicity director. Back then, Morgan was not a good fielder. He had trouble with ground balls to his right and he could not turn the double play very well. But he worked hard and became extremely proficient in all phases of the game. He ended up winning five consecutive Gold Glove Awards in the 1970s—all with one of the smallest gloves you will ever see on an adult's hand. He felt it allowed him to get the ball out more quickly.

Pat Gillick was the assistant farm director for the Colts back then, and he will tell you that—despite being only 5'8", having a relatively weak arm, and "hard hands" when it came to fielding ground balls—they were not surprised when Morgan became a very successful big leaguer.

"It was his attitude that made him stand out more than anything. He knew what he had to do to succeed," Gillick will tell you. "He was very aggressive and had the kind of cockiness you like to see. He always thought positively. Even when things didn't go well, you knew that Joe was thinking 'How can I solve this problem in the future?'"

"Little Joe" was his nickname because of his height, but there was nothing little about his performance, his production, or his professionalism. Not only could he play the game well, he was also very intelligent in how he went about his business—a trait that would pay off very well after he retired.

One of my better player acquisitions was trading pitchers Mike Krukow and Mark Davis to San Francisco for Morgan and closer Al Holland on December 14, 1982. Without Morgan and Holland, we would not have been in the 1983 World Series. Morgan, who was at the end of his career, did not have a great overall season. He hit only .230, but he was terrific in September when it really counted—when the Phillies won 75 percent of their games and took the division.

Of all the great stats you can relay about Morgan—the on-base percentage, the stolen bases, the surprising power, the runs scored, the awards—one set of numbers stands out above all the others—the record of his team the year they acquired him.

Morgan changed teams five times in his career. At every stop, his team got better immediately and three times made the postseason—and that's no coincidence. He was a great leader and made the players around him better:

1972 Reds—After going 79–83 and finishing fourth in 1971, the 1972 Reds improved to 95–59 and went to the World Series, taking the A's to Game 7.

1980 Astros—After going 89–73 in 1979 and fading badly down the stretch, the Astros went 93–70 in 1980 and finished first for the first time in their history. They lost to the Phillies in the greatest postseason series ever played.

1981 Giants—After finishing 11 games under .500 in 1980, the Giants finished over .500 for only the second time in eight years.

1983 Phillies—After finishing second at 89–73 in 1982, three games off the pace, the Phillies won 90 games and took the division with Morgan as their 39-year-old second baseman.

1984 A's—Even at the age of 40 and in his last stop, Morgan's streak held. The 1984 A's won three more games than they had the previous year.

Morgan has distinguished himself in his postbaseball career as well. He became an entrepreneur, purchasing restaurants and a Coors distributorship. He was working 70 hours a week while going to Cal State Hayward's evening college to get his undergraduate degree. He later sold all of his business ventures and concentrated on his baseball-broadcasting career as ESPN's number one baseball color guy, and he has for several years been the analyst with Jon Miller.

Morgan would have been a great manager or general manager and was offered either of those jobs by Houston Astros owner John McMullen in 1982. Joe declined, and the rest is history. He is the model of a driven and successful person.

I admire Joe very much.

The Exciting Juan Samuel

Juan Samuel was another second baseman who was a real favorite of mine. "Sammy" was a very exciting player to watch. I personally scouted him when he was playing Triple A baseball at Portland, Oregon, in the Pacific Coast League and made the decision to bring him up to the big leagues.

Watching Juan Samuel play was a real treat. Sammy was a terrific athlete, and he exhibited a real joy when he played. He could run and had surprising power. He not only hit a lot of doubles and triples and quite a few home runs as well, he was also a proficient base stealer. You won't find many players who reach double digits in doubles, triples, home runs, and stolen bases—and he did it four seasons in a row!

His defensive skills as a second baseman, however, did not match his offensive prowess. After a few seasons, the Phillies decided to move him to center field, and ultimately, general manager Lee Thomas traded him to the New York Mets for Lenny Dykstra and relief pitcher Roger McDowell. This was a trade that I would not have made because I really loved his personality and the excitement he brought to a game. His big smile and happy persona made him very special to be around.

But the trade worked out extremely well for the Phillies as Dykstra led us to the World Series in 1993 while McDowell did a good job out of the bullpen. Samuel's career started to go downhill after the trade. His decline actually began before the trade, and I have a theory that moving Sammy to center field really hurt his pride and contributed greatly to his falloff in production. When he was a second baseman, he was regarded as one of the top players at that position and made the All-Star Team a couple of times. But as an outfielder, he was just ordinary—one of many good outfielders in the game. He never made the All-Star Team as an outfielder.

The Clubhouse Impact of Dutch Daulton

What a man!

Catcher Darren Daulton was and always will be one of my heroes. When the Phillies signed him, he was a scrawny 17-year-old kid from Arkansas City, Kansas. He made himself a great player by hard work and his dedication to becoming a winner. He progressed nicely through his minor league career and finally made it to "prime time" in 1983.

He struggled to stay healthy throughout the 1980s, and his performance suffered. We ended up bringing in Lance Parrish to catch because we weren't certain Daulton would ever be able to hold up as a full-time player. "Don't give up on me," Daulton told me. "I'll be a player one day."

We didn't, and he was right. He survived a serious car accident in May 1991, and seven knee operations. A number of Phillies players had attended a bachelor party for teammate John Kruk. Daulton left the party in outfielder Lenny Dykstra's Mercedes. Dykstra lost control of the car, and they crashed into a tree. Both players were seriously hurt, with Daulton suffering a broken left eye socket and scratched cornea. He spent almost two months on the disabled list and some rehab time in the minors. He was only able to play 89 games that season and batted just .196.

Dutch came roaring back the next season and led the league with 109 runs batted in, becoming only the fourth catcher in baseball history to lead the league. The other three—Roy Campanella, Johnny Bench, and Gary Carter—are in the Hall of Fame. Daulton was an All-Star in 1992, 1993, and again in 1995, but more importantly he was the real leader of the team and the stabilizer for young pitchers like Curt Schilling and Tommy Greene.

"You can ask any player on the 1993 team, and they will tell you that the Phillies would not have been in the World Series without Darren Daulton," said manager Jim Fregosi.

"He is simply the best catcher in baseball," general manager Lee Thomas said in 1994.

"He's like E.F. Hutton," said pitcher Larry Andersen. "When he speaks, everybody listens. It's like he is the godfather, and we're all a bunch of thugs."

Curt Schilling appreciated how focused he was on being a catcher, even though it came at the expense of his hitting. "I never once heard him talk about his hitting during the game. That's unusual. The regulars, the position players, that's all they ever talk about, all game long. But Dutch just kept focused on his pitcher. He devoted all his energy and attention to making the pitcher successful. That's putting the team ahead of yourself."

As great a leader as Daulton turned out to be, it was a role he originally resisted because he was actually fairly quiet and reserved and preferred to be just "one of the guys." "There aren't a lot of players in today's game who would do what Dutch did," Fregosi observed years later. "They just want to play the game, make the money, and go home. They don't want to accept the responsibility of being there for their teammates."

Unfortunately, a foul tip off Jeff Conine's bat on June 29, 1994, broke Dutch's right clavicle, and his career started to go downhill. Dutch retired after the 1997 season, after hitting .389 for the Marlins in their World Series triumph over the Indians.

Darren Daulton will always be one of my truly favorite players—competitive, tough, and a real leader of men.

The Wit and Wisdom of John Martin Kruk

John Kruk was another one of the leaders on the 1993 championship team. He became a good personal friend and golfing buddy.

He also demonstrated a quick wit and a great sense of humor. "The Krukker" is one funny guy.

In 1992 at the All-Star Game in San Diego, he and Daulton had forgotten to bring their warm-up jerseys.

"That was kind of embarrassing," Kruk said. "We tried to buy Phillies souvenir shirts at the concession stand, and they didn't even sell them. That's when you know you really stink."

A Denver sportswriter, noting his .368 batting average at Coors Field, asked him how he liked playing there.

"I don't think I like playing here too much."

"Why not?"

"I can't breathe," he said. "Why would I want to play here if I can't breathe? If I can't breathe, I'll die. The beer doesn't even taste good up here. Even if it did, I don't have enough energy to drink it. There's nothing wrong with the team. I'm not saying I wouldn't play for their team. I just can't breathe. So I'd die, and I couldn't help them."

When he was asked about leading the voting for first baseman for the All-Star Game in 1993, he observed, "It's amazing the fans want to see me play. It's scary. What's our society coming to?"

Kruk made it to that All-Star Game in 1993, where some guy stuck a microphone at him and asked, "If I told you at the beginning of spring training that you'd be standing here, the National League starting first baseman, with your team in first place by five games at the All-Star Break, what would you have said?"

Kruk looked at him and said, "I'd have said you had a dependency problem and that you must be using something we've never heard of."

When Mitch Williams played for the Cubs, he wore No. 28—the same number Kruk wore for the Phillies. When we acquired Mitch, Kruk gave him his uniform number.

"Mitch's wife had all this jewelry with 28 on it," Kruk explained, "so I gave my number to him for two cases of beer. Mitch got divorced, and now he wears No. 99. The two cases of beer are gone. It's a sad story."

One of Kruk's most memorable at-bats was against intimidating, 6'10" left-hander Randy Johnson in the 1993 All-Star Game. During the regular season, most left-handed hitters such as Kruk would come down with a 24-hour virus anytime Johnson was pitching—primarily because of a slider that he threw from a near-sidearm motion, which looked like it was going to hit them in the back of the head. For Kruk that particular night, on national TV, sitting it out was not an option. He had nowhere to go but the batter's box.

So when the first pitch actually was behind Kruk and almost hit him in the head, he got a bit...disconcerted. Krukker bailed out on the next three pitches, striking out feebly.

After the game he was asked about that at-bat.

"It would be embarrassing to die on national TV," he said. "I'll only come back to this game again if they put in writing that Randy Johnson ain't coming. If he was gonna get me, he was gonna have to hit a moving target. I don't know where the first pitch was, and I didn't give a damn where the next three were, as long as they missed me. I was giving up the at-bat to save my life."

Kruk was certainly one of the rounder players to ever don a major league uniform—and perhaps the roundest to ever bang out 1,000 hits. He had what George "Boomer" Scott, the rather large first baseman who tried gamely to squeeze into the polyester doubleknits of the Boston Red Sox back in the 1970s, called a "Dunlop."

"What's a Dunlop?" Boomer was asked.

"That's when your belly done lopped over your belt," Boomer replied.

After the 1991 season Kruk tried to get in better shape, and he actually came to camp in 1992 without his Dunlop. And he didn't hit nearly as well. Tired of watching him come back to the dugout after making an out, Fregosi said, "Get fat again."

Kruk was certainly known far more for his straight talk than his training habits. A female fan saw him smoking a cigarette and she scolded him.

"You're a professional athlete!"

"Lady, I'm no athlete," Kruk replied. "I'm a ballplayer."

That was John Kruk, always keeping things in perspective. When the players filed sadly onto the plane to leave Toronto after losing the World Series, Kruk was the one with a hot dog in each hand.

He finished his career with the Chicago White Sox, hitting a single on July 30, 1995, running to first, and abruptly retiring on the spot. That hit allowed him to leave the game with a .300 career batting average.

If Only Tug McGraw Could Have Just Lightened Up and Had More Fun

Fun-loving players such as John Kruk always add to the joy of working in major league baseball. While some players feel they need to be intensely serious to be successful, Frank "Tug" McGraw did not have that problem. He was about having fun as well as being a terrific relief pitcher and tough competitor.

In the heat of the pennant race in 1980, he came into a game against the Cincinnati Reds in the bottom of the ninth. There were two outs, and the bases were loaded with slugger Tony Perez at the plate. McGraw struck him out and was asked after the game if he was nervous in that situation.

"I read the other day that 10,000 years from now the earth will be a big ball of ice," McGraw replied. "When that happens, no one is going to care what I did against Tony Perez."

He had a name for all of his pitches. His change-up was called "Peggy Lee" in honor of the singer who had a hit song called "Is That All There Is?" He named one of his fastballs "Bo Derek" because it had a "nice tail" on it. Tug called his sailing fastball "Cutty Sark" and his straight fast ball "John Jameson." When he gave up a home run, he called it a "Sinatra Ball"—"Fly Me to the Moon."

Like a lot of fun-loving guys, Tug would have a few drinks now and again. When he had a few too many the night before, you would often find him asleep on the trainer's table during the game. But he was always awake by the seventh inning, when we might need him.

He was once asked how he would spend his salary. "Ninety percent I'll spend on good times, women, and Irish whiskey," he replied. "The other 10 percent I'll probably waste."

When the Phillies were to open the final season at Veterans Stadium in 2003, the plan for Opening Day was for me to drop the first ball of the season from a helicopter to Tug McGraw. We decided to practice the act in spring training near our new facility at Bright House Networks Field. It was a very windy day, and I was kind of hanging out the door of a helicopter. I was scared to death, but I managed to drop the ball to the "Tugger." Not only did he catch it, he caught it with his glove behind his back. Unfortunately—or maybe fortunately—the wind was so strong on Opening Day that we had to scrap the mission.

One of my last remembrances of the Tugger was when I was lying in a hospital bed in November 2003, at Bryn Mawr Rehab Hospital, recovering from a hip replacement. True to his impish nature, he and Larry Christenson snuck into my hospital room to bring me a double vodka martini. No one realized at the time that Tug was very ill. Sadly, he died a few months later from a brain tumor.

Tug's passing was a real loss for the Phillies and for major league baseball.

Memorable Owners

When I first began attending functions of major league baseball owners, it was like going to the good ol' boys' hunting lodge. Nowadays, these sessions look more like business meetings, right down to the PowerPoint presentations. One thing hasn't changed: there were some characters running franchises back then, and there are still some characters running them now.

In the 1950s, there were only 16 major league teams, and the owners would meet and socialize by league—National League owners with other National League owners, and the American League owners in their own group. I attended a number of National League dinner parties with my father, and they were quite entertaining. Almost every owner would stand up and tell a funny story during the course of the evening. There was no talk about revenue sharing, luxury tax, players unions, or long-term player contracts. The conversations usually centered on hunting and fishing experiences. Perhaps 20 people would attend. I can still remember that Don Grant of the New York Mets was the champion joke teller and Gussie Busch of the St. Louis Cardinals was often leading the group in song.

Fifty years later, after several stages of expansion, after the birth of free agency and arbitration, and after the power became centralized with the commissioner's office, these social functions included both leagues and were attended by 100 or more baseball executives who gathered to discuss mainly business issues with very little levity.

By now you know all about Judge Roy Hofheinz. I have met dozens of other owners throughout the years, and here are a few stories about some of the most memorable ones.

The Candidness of Robert Edward Turner III

When Ted Turner purchased the Atlanta Braves in 1976, he was not the gray-haired, well-dressed media tycoon that we know today, but a brash 37-year-old millionaire known as "Captain Outrageous" and "the Mouth from the South."

Shortly after he bought the team, he called me on the phone.

"I understand you are the best marketing guy in the game," Turner said. "We can't even draw a million people, so I would like to come to Philadelphia and pick your brain."

When he arrived at my office, he started off by telling me a bit about himself.

"Before you tell me how to sell tickets, I want to tell me a little bit about myself," Turner said in his Southern drawl. "My dad sold billboards and committed suicide. I plan to conquer the world with cable television and then commit suicide."

That was a bit of a shock to hear, but I found Turner to be a very entertaining guy. Given that first meeting, I couldn't say I was all that surprised when he:

- Gave the high-profile free-agent pitcher he'd signed (Andy Messersmith) the number 17 in order to help publicize his cable channel of the same number. If that wasn't enough, he put the word "Channel" rather than "Messersmith" on the back of the jersey.
- Got too aggressive going after free-agent Gary Matthews after the 1976 season and got suspended for a year for tampering.
- Got frustrated by the lousy play of his team in early May 1977 and, while his suspension was being appealed, decided to name himself manager. "Managing ain't that hard," he

said. "All you have to do is score more runs than the other guy." The team went out and lost their 17th in a row. Because league rules prohibit an owner from managing his team, his tenure lasted only one game. Two days later, the manager he'd temporarily relieved (Dave Bristol) was back on the bench.

- Came in as an outsider to the old-money world of sailing and skippered his yacht, *Courageous*, to an America's Cup victory in 1977—then showed up at the postrace press conference drunk and not exactly trying to hide it.
- Eventually did conquer the world with cable television.

I loved how candid Ted was, even about his personal life.

I asked him once, "What's it like to be married to Jane Fonda?"

"It's a pain," he said. "She never lets me out of her sight. My first wife never cared where I was or what I was doing."

I was not surprised when they got a divorce.

Turner was very smart, very funny, and very outspoken. I really enjoyed it when he would come to the league meetings because he told it like it was.

With Ted, what you saw was what you got. He was a guest on the CNN show *Crossfire* in the late 1980s when the topic for debate was Turner's controversial practice of colorizing classic black-and-white movies he'd acquired when he bought MGM. He addressed the issue simply and directly: he owned them, so why couldn't he do what he wanted with them?

Though *Crossfire* is known for its heated debates, the only time Turner even came close to losing his cool that day was when the cohost, Pat Buchanan, continued to address him (his boss, after all) as "Mr. Turner."

"Call me *Ted*!"

As CNN continued to grow throughout the 1980s and 1990s into one of the most recognizable brands on the planet, I never forgot what he had told me: "I am going to conquer the world with cable television."

The Craziness (Like a Fox) of Charles Oscar Finley

As outrageous as Ted Turner could be, he was as quiet as a church mouse compared to Charles "Charlie O." Finley.

Charlie O. was ahead of his time in many ways, championing ideas that were considered revolutionary at the time: divisional play, World Series and All-Star Games at night, colorful uniforms, inter-league play.

"Play four games against each team of the other league. Great rivalries, including Yankees-Mets, White Sox–Cubs, and Indians-Reds would help at the gate surely.... Without interleague play, baseball gives fans only half the show."

That was Finley—in 1965.

Finley also had a few ideas that are, at best, still ahead of their time and, at worst, just plain goofy. He changed the right-field dimensions of the Kansas City Athletics ballpark to match the short porch of Yankee Stadium on the theory that New York's dynasty had more to do with park dimensions than guys named Mantle, Berra, and Ford. He introduced a mechanical rabbit behind home plate to deliver balls to the umpire. He pushed for orange baseballs to improve visibility. To speed the game up, he wanted three balls, two strikes, and a "20-second shot clock" for pitchers. Though one of the many beauties of baseball is the absence of timekeeping, I have to admit that there are certain pitchers who I wouldn't mind seeing get flagged for "delay of game."

"We've got guys out there who throw once every half hour. Let's put up a 20-second clock in every ballpark," Finley suggested. "If it runs out before the pitcher throws, charge him with a ball. That'll speed things up."

And that was more than 30 years ago! Poor Charlie would be beside himself during some of today's marathons.

Some of Finley's brainstorms remain controversial to this day, none more so than the designated hitter. With both attendance and runs scored trending down, Charlie led the charge for the DH, which became effective in the American League on an experimental basis in 1973.

"Baseball has dragged its feet in making changes. We're favoring the defense when it's offense the fans want to see," he said.

Finley was indeed innovative and flamboyant. A designated hitter wasn't enough for him, so he signed a college sprinter named Herb Washington and turned him into baseball's first and only "designated runner." Washington's only purpose was to pinch-run and steal bases. Washington was so fast that he was even responsible for the development of a new play—the pick-off steal—in which he would simply take off for second when a pitcher threw to first. Washington stole 29 bases in 1974 and retired after the 1975 season with career totals of 33 runs scored and zero plate appearances.

When Finley signed young prospects, he immediately christened them with a nickname. Jim Hunter became "Catfish." John Odom became "Blue Moon." Vida Blue—whose name was great to begin with—turned down a cash offer to change his name to "True." He also gave bonuses to his players for growing long hair and mustaches.

Unfortunately, Charlie O. had a well-deserved reputation for being cheap and mean-spirited, too. Finley attempted to "fire" his second baseman, Mike Andrews, during the 1973 World Series for a couple of errors that cost the A's a game. He went so far as to force Andrews to sign a false affidavit claiming an injury so that he could be replaced with a healthier player. Commissioner Bowie Kuhn would have none of it, and the A's players put Andrews's No. 17 on their sleeves in tribute.

A common hatred for Finley is credited with unifying a very divided clubhouse in Oakland, as the A's rolled to three consecutive championships from 1972 to 1974. His fellow owners didn't think much of him, either. Though I admired Finley in many ways, my father despised him.

Warren Giles just did not go in much for promotions. Not surprisingly, he didn't care much for Bill Veeck either. And though he liked most of what I did—because he felt I made certain that the baseball game always came first—he did not care for the Phillie

Phanatic one bit. About the only promotion I could remember my father doing in Cincinnati was bringing in a guy named Jackie Price who used to take batting practice while hanging upside down. For my father, it was all about respecting the traditions and the integrity of the game—something he didn't think Finley was doing.

Another reason my father thought poorly of Finley was the Oakland A's mascot—a mule named "Charlie O." The mule was one of the cleanest and best-looking four-legged animals I have ever seen. I was attending a pregame cocktail party prior to a World Series game in 1972 in Oakland, and this beautiful mule was walking around the party just like any other guest. My dad had a martini in his hand talking to Finley, and "Charlie O." came up behind him and started to sample my father's drink!

Despite Finley's revolutionary ideas and his team's great success in the early '70s, the A's dynasty began to collapse. Ironically, the team was the first and most obvious victim of someone else's revolutionary idea: free agency. Not wanting to pay what he felt were inflated and unaffordable salaries to his star players, Finley tried to sell them to the highest bidder—Joe Rudi and Rollie Fingers to the Red Sox, Vida Blue to the Yankees. Commissioner Kuhn, invoking his power to make decisions "in the best interests of baseball," voided the sales. As a result, Finley wound up losing the players to free agency without any type of compensation.

Bowie Kuhn wasn't Charlie Finley's biggest fan, either.

He might have been crass, cheap, and obnoxious, but Charlie Finley was also a very savvy businessman who understood basic economics. When free agency became reality, his idea was to "make 'em all free agents" because he understood that a large supply would serve to hold down prices. His fellow owners were aghast at such a notion and moved to place restrictions on free agency, which was exactly what Marvin Miller wanted. B.J. Ryan and A.J. Burnett—very wealthy beneficiaries of the law of supply and demand—are just two recent examples of the very many players who should be eternally grateful that this idea was never seriously considered.

George Walker Bush—Way Back When

George W. Bush, the 43rd president of the United States, was part owner and co–general partner of the Texas Rangers from 1989 to 1994. His strategy to become an owner of a baseball team was actually similar to mine.

He arranged a syndicate to purchase controlling interest in the Rangers for $89 million. He borrowed $500,000 from a bank to buy a small stake in the team and convinced the investing group to make him a general partner and the public face of the team. His co–general partner, Rusty Rose, assumed control over the financial side. Bush received a reported salary of $200,000 and, using his political connections, began lobbying for a new stadium for his club.

In November 1994, Bush was elected governor of Texas with 53.8 percent of the vote, defeating popular incumbent Ann Richards. Frankly, when this occurred I was shocked. I could not picture George Bush as a governor, let alone president of the United States. I pictured Bush more as the perennial social chairman of a college fraternity. He was fun to be around—telling funny stories, smiling a lot, personable, and good-looking. He was very likable, but he did not seem the statesmanlike type.

However, Bush was always very logical, sensible, and outspoken when discussing major issues in baseball, and he was particularly active in revenue sharing and scheduling matters.

When Tom Hicks purchased the Rangers in 1998, the ballpark in Arlington was a reality, and the value of the franchise had increased dramatically. Hicks wound up paying $250 million (for the team, that is—paying that much for a shortstop came later). Bush pocketed $14.9 million for his initial investment of a borrowed $500,000.

Not bad work if you can get it.

You might hear his name mentioned more and more as a possible commissioner after he leaves office in 2009. After all the stress that comes with life in the Oval Office, mediating disputes over revenue disparity will probably seem like a walk in the park.

The Danger of Standing between Ray Arthur Kroc and His Seat

Ray Kroc, the founder of McDonald's, became a local hero in 1974 when he purchased the San Diego Padres and kept them from moving to Washington D.C. If he hadn't done this, my life would have been very different; food magnate Joe Danzansky was trying to buy the Padres in order to move them to Washington D.C., and I was campaigning to become the general manager of the new Washington team.

Kroc was like a bantam rooster—short in stature, highly energized, and at times very loud. In his first year as owner of the Padres, he won favor with the fans of San Diego—but not the players and coaches—when he took over the public-address system during a losing streak.

"Ladies and gentlemen, I suffer with you," Kroc announced. "I have never seen such stupid baseball in my life."

He was also a man who liked things to go his way. I hosted a special party in the Phillies' executive dining room for President Gerald Ford before the 1976 All-Star Game at Veterans Stadium. When the president was leaving the party, the Secret Service asked me to stand at the exit and not allow anyone to leave for 10 minutes. As I was doing what I was told and blocking the doorway, Kroc came over and demanded to be let out.

When I told him he had to stay put, Kroc actually started jumping up and down.

On my feet!

"No goddamn president is going to keep me from seeing the game!"

The PR Genius of George Michael Steinbrenner III

An owner with a similar style to Kroc is a guy named George Steinbrenner. George is one of the few people in the baseball world who can be called by his first name alone. Known for being outspoken and a bit of a bully, he was always very nice to me. The stories I have heard from people who worked for him, on the other hand, are rather disheartening.

When Gabe Paul was general manager and part owner of the Yankees, he said to me, "Bill, the most limited thing in the world is being a limited partner of the Yankees."

Gabe couldn't even get tickets to Yankees World Series games until the day of the game.

"The Boss," as George is still known, once fired a secretary for taking 10 minutes too long on her lunch break.

But George didn't just make the secretarial staff watch the clock. Woody Woodward, whom I hired as the Phillies general manager in 1987 after he left the same post with the Yankees, told me that George would ask him to be by a telephone every Saturday at 2:00 PM and to expect a call. Woody did what he was told. George seldom, if ever, called.

God help Woody, though, if he wasn't there the one time he did.

Dallas Green told me about a fellow who worked in the Yankees front office, commuting in from Pittsburgh to spend the workweek in New York and then flying back home on Friday for the weekend. One Friday, this guy had the misfortune of grabbing an early flight home on the same day that George happened to call for him at a few minutes before 5:00.

George issued an order that this individual be greeted at the airport in Pittsburgh with the following message: turn around and fly back to New York for a possible weekend meeting.

Dallas will also tell you about how incredibly loyal George is to people who have worked for him or played for him, keeping countless numbers of them on the payroll when they really didn't have much, if anything, to do.

George also appears to have mellowed as the years have gone on. The same man who made 20 managerial changes in his first 20 seasons, including hiring and firing Billy Martin five separate times, has actually had only two managers over the past 15 seasons. He is even allowing Joe Torre to approach Ralph Houk's team record of seven consecutive seasons without winning a championship. Among active managers, Torre's tenure is exceeded only by Bobby Cox—so I guess that makes George the third-most patient owner in baseball today.

George, however, is definitely my hero when it comes to public relations. The man is a genius. I do not believe that there are many days during the course of a year that there is not a story about the New York Yankees in some publication. He tries to stir up interest all the time. He used to do it by threatening managers, firing managers, rehiring managers, coming up with derisive nicknames for his high-priced players, and generally creating turmoil in the clubhouse—all of which created more interest in his Yankees. Now he uses other targets, like the World Baseball Classic, to stir up controversy. George was very ticked off that his three biggest stars—Jeter, Damon, and A-Rod—were not playing for the Yankees in the team's spring-training games, and he was not shy about letting people know that.

I tried to take a page out of his book and generate publicity in unconventional ways when I was CEO of the Phillies. I preferred controversy to apathy and would occasionally get a trusted reporter on the phone and "plant" a story about a trade we were pursuing.

"We're trying to get Eddie Murray from the Orioles."

Sometimes I looked a little stupid, but at least I got the fans talking about the Phillies.

George doesn't show up much at owners' meetings anymore, though I'm not certain why. Maybe he doesn't want to catch too much face-to-face grief about his payroll. Of late he's made it a point not to be the owner who hands out the largest contract in baseball—but since 1999 or so, he certainly hasn't hesitated to set the bar when it comes to team salary.

The Late, Great Walter Francis O'Malley

Back when George was attending the owners' meetings more frequently, his archenemy was Walter O'Malley of the Dodgers. It was somewhat ironic, given that they both went to the same military academy in Indiana. To hear them sarcastically cut each other up in the meetings was sometimes embarrassing, but it was never dull.

O'Malley, a jowly and heavyset man who frequently had a cigar in his mouth, was very close to my father. He was clearly the most powerful member of the owners group. He dominated the meetings and usually got votes to go his way. Other owners both respected and feared him. Frankly, it would have been a lot easier for me to picture O'Malley in the Oval Office than Bush.

O'Malley was a real visionary. He saw the future when it came to new markets, uprooting the wildly popular Dodgers from the largest market in the nation because he saw greater potential in Southern California—while also convincing Horace Stoneham, owner of the archrival Giants, to make the same leap of faith to Northern California. O'Malley reaped all the benefits of not having to go it alone, but he still got to keep the best market for himself. Pretty sweet.

Yes, Walter O'Malley was a real deal maker. Once in Los Angeles, he persuaded the Union Oil Company to pay him $20 million to build Dodger Stadium in exchange for 10 years of exclusive advertising in the stadium. Though he didn't allow Union Oil to put their name on the stadium, as is so common today, this was essentially the beginning of naming-rights deals that are now so prolific in all sports.

He was only about 30 years ahead of his time on that one.

Walter O'Malley also saw the future when it came to television broadcasts. There was great controversy about the practice of televising home games. My father and many owners thought it was a huge mistake and could turn baseball into a studio game with no one in attendance and everyone watching on TV. Given how difficult it was to get to some parks by car back then, this was a valid concern. O'Malley and Mets chairman Don Grant, however, believed that televising home games would increase attendance. You could show fans having a good time at your park and cheering for the home team. Obviously, it turned out that O'Malley and Grant were right.

Walter O'Malley was truly one of the most influential owners in the history of major league baseball. When my father retired as National League president in December 1969, he wrote a letter of appreciation to O'Malley, which read as follows:

Dear Walter,

There is no one in the league with whom I have had closer contact—officially or personally. You have been helpful to me as counselor on so many occasions. You contributed immeasurably to discussions in our Executive Council meetings, our league meetings, and joint meetings. (I remember well your presentation regarding the 162-game schedule at our recent joint meeting in Chicago.) Very important to me has been the close personal relationship I have enjoyed with you and your wonderful family.... I am grateful to you for being understanding of my errors, helpful with advice when requested, and an opportunity to know and be with your family.

The Commissioners

Major League Baseball is, by its very nature, a fairly conservative institution. Unlike the NFL, which tinkers with its rules on an annual basis, there have been few immediate, league-wide changes of any significance in its 100-plus year existence. The ones that do come to mind—the livelier ball of the 1920s, the expansion of the early 1960s, the designated hitter in 1973, and drug testing today— were not driven by abstract speculation or leaps of faith but as pragmatic responses to very real problems.

A Role Born Out of Crisis

One of the most significant changes baseball ever made was establishing the office of commissioner in 1921, which was prompted by perhaps the greatest crisis the game has ever faced: the revelation that the 1919 World Series had been fixed.

All baseball fans have heard that story so often that the words "fixing the World Series" have lost some of their impact. To understand how big a mess baseball had on its hands, it might help to put it in modern terms. Instead of gamblers, let's cast agents as the bad guys. Imagine an agent was colluding with the hitters and pitchers he represented to positively influence each other's statistics during the last years of their contract.

"I'll get my pitchers to throw you first-pitch change-ups out over the plate," the agent tells his free-agent hitters. To his pitchers who are about to go out on the market, he says, "I'll get my hitters to give up some at-bats when you're pitching. We'll all make out like bandits."

If you think steroids have created a firestorm, this controversy would actually raise the issue of whether players "play to win." The outcry would be deafening. The government, the media, the court of public opinion—the pressure on baseball to make dramatic changes to keep this from ever happening again would be enormous. And with $5 billion in revenue at stake, dramatic changes would happen.

That's what it must have felt like in 1919 for the three-man commission that had been overseeing Major League Baseball since 1903. When the whispers about the integrity of the 1919 World Series—which started in the first inning of the first game—grew louder and more public, that commission was as good as dead. When something like that happens on your watch, there is no rebuttal to the claims that you are ineffective.

A New Sheriff in Town

Because the owners had to make a strong statement to the public that they were intent on cleaning up the game, a federal judge named Kenesaw Mountain Landis was appointed as baseball's first commissioner. He was famous and flamboyant and certainly looked the part of a tough new sheriff in town. But one of the real reasons that Judge Landis was selected—though this wasn't put out there for public consumption—is that he had helped the owners several years previously by delaying a ruling on an antitrust lawsuit brought against Major League Baseball by the new Federal League. The new league did not have time on its side and, as a result of this delay, it collapsed before it got its day in court.

Judge Landis demanded and received from the owners significant power to make rulings in the best interests of the game. He served as baseball's first commissioner from 1921 until his death in 1944 and was greatly respected by the public, the press, and my father—primarily for his handling of the great crisis that brought him into office.

The Black Sox Scandal involved eight key players on the 1919 Chicago White Sox, including star Shoeless Joe Jackson, who conspired to take bribes from gamblers to lose the World Series to the Cincinnati Reds. Despite signed confessions by both Jackson and pitcher Ed Cicotte and testimony from some of the gamblers, the courts failed to convict the eight players. Despite the verdict, Judge Landis permanently suspended from baseball all eight players, based on the notion that the integrity of the game was sacred and any action that compromised or potentially compromised that integrity could not be tolerated.

Many people still believe that Shoeless Joe Jackson should be in the Hall of Fame because he was an unwilling participant in the scandal, having hit .375 and the Series' only home run—as everyone who has seen *Field of Dreams* knows. One of the suspended players, Buck Weaver, never accepted any money and fought all his life to have his named cleared—as documented in *Eight Men Out*. Even after his death, his family has taken up Buck Weaver's cause. The reasoning behind his inclusion in the suspensions—that he knew of the conspiracy yet did nothing about it—is a powerful lesson.

No person who ever served as commissioner, however—not even Landis—has escaped significant criticism. Although Landis got high marks for maintaining the integrity of the game, he received much criticism for being a racist. Despite increasing pressure from the black press and activist groups, including the American Communist Party, to integrate the game, Landis was steadfast in not permitting Negro Leagues players to play in Major League Baseball—although he never would admit that there was any rule or policy prohibiting blacks to play in the big leagues. This was the unwritten rule, the so-called "gentlemen's agreement."

Happy Chandler Makes the Owners Angry

Following his death after 24 years in office, Landis was replaced by A.B. "Happy" Chandler in 1945. Chandler, a senator from Kentucky, was a gregarious good ol' Southern boy. Ironically, it was the "Southern boy" who was commissioner at the time that Branch Rickey integrated baseball. Chandler's view, held by many but most importantly by him, was that if African Americans could die for their country in World War II, they certainly should be allowed to play major league baseball.

Chandler gained the public support of many players on April 4, 1947, when he announced adoption of a major league player pension plan offering annuity and life insurance benefits. His handling of the Mexican League issue was not as popular.

Shortly after Chandler took office, more than a score of players leaped to the Mexican League, lured there by fabulous financial offers. The list included, among others, Max Lanier, Mickey Owen, Fred Martin, Sal Maglie, Lou Klein, and Danny Gardella. Chandler, alarmed at the mass exodus, plastered a five-year ban on any player signing with the Mexican League. Lawsuits were filed by the renegade players but never came to trial, and in 1949 Chandler agreed to reinstate the Mexican "jumpers."

In 1951 five or six owners, led by Fred Saigh of St. Louis and Del Webb of the Yankees, managed to get Chandler fired. Saigh was furious because one of the banned jumpers, Danny Gardella, had filed a lawsuit threatening baseball's vital reserve clause, and Saigh blamed Chandler for the suit. Webb was upset because Chandler had blocked his Yankees from signing high school players. Chandler also upset a number of owners by suspending Brooklyn Dodgers manager Leo Durocher for a full year (1947) for detrimental remarks toward baseball and for his association with known gamblers.

Ford Frick's Disappearing Act

A real donnybrook took place among the owners as they tried to find a new commissioner. Eventually the list of candidates was pared down to three finalists: a guy named Richard Nixon, then a highly thought of lawyer in Washington D.C.; Ford Frick, a former sportswriter who was then president of the National League; and my father, Warren C. Giles, then president of the Cincinnati Reds.

After further discussion, the owners eventually got down to two candidates—Frick and my father.

You needed a 75 percent majority (12 out of 16) to be elected commissioner, and, after 17 ballots and much debate, neither Frick nor my father could muster more than nine votes. At that point, the decision was made to ask one to withdraw his name and to pay both candidates $55,000 a year—one as commissioner and one as president of the National League. Having no better way to make the decision, the owners did what we all do in such situations. They flipped a coin.

Ford Frick "lost." He would be asked to withdraw, and if he was willing to do so, then Warren Giles would become the third commissioner of baseball. Frick was having dinner at a restaurant in Fort Lauderdale with his assistant, Charlie Segar. Someone tipped off Segar what was going on, so when the call came, Segar answered instead of Frick.

"No, I don't know where Mr. Frick is," Segar said on the phone, though Frick was sitting a few feet from him at the table.

Not being able to get in touch with Frick, the owners then got in touch with my father.

"I'll withdraw," Warren Giles said, "on one condition."

"What's that?"

"I want to move the National League office from New York to Cincinnati."

My father wanted to move into Happy Chandler's office, which was located in Cincinnati. I was a junior in high school, and my dad did not want to move me away from my friends and school. The owners agreed, and the Giles family was able to stay in Cincinnati.

My dad never thought much of Charlie Segar after he found out about what happened at the Florida restaurant. Will Harridge was president of the American League at the time, and both league presidents were more powerful than the commissioner because the leagues made the majority of business decisions. The commissioner had more of a judicial position, which involved mainly settling disagreements between leagues, taking necessary disciplinary action, and upholding the integrity of the game.

The integrity of the game was something that my father constantly preached to me and to everyone. For example, he would never allow incentive clauses for any accomplishment a player might earn that the opposition could control.

"I don't want Willie Mays to get a $100,000 bonus for hitting 55 home runs," he said, "because there would be a temptation or a suspicion by the fans and media that Mays might take the opposing pitcher out to dinner before the last game and offer him money to throw every pitch down the middle of the plate. Plus, the owner might ask the manager to sit a player if he was on the verge of getting a big bonus."

When it came to meting out discipline, the league presidents had much more power back then. One of my favorite stories involved Maury Wills.

My dad had fined shortstop Maury Wills $50 for arguing with an umpire. Wills got $50 worth of pennies and dumped them through the mail slot of my father's office in Cincinnati, and the pennies flew all over the floor. My father immediately called Dodgers general manager Buzzie Bavasi and told Bavasi that if Wills did not come over to pick up all the pennies and to bring a $50 bill within two hours, Wills would be suspended for 10 games. Wills complied.

Clearly, it was a lot easier to make a point when you didn't have to worry about players running to Don Fehr or Gene Orza to complain.

Each league did their own scheduling and had a different method of sharing revenues. The umpires in each league were hired and managed by the league, and over time both the equipment worn and the way the strike zone was interpreted was different in the American League and the National League.

Commissioner Ford Frick is best known for attaching an asterisk to Roger Maris's 1961 home-run record. Frick had been Babe Ruth's ghostwriter and was loyal to Ruth and his wife and didn't want to see Ruth's record broken. Ruth set the record of 60 home runs in a season of 154 total games, while Maris hit 61 in a season that totaled 162 games.

That asterisk has since been passed on—in the court of public opinion—to Mark McGwire and Barry Bonds, while Maris's feat, ironically, is more celebrated now than when he accomplished it.

Frick did, however, help to guide the geographical expansion of major league baseball beyond the northeast quarter of the United States. At the opening of the 1956 season, Commissioner Frick stated, "I think our [baseball's] greatest achievement in recent years has been that we have adopted the forward look. We have torn away from outmoded beliefs that there should be no tinkering with franchises or procedures. We have opened up new frontiers, we have become more modern in our thinking and our dealings with each other and, personally, I will not be happy until we have a major league set up in the United States stretching from California to New York and from Canada to the Gulf of Mexico."

Frick believed that big population centers in the west and south must be brought into the major leagues. During Frick's tenure, the Philadelphia A's moved to Kansas City, expanding the league's western boundary by some 300 miles beyond St. Louis. In addition, the Boston Braves took off for Milwaukee. And then, at the end of 1957, the Dodgers and Giants left New York City for new, uncharted territory in Los Angeles and San Francisco. Finally, Frick oversaw baseball's first expansion since 1903, when two American League teams were added in 1961, followed by two new teams for the National League in 1962.

Frick also pushed for healthier minor leagues—minor league attendance had plummeted during the 1950s because of the advent of both television and air-conditioning, among other factors. He also wanted improved ballparks with better parking facilities. The growth of the suburbs ushered in the importance of the car in post-war America, and people driving from suburban homes to urban ballparks needed safe places to park their cars.

The Wrong Man for the Job—Literally

When Ford Frick resigned on September 21, 1965, a search began to find a new commissioner. Pittsburgh owner John Galbraith was chairman of the search committee. The owners decided in November 1965 to name General William Eckert the new commissioner, and they gave him a seven-year contract. It is important to note that the real power still resided with the league presidents. The owners wanted a commissioner they could control, and a three-star general who lacked any baseball or sports experience certainly fit the bill.

It turned out that the general that baseball really wanted to hire had a similar name—General Eugene Zuckert, the former secretary of the air force. William Eckert was commissioner of baseball by mistake.

It did not take too long for the owners to realize that they had hired the wrong man. William Eckert was a very well-dressed man who always wore well-groomed suits and very highly starched shirts. Unfortunately, he came across as a "stuffed shirt." He had no personality, no passion, and not much knowledge of baseball. On one occasion he was giving a speech to all the baseball managers and public relations men in baseball, including myself, when he pulled out some four-by-six-inch index cards from his suit pocket and started talking about aerodynamics, rudders, and lift on the wings of airplanes.

"What is he talking about?" we all said to ourselves.

It turns out he was scheduled to speak to a group of United Airline executives later in the day and had pulled the wrong cards out of his suit.

Joe Reichler, the very knowledgeable MLB PR man, tried to coach and train Eckert about baseball, but it was a lost cause. Three years into Eckert's seven-year contract, an ownership committee negotiated a termination agreement.

Bowie Kuhn and the Billion-Dollar Clock

Bowie Kuhn took over as commissioner in 1969. Kuhn had been legal counsel for the National League for a number of years and was well respected. He was tall, intelligent, and maybe a bit "stuffy," but he really loved the game and cared a lot about the fans. I liked and respected him.

Kuhn is perhaps best known for baseball's most controversial rule change, even though it was a league decision. Beginning in 1973, the American League adopted the designated hitter because pitching was dominant in the late 1960s and early 1970s and owners were concerned that lack of offense was hurting fan interest.

The designated hitter rule has been a source of controversy since its inception. Baseball purists hate the rule, arguing that baseball has always been a game of generalists, in which every player had to have both offensive and defensive skills. Many argue that much of the in-game strategy regarding the utilization of pitchers, the use of pinch-hitters and the good old "double switch" is lost when each team has a DH. The advocates reply to that, "I'd rather see a hitter hit than a manager think."

There were also many questions initially about how to implement the rule. For example, how should the DH be employed in the All-Star Game and the World Series when one league employs a DH and the other league does not? The DH has been used in the All-Star Games played in American League parks since 1989, but in the World Series the decision initially was made to use the DH in alternate years for both teams. I did not think that this policy for use of the DH during the World Series was fair, and I eventually persuaded the owners to have the DH in the World Series every year, but to use it only at the American League home games.

If Ruly Carpenter, the president of the Phillies, had not been fishing in the Atlantic Ocean in 1977, both leagues would have the DH. Ruly had asked me to represent him at the National League meeting in 1977 and to vote for the DH because he and Phillies general manager Paul Owens felt that the Phillies would be a better team with the DH. The Phillies had two very good hitters—Greg Luzinski and a minor leaguer, Keith Moreland—who were not very good defensively.

When I got to the meeting, I was informed that the DH would not become effective until the next season because the players union had to approve it, and they never approved an owners' unilateral decision. The owners could implement this kind of decision in the next year.

The National League needed seven votes (out of 12 teams at the time) to pass the DH. There were six teams in favor and four against when the vote came around to Philadelphia and Pittsburgh. Harding Peterson, the GM of Pittsburgh, was told by owner John Galbraith to vote the same way as the Phillies because the teams were big rivals at the time. I tried to reach Ruly by phone but was told he was out in the ocean fishing. I did not know how to vote because of the year delay in adopting the rule, so I abstained and the Pirates abstained. An abstention is the same as a no vote, and as a result of my inability to reach Mr. Carpenter that fateful day, there is no DH in the National League. The issue has never come up for official vote again and, if it did today, the result would more likely be the elimination of the DH in the American League.

My father and I were not big fans of the DH anyway, so I was happy with the outcome. Today I actually like the fact that one league has the DH and one does not. It creates healthy debate and permits some popular players the opportunity to stay in the game when their defensive skills have deteriorated.

Bowie Kuhn is remembered for many things other than the DH, not the least of which is the fact that he never wore a topcoat at World Series night games no matter how cold it was. There was a lot of criticism about playing World Series games at night, a policy that began in 1971—with all games played at night by 1985. The critics claimed that it would be too cold and that children would not be able to watch because the games would end too late. So Bowie wanted to give the impression that it was not cold. Some skeptics believed that while the commissioner didn't wear a topcoat, he made sure to wear insulated underwear!

Another key event during Kuhn's tenure was the spiking of television rights revenue. In 1982 I was appointed chairman of the National League Television Committee, and Eddie Einhorn, co-owner of the Chicago White Sox, was appointed head of the AL TVC. The task of working out a new television rights deal between the networks and MLB turned out to be one of my most interesting and rewarding negotiations. The three of us got along real well and we called ourselves "KEG" (not to be confused with EKG) for Kuhn, Einhorn, and Giles.

According to the agreement then in place, ABC and NBC had paid $300 million each to split the baseball "jewels"—the All-Star Game, the League Championship Series, and the World Series. Our goal was to get a total of $1 billion for the rights to telecast these events for six years—$500 million each from ABC and NBC. The problem was that ABC had told us they would pay only $350 million for their half.

We went to NBC's Art Watson, a great and fun guy, and laid out the deal.

"Art, the whole package is NBC's for $1 billion," Einhorn said. "But if you don't take it, we're going to ABC to offer them half for $500 million. If they balk at that, it's yours for $900 million. So you can either take half, roll the dice you get it all for $900 million, or take ABC out of the picture right now for $1 billion."

Now Einhorn isn't the easiest guy to understand, especially when he's throwing numbers around. So at this point in the negotiation, Art would pull me aside and ask me if I had understood a word that Eddie had said. When you're dealing with this kind of money, you want to make certain you've got the right number of zeroes.

We made the deal with NBC as we all were having dinner at a table set up in the kitchen of the '21' Club in New York City. It was quite a scene. And, as with most deals, it ended up taking its own course. We eventually ended up getting the billion dollars we had originally targeted, with NBC paying $525 million and ABC $475 million, and with NBC getting a slightly better schedule of games. Our KEG group was highly praised, and baseball gave each of us an attractive grandfather clock with a plaque, thanking us for our good work.

It's a shame we didn't end up using a small portion of that billion dollars to make a speculative investment that I pitched to Kuhn in 1982.

"We have the opportunity to buy into this cable channel that could really end up being something," I said. "We can own half for only $30 million."

"Bill, there is no way this group of owners would do that," Kuhn replied. "Forget it."

So that's how Major League Baseball missed out on owning half of ESPN.

Not all of Bowie Kuhn's activities as commissioner involved negotiating TV contracts and attending night games in October sans topcoat. One of the recurring issues during Kuhn's tenure was labor relations. Marvin Miller had been appointed the director of the Major League Baseball Players Association in 1966 and set out to make the association into a real union. Over a period of 15 years, Miller was able to place the players on an even plane with the owners, primarily by incorporating a grievance procedure into the basic labor agreement. It was this grievance procedure, and the hearing by an independent arbitrator, that brought about free agency in December 1975, as the Seitz ruling declared that the reserve clause did not bind a player to one team in perpetuity. Of course, major league baseball was never the same.

In an attempt to regain some of the power they had lost, and to try to mitigate the impact of free agency, the owners sought to have compensation in the form of players and not just draft picks introduced into the basic labor agreement. The lack of agreement on this led to the two-month strike in 1981, but the two sides agreed to continue discussing the issue. There was no agreement by spring 1982, and as a result, this was a difficult one for baseball and for Commissioner Kuhn.

Donald Fehr had taken over as the new director of the Players Association, Marvin Miller having retired on July 31, 1981, in the middle of the players' strike. During the winter and spring of 1982, the owners and the players continued working on a new collective bargaining agreement but without success. The key sticking point was the owners' demand for compensation in the form of players for the loss of free agents.

With no progress being made, the owners locked the players out of spring training in March 1982. The hardline owners, led by August Busch of the Cardinals, felt that we should continue locking out the players until we got a deal more favorable to ownership. Peter O'Malley and I were urging Kuhn to open spring-training camps because we feared the fans' backlash was building and it was becoming very difficult to sell tickets and sponsorships.

Kuhn finally did order spring camps opened in mid-March of 1982 without an agreement. The hardliners were upset because the owners did not end up with as good a deal as we might have received, even after the lengthy strike that split the 1981 season in two. They felt that holding firm in 1981 had been for naught.

When it came time to extend Kuhn's contract in November 1982, the hardliners had enough clout to oust him. Kuhn did stay on until a successor was found.

Peter Ueberroth's Really Bad Idea

Peter Ueberroth, an entrepreneur, was elected commissioner on March 3, 1984, and took over on October 1, 1984. Ueberroth had received worldwide acclaim for running the 1984 Olympics in Los Angeles. Those Olympics were a huge success, both artistically and monetarily, and the tactics used by Ueberroth, including signing a large number of sponsors and using huge numbers of unpaid volunteers, represented a sea change in the way the Olympics have been run since.

Ueberroth was an impressive man. He was bright, physically fit, had a good public persona, and was always well dressed. He negotiated a clause in his contract that was significant for baseball, insisting that baseball change the voting rules for electing or reelecting the commissioner from a 75 percent vote to a simple majority. He felt that if any man was to do the right kind of job as commissioner, he would have to upset some owners and that the game would be better served with the rule change. I believe he was right.

He was challenged right away during the League Championship Series. First, he acted quickly to placate the networks—upset that the Cubs, who still played only day games, were scheduled for three home games in the NLCS—by giving the home-field advantage to the Padres. As unpopular as this made him in Chicago, had he done what had also been suggested—moving the games to Busch Stadium or Comiskey Park—he wouldn't ever have been able to set foot in Chicago again.

If that wasn't enough, the umpires went on strike during the League Championship Series and college umpires worked the games. Ueberroth personally negotiated a deal that brought the umps back for the World Series. He was a big fan of the umpires and tried to get them better pay and working conditions.

Ueberroth also fundamentally changed how owners' meetings were run. First of all, he changed the style of the meeting configuration from a round-table setup to a classroom style, where all owners would face him. At only the second of those meetings, with all 26 owners facing him, he made a very profound statement.

"I have been your commissioner for only six months, and I have discovered the problem with the economics of the game," Ueberroth said. "If I gave each of you a red button and a black button and told you that if you wanted to win the pennant but lose $4 million you press the red button, or, if you wanted to finish fourth and make $4 million you press the black button, you would all press the red button." He was right.

It had been almost 10 years since the advent of free agency. Player salaries were getting out of control, bidding for free agents was skyrocketing, and the industry was losing money. Ueberroth devised a plan for the 1985 signing season where teams were not to make any significant offer to a free agent if the team that had that player under contract wanted to keep him. The plan did help slow down escalating salaries in 1985, 1986, and 1987. Unfortunately, the plan also happened to be illegal and blatantly obvious.

The union later sued the owners for collusion and won their case. Baseball had to negotiate a settlement of $280 million, with the money distributed to players who were financially affected by the owners' collusion. More importantly, the level of trust by the players of the owners was severely—and almost irrevocably—damaged.

I was one owner—and there weren't many—who bucked the

system in what was the most stressful period of my career as a CEO. I did not believe that the Ueberroth rules were sound or legal, and I wanted to sign catcher Lance Parrish from the Detroit Tigers. In 1987 I felt the Phillies were very close to having a championship-caliber team and that we needed a quality catcher to get us over the top and in real contention to win everything.

During the winter of 1986–87, Mike Schmidt and a couple of other players called me frequently to push me into signing Parrish. At the same time, I was getting calls from a number of owners telling me not to sign Parrish. I was really in the middle, and I did not know what to do.

I called my friend Peter O'Malley, the son of the late Walter O'Malley and the owner of the Los Angeles Dodgers.

"I need your advice, Peter," I asked, and told him my situation.

His response was simple and sound. "Do what you think is right."

I also called my friend, Lou Hoynes, who was the attorney of the National League at the time.

"I think baseball is in trouble with this strategy," he said, "so it might be a good thing if you signed Parrish."

I made the decision to sign Parrish, provided it did not cost much more than the $1.1 million the Tigers had offered him. I negotiated a deal in late February of 1987 with his agents in Tampa to pay Parrish $1.2 million in 1987 with an easy-to-reach incentive of $250,000.

At the end of the day, the biggest problem with the Parrish signing was that he was a big disappointment on the field. I think the stress of the entire episode really got to him. He not only did not hit well, but he also dropped many, many balls and did not throw well. When his lovely wife came to a home game, the fans would yell nasty things at her and that just made Lance more stressed out.

Things got so bad that the entire Phillies defense started to make a lot of errors. I hired a psychologist to advise me on what might be going wrong with the defense of the Phillies. He explained to me that the catcher is the focal point of the entire team, and when he is not performing defensively it will affect the other eight players. It appeared that he was correct.

Despite all of that, Ueberroth did have a lot of good qualities—but he was not really in love with baseball. I always believed that he wanted to be a successful commissioner so that he could put another gold star on his lapel in order to reach greater heights—maybe even president of the United States.

I had dinner with him at the '21' Club in New York toward the end of his term as commissioner and asked, "What do you plan on doing next?"

"The Republican Party of California wants me to run for senator," he said, "but I am only interested in becoming governor or possibly a vice presidential candidate."

How exactly does one respond to that?

Despite his relatively short tenure and his desire to move on to a position of greater significance, Ueberroth had many accomplishments, including introducing sponsorships to major league baseball and reinstating Mickey Mantle and Willie Mays after Bowie Kuhn had banned them because they had been hired as glad-handers by casinos, basically to play golf with high rollers.

In 1985 Ueberroth reinstated the players, saying, "I don't think it is the role of commissioner to decide who former players play golf with."

Ueberroth also extended the LCS from five games to seven, created a drug-testing policy for minor leaguers, and tried to get one in the major leagues. In 1985, he had all World Series games go to night games, negotiated a TV contract on an exclusive basis with CBS, and almost created a baseball channel on cable TV.

I was always urging baseball to have our own cable channel, all the way back to that opportunity to get in on the ground floor of ESPN. I was a big believer in cable and, with the Flyers and Sixers, helped form PRISM, one of the nation's first multisport regional sports channels. It went on the air in September 1976. Ueberroth was one of the few who did believe in a baseball cable channel. Peter, Paul Kagan, Paul Bortz, and I created some income and expense projections and spent a lot of time analyzing the pluses and minuses of an exclusive cable channel for baseball. The bottom line was that in five years the channel would have been profitable, but the owners would have to give up a minimum of $42 million annually that was being paid by ESPN.

The Executive Council of MLB voted against taking the chance—another mistake. However, in 2006, major league owners did vote to approve a baseball channel on a digital sports tier, which would allow MLB to continue their lucrative deals with ESPN and TBS while still having their own channel.

The Only Poet Ever to Hold the Position

In 1989 Ueberroth decided not to run for reelection and Bart Giamatti, a professor of English literature by trade, native New Englander, and Boston Red Sox fanatic, was elected commissioner. Giamatti, the former president of Yale University, had been president of the National League for a couple of years prior to his promotion to commissioner. The man hired to replace Giamatti as NL president was Bill White, formerly a fine ballplayer with the Cardinals and Giants. He was the first African American to hold that high of an office in Major League Baseball.

Most everyone loved Giamatti, including me. He was a real romantic about life and particularly baseball. He wrote a number of beautiful essays about the great attributes of our national pastime. He was an exceptional man with prose and spoke eloquently about the game. His book, *A Great and Glorious Game*, is a compilation of his essays about baseball. It was published posthumously and was compiled by his colleagues and friends.

Giamatti's essay titled "The Green Fields of the Mind" begins, "Baseball breaks your heart. It is designed to break your heart. The game begins in the spring when everything else begins again, and it blossoms in the summer filling the afternoons and evenings, and then as soon as the chill rains come, it stops and leaves you to face the fall alone."

His ability to capture the emotion and the beauty of baseball is unparalleled.

The following are remarks made by Giamatti at a CBS TV affiliates meeting on June 4, 1989. Similar sentiments about the cultural significance of baseball also appear in *A Great and Glorious Game,* and it is a passage that I just love.

> It is very difficult for America to imagine a time without baseball. A soldier at Valley Forge records in his diary that he played in a game of "Baste." The first modern rules were used on June 19, 1846, and their basic grid has not changed. Currier and Ives show soldiers playing on a diamond in a Confederate prison camp during the Civil War. Successive waves of immigrants from the 1870s to today have learned about America, about what it is to make oneself into this uniquely free creature that is an American, through watching and playing baseball.
>
> The game spread across the continent with industrialism and animates our largest cities to this day, uniquely binding the community and the region, as few other social bonds can. It is still played in towns and villages, on greens and commons and cleared spaces, on Sunday afternoons, on soft evenings in summer, as it always has been. Baseball has a history which renews itself with each pitch, in every game, over every season—a history it is profoundly aware of. A history that is radically and intimately connected to our history, the history of a diverse people struggling to find a precious unity. Whether we think of baseball as a game or as a business—and it is often, though not always, both—it is finally an institution, a free-standing American idea that transcends any given individual, even as it cherishes individualism. No game of ours is as much a part of America's history as baseball. No other American game has always been as different from other games. Baseball is not a territorial game; it is not about conquering; I do not send a team out to capture the other team's goal or ground. Baseball may not even be truly a team sport; it may really be a game an individual plays with a group.

It may be that America has cared so deeply about base-ball for so long precisely because baseball reproduces, again and again, that interplay of individual and group, of personal freedom and communal responsibility, that Americans so love, that we have built into our Consti-tution and into our internal mythology of checks and bal-ances, into our national quest for a unified diversity....

At its core, baseball is about homecoming. That is why it is always thought of in terms of nostalgia.

Unfortunately, Giamatti inherited an investigation involving Pete Rose betting on baseball that had begun with Commissioner Ueberroth. On August 24, 1989, Giamatti banned Pete Rose from baseball for betting on his own team, the Cincinnati Reds, when Rose was managing them.

Giamatti said at the time, "The matter of Mr. Rose is now closed. Let no one think it did not hurt baseball. That will pass, however, as the great glory of the game asserts itself and a resilient institution goes forward. Let it also be clear that no individual is superior to the game."

One week later, Giamatti died of a sudden heart attack. Many pundits felt that the stress relating to the Pete Rose ban may have caused the heart attack. He was but 51 years of age when he died. His legacy—and his words—live on.

Fay Vincent Jr., who had been Giamatti's right-hand man, was quickly asked to serve Giamatti's term as commissioner. Prior to his role in the Commissioner's Office, Vincent had held important posts with Columbia Pictures and Coca-Cola and was well respected in the business world. People said that Giamatti never made any decision—including what tie to wear—without first asking Vincent. Many believed that the banning of Pete Rose from baseball was more of a Vincent decision than a Giamatti decision. I know that I do.

Like his two predecessors, it did not take long for Fay Vincent to be in the center of a difficult situation. At 5:04 PM (PST) on October 17, 1989, a horrific earthquake measuring 6.9 on the Richter scale hit the San Francisco Bay Area just prior to the start of Game 3 of the World Series between the Giants and the Oakland A's.

I was there.

When the earthquake hit, I was walking in the parking lot from a hospitality tent to the game in Candlestick Park with Phillies manager Nick Leyva. The first thing I noticed was that cars in the lot were starting to move up and down.

I told Leyva, "I'm having a heart attack."

"No you're not, Bill," Leyva responded. "This is just a little earthquake. We have them all the time out here."

Leyva had been brought up in the Bay Area. He was right about the earthquake, but wrong about the little. Many people were killed, homes, businesses, and even bridges were destroyed, roads buckled, electricity was lost, and structural damage occurred at Candlestick Park. It was obvious that being able to complete the World Series in San Francisco was by no means a given.

It was a tough decision for Commissioner Vincent. I spent a few hours with him and some TV folks in his hotel suite during the delay, discussing our options. Should we cancel the Series and declare the A's the winner? Should we move it to Los Angeles? Should we finish it prior to the beginning of the following season? Or should we resume it when the ballpark was declared safe? I argued for the latter, which was the course of action he eventually took.

I thought Vincent handled the tough decision very well. He felt it was a good thing to resume the Series to allow the people in the Bay Area to get their minds off the trauma of the earthquake. The damage to Candlestick Park was repaired quickly, and the World Series resumed 10 days later. The A's, on a roll before the quake, picked up where they left off and took out the Giants in four straight games.

More controversy occurred during the following spring when, during yet another stalled labor negotiation, the owners again locked the players out of spring training. Training camps did not open until March 20, with the season starting a week later.

As time went by, several owners in the game became disenchanted with Vincent, particularly because of his approach to labor relations and the players union, as well as his handling of expansion realignment and his allocation of the expansion proceeds. To the more hardline owners, Vincent appeared soft on labor matters, too much of a "dove" when the owners wanted a "hawk" to deal with Don Fehr.

A Coup D'Etat

In 1992 Milwaukee owner Bud Selig, Jerry Reinsdorf of the White Sox, Peter O'Malley of the Dodgers, and Stan Cook of the Cubs started a coup to oust Vincent as Commissioner of Baseball. Selig and Reinsdorf had worked the phones to find out which owners were in favor of ousting Vincent. They orchestrated an owners meeting in September 1992 to discuss and hopefully get enough support to get Vincent to resign. They even had a special seating chart at the meeting whereby they put an anti-Vincent owner next to any owner on the fence so that they could persuade enough owners to join the coup.

It worked!

The owners voted 18–9 to call for Vincent's resignation. I voted with the majority. A decision was then reached to let the Executive Council of 12 owners run the Commissioner's Office until a permanent commissioner could be found. Selig was named president of the council, and the National League owners voted me onto it.

The Executive Council's Big Challenges

The Executive Council embarked on a very thorough and important agenda to see how they could solve many problems facing the business of baseball. Many committees were formed to study the problems. The idea was for the council to try to solve the problems before we hired a full-time commissioner.

The industry was losing money and the losses were continuing to grow. The issues we needed to address, and the manner in which we did, represent the biggest changes in the administration of the game since Judge Landis was appointed in 1921.

Some of the key issues we were addressing were as follows.

Governance

Should the power of the leagues be diminished, and should we centralize more business decisions in the hands of the commissioner?

A decision was made to centralize in the Office of the Commissioner all scheduling matters, all matters related to umpires, discipline, and labor, and almost all business decisions. Few business decisions would be made in separate league meetings, with most meetings becoming "meetings of the whole." Eventually separate league meetings were abandoned entirely, and full-time league presidents were eliminated.

Labor Relations

Should baseball change the structure of its separate labor relations committee?

Eventually the committee was disbanded. The director of labor relations worked directly for the commissioner and became a member of his cabinet.

Schedule Format and Divisional Alignment

How many divisions? Should teams change divisions? What about interleague play? Expansion? The wild-card? The number of post-season games?

I became very involved with this committee. At my urging, we created interleague play and a wild-card team in each league. Whether you like or loathe these innovations, I deserve much of the credit or blame for them. We also introduced an unbalanced schedule, whereby teams played more games within their own division, and expanded from 26 to 30 teams.

In my opinion, all those decisions had a positive effect on the popularity of the game and increased revenue. I particularly like how the wild-card has worked out because it helps to maintain fan interest even if one team is running away in a division.

However, expansion, in my opinion, has been a mixed bag. Arizona and Colorado received good fan support, but Florida and Tampa Bay have really struggled. Expansion also made it almost impossible for any existing franchise to move to a new location if they were struggling from lack of fan or political support. Ironically, an expansion team—the Florida Marlins—are really feeling the effect of that right now as they try to get a stadium built in South Florida.

When expansion took place, there were many committee meetings and league meetings regarding the alignment of teams in the various divisions and how many teams would be in each league. I was in favor of two leagues with 15 teams each. However, that plan would have necessitated each team playing 30 interleague games, which many teams did not want. Some teams wanted to put all teams in the Eastern time zone in one league. The Chicago Cubs wanted to be in the eastern division, thinking they would get more TV money because earlier games lead to larger audiences. I wanted Pittsburgh and Cincinnati in the east division with the Phillies, Mets, and Braves. Tampa Bay wanted to be in the central division so that they did not have to compete with the high payrolls of the Yankees and Red Sox. Arizona wanted to be in the National League, but many teams thought it made more sense for them to be in the American League. There were other disagreements, but Bud Selig was able to do a good job of mediating the debate, and we are where we are.

The Physical Offices
Where should they be? What should they include?

I was very involved in insisting that the league offices and commissioner's office be moved into a more vibrant and high-energy office space in New York City. The old offices were short of space, with cardboard boxes all around, and generally gave you the impression of walking into some down-and-out law office. The new offices at 245 Park Avenue have some excitement, with a lot of great artwork and historic pictures on all the walls, plus some audio and video presentations thrown in. All of this showed progress and futuristic thinking—which is what we need to capitalize on all the new growth opportunities that are available to us if we put our minds to finding them.

Licensing, Sponsorships, and International Interest

How best to organize and govern to maximize the popularity of the game and create the most revenue for the game?

Eventually, an MLB enterprise board was formed to manage these matters. Each team became a shareholder so that baseball could share equally in all revenue instead of having the most popular teams, like the Yankees, do their own licensing and marketing

This decision was quite successful, particularly with new technology coming on board. The MLB.com website, satellite radio, a digital cable channel, and a World Classic of International Baseball have all been the result of this decision. The latter is especially promising.

In 2006 Major League Baseball organized its version of a World Cup—the WBC, or World Baseball Classic. This tournament featured teams from 16 different countries and was played in March during spring training. Japan beat Cuba in the finals. While interest was somewhat tepid in the United States—partly because fan interest in March is focused on spring training and the NCAA basketball tournament—it was very strong worldwide, particularly in Latin America and in the Far East. While the results were disappointing for the U.S. team and its fans, the tournament fulfilled its primary purpose of raising interest in baseball worldwide.

Not every owner, of course, was in favor of the classic. George Steinbrenner, in particular, was critical of the tournament. His three big drawing cards, A-Rod, Jeter, and Damon, risked injury by participating. Just as important to Steinbrenner, whose Yankees consistently draw sellout crowds in spring training, was the absence of these stars from those games.

In fact, this is my big complaint with the World Baseball Classic. In our first spring-training game, I went to see the Phils play the Yankees in Tampa Bay and sat next to an unhappy woman.

I overheard her saying, "I can't believe this. I spent thousands of dollars to bring my family to Florida just to see baseball, and we can't see Damon, Jeter, Rodriguez, Abreu, or Utley."

I'm sure George heard his share of that, too. By criticizing the classic, George is attempting to deflect the blame: it is not my fault that you are not seeing our stars—the commissioner and the WBC took them away.

I agree that this is a problem, but all in all I feel that the pluses of the WBC outweigh the minuses.

The Best Commissioner the Game Has Ever Had

With all the major issues of the business of the game having been dealt with, and with the enterprise of baseball heading in the right direction, it was time to find a new and permanent commissioner. A search committee was formed and a list of candidates investigated, but I do not believe the search was really serious. Bud Selig and his "kitchen cabinet" knew that Selig was going to be the next commissioner from day one.

I respect Selig in a lot of ways—he really loves and cares about the game, he is smart, he accomplished a lot as president of the Executive Council, and he is a great politician. It was amazing to see how effectively he could work the phones and convince owners to vote for things he wanted to accomplish. He would give almost every owner something important for his or her own franchise in order to gain support and it worked for him. Bud Selig really understands how to garner and utilize power.

I was in favor of creating two leaders for the game: a commissioner to be baseball's spokesman and to uphold the integrity of the game, while Selig retained his position as president of the Executive Council to manage the business of the game. This position was seriously discussed—for which I would have nominated Senator George Mitchell—but when it came down to a vote, Selig was unanimously elected commissioner on July 9, 1998.

Those who criticize him for what he doesn't do, or how quickly he doesn't do it, simply don't understand how difficult a role he has. Those who want him to be a "tough cop" like Judge Landis are conveniently forgetting that Landis didn't have the most powerful union on the planet weighing in on every decision he tried to make.

We all have ideas that we feel would make major league baseball even better than it already is. If I were king for a day, I would love to institute a minimum and maximum team payroll, put a three-year limit on guaranteed contracts, grant more compensation for lost free agents, and help competitive parity through more revenue sharing. I'm grounded enough in reality, however, to know that none of these changes would be what you'd call a slam dunk to implement.

Selig has accomplished more in his tenure than any other commissioner. In fact, I believe he is the best commissioner the game has ever had. He is a genius at getting votes for key issues that he favors, and he always knows where each owner stands on all issues. Most importantly, Selig has done an astounding job straightening out the economics of the game. One of the ways he's done that is by hiring excellent people to work for him, including Bob DuPuy, the president of MLB, a smart man in an important position who usually gets things done in an effective way; Rob Manfred, vice president of labor relations, who has been outstanding in his role, rebuilding the trust of the players; and Tim Brosnan, executive vice president of business, who has done a terrific job marketing the game, negotiating TV deals, and overseeing international baseball and the Enterprise Board. I really admired these men and their accomplishments, which have made MLB better and stronger, benefiting everyone—owners, players, and fans.

In 2001 Commissioner Selig named me honorary president of the National League. I get to represent the NL at the All-Star Game, though it has not been "like father, like son" as far as our success on the field is concerned. My father won 17 of 23 during his tenure as National League president, while I'm 0 for 6 so far. Back when my father was running the National League, major league baseball was still very much composed of two distinct leagues with two very distinct identities. It was very important to him that the National League be recognized as a superior league to the American League, and he gave impassioned speeches to the players in the clubhouse before each game. He also went so far as to insist that the charter flight that carried the National League executives to the World Series take off and land before the American League plane.

I also represent the National League at the World Series and get to present the Warren C. Giles Trophy to the winner of the National League Championship Series.

I'm very honored by this, and, though it wasn't the most difficult or significant decision any commissioner has ever had to make, it's certainly one of my personal favorites.

And I look forward to presenting my father's trophy to myself someday.

GRADING THE COMMISSIONERS

Landis—B: Great job on the Black Sox Scandal. Dropped the ball on integration.

Chandler—C: You'd think a guy named Happy would be more aware of the feelings of his constituents.

Frick—C-: When you're best known for an asterisk, that's generally not a good thing.

Eckert—F: The wrong man for the job—literally.

Kuhn—B: Successfully ushered baseball into the modern age.

Ueberroth—B: Had some good ideas—and one really bad one.

Giamatti—B: His time was over far too soon.

Vincent—D: His soft stance on labor issues helped usher in a very bleak period in baseball's financial history.

Selig—A-: Slow and steady wins the race.

Richie Ashburn:
A Philadelphia Icon

September 9, 1997

Don Richard Ashburn was arguably the most beloved person ever to live in the Delaware Valley, at least since Ben Franklin—and Franklin couldn't hit a slider. Ashburn was a part of Philadelphia baseball for almost 50 years. In the days after he died of a heart attack at 5:45 AM on September 9, 1997, at the Grand Hyatt in New York City, more than 40,000 people mourned his death and expressed their love in person. The outpouring of affection for the farm boy from Tilden, Nebraska, was overwhelming and something the city of Philadelphia had not seen before and probably will never see again. I was vacationing in the United Kingdom with my wife, Nancy, and good friends Sara and John Mashek on September 9. I received a fax from my assistant, Nancy Nolan, telling me that my good friend Richie Ashburn had passed away. I was in shock and wound up taking a two-hour walk through the beautiful green pastures and streams in the Wales countryside. With tears in my eyes, I reflected back on my wonderful relationship with a man I truly loved.

On the Golf Course with Richie

I do not believe that I was ever in his company when he did not make me laugh or at least bring a big smile to my face. He didn't really try to be funny; it just came naturally to him. To spend four hours riding in a golf cart playing 18 holes of golf with Richie was about as good as it gets. He always had a hat on his head (he must have had hundreds of hats) and a pipe in his mouth. He always carried a plastic bag in the cart with lots of candy in case he got into trouble from his insulin shot that he would take for diabetes. After teeing off we would drive out to his ball (he was a singles hitter off the tee just as he was in baseball), and he would always ask me how far he was from the hole because he didn't like to look around for the distance marker on the sprinkler head. He would always go to his golf bag and say:

"Bill, I have the perfect club for this shot."

At which point, he would often proceed to hit the ball into a trap or slice it into the woods.

On any putt less than five feet he would say:

"Bill, I never miss a putt from this distance."

At which point he would miss, sometimes badly, and would say:

"How come that ball didn't go in the hole?"

The Ashburn Family Welcome Wagon

When I moved to Philadelphia, I was advised by Phillies executives to purchase a home in South Jersey because it would be an easy commute to Veterans Stadium. Richie told me that I should consider buying a home in Gladwyne, a suburb to the west of Philadelphia along the famous Main Line. Richie would get me into the Philadelphia Country Club so we could play some tennis, golf, and squash together. My wife, Nancy, and I fell in love with Gladwyne and purchased a home there.

I spent many days playing golf or tennis at the country club with Richie and I enjoyed every minute of it. He was an 18 handicap in golf and I was a 16, but in tennis he would beat me about 75 percent of the time. Richie Ashburn is a Hall of Fame center fielder and, of course, a great athlete. He was a very accomplished squash player and he won tournaments in the Philadelphia area. I had never played the sport before moving to Philadelphia, so I decided it was not a good idea to challenge him on the squash court.

Richie's family—wife Herbie, daughters Jan, Jean, and Karen, and sons Richard and John—were all very helpful to my family when we moved into Gladwyne. They introduced us to some of their good friends and introduced their kids' friends to our three sons. Karen Ashburn became the primary babysitter for us.

Foul Balls and Odd Plays

I only saw Richie play a few baseball games with the Phillies, having lived in Cincinnati during most of his career. I do remember my father presenting him with the Mel Ott Award for leading the National League in hitting in 1958 with a .350 batting average. Richie was always a bit overshadowed, playing the same position during the era as Mickey (Mantle), Willie (Mays) and the Duke (Snider). But he did have a great 15-year career as a fleet-footed center fielder, retiring after the 1962 season with a lifetime batting average of .308, amassing 2,574 hits and 234 stolen bases. He certainly had more good years left and could have likely gotten the 426 hits necessary for the magic 3,000 level, but after a season with the hapless (40 wins and 120 losses) expansion Mets, he was ready to hang 'em up.

Ashburn really wanted to manage the Phillies after he retired. He would often ask me to talk to Phillies owner Bob Carpenter about his desire to do so. I would advise him not to pursue a managing career.

"Richie, I am sure you would do a good job," I said, "but I am also sure you would eventually be fired and then where would you be? You are truly loved by everyone as a broadcaster and newspaper columnist, and you have a lifetime job."

Although I did not see him play much, I sure heard a lot about his career from Richie—usually at the "19th hole" after a round of golf. Many of his stories were legendary. He was notorious for hitting foul balls into the stands, particularly when he was trying to get a walk. When Richie was playing for the Chicago Cubs in 1960, the

Cubs had a pitcher named Jim Brewer who was having a lot of trouble with his wife, whose name was Babs.

"Hey, Richie," Brewer said, "Babs is at the game today, and I will give you $500 if you hit her with a foul ball."

On Richie's first at-bat, he hit a foul ball not far from Brewer's wife. Brewer stepped out of the Cubs dugout and yelled, "Richie, three seats over and two rows up and you got her."

On August 17, 1957, a woman by the name of Alice Roth was attending a game at Connie Mack Stadium when Richie hit her in the face with a foul ball. As the paramedics came to help Miss Roth, and as they were carrying her off on a stretcher, Richie hit another foul ball that hit Roth lying on the stretcher.

When Richie played his final season in 1962 with Casey Stengel's woeful New York Mets, he was having frequent difficulty communicating with the team's Latino shortstop, Elio Chacon, on pop-ups hit to short center field. Chacon ran into Ashburn a few times when Richie was yelling, "I got it."

During the season, the Mets acquired a bilingual outfielder named Joe Christopher. From him, Richie learned that "*Yo la tengo*" meant "I got it" in Spanish. Soon after gaining that piece of knowledge, Ashburn came running in on a short fly yelling, "*Yo la tengo*." Chacon got out of the way, but burly left fielder Frank Thomas from Pittsburgh—who didn't know "*Yo la tengo*" from yellowfin tuna—came charging in, knocking Ashburn over.

The Mets were bad, so bad that Jimmy Breslin wrote a book about their inaugural season titled *Can't Anybody Here Play This Game?* But they were entertaining. They had a cast of characters, led by famous manager Casey Stengel.

During that 1962 season, truly one of the most unique plays ever seen on a baseball field occurred, and it probably could have only happened to the 1962 Mets. Choo-Choo Coleman, who was one of the most entertaining players I have ever seen, was catching. Phillies first baseman Dick "Dr. Strangelove" Stuart was on second base and a single was hit to center field. Stuart and the throw arrived at home plate at the same time. Stuart missed tagging home plate and Coleman missed tagging Stuart. The umpire made no call, and Stuart ran to the far end of the Phillies dugout. Catcher Coleman could not remember who the base runner was, so he ran into the Phillies dugout and started tagging the Phillies players one by one. Stuart saw Coleman coming and started to run to home plate. Coleman threw the ball to the pitcher standing at the plate, and they got Stuart in a rundown between home plate and the dugout, where he was eventually tagged out.

The beginning of Richie's baseball career was a lot like that rundown. Going back to the beginning of his career, it is interesting that Richie actually signed two illegal baseball contracts before finally signing a legal contract with the Phillies in February 1945. At the age of 16, while still in high school, the Cleveland Indians sent him a professional contract in the mail. Although his father, Neil, thought it was illegal, Richie signed it anyway because he was so excited about playing professional baseball. Commissioner Landis voided the contract because Richie had not graduated from high school yet, and he fined the Indians $500. But Landis took a liking to Ashburn and let the young catcher keep his $1,000 bonus. Yes, Ashburn was a catcher until Phillies manager Eddie Sawyer observed his great speed and moved Richie to center field when he was in AA ball.

Upon Richie's high school graduation, the Chicago Cubs signed him to a pro contract. The contract contained a clause that stated that Richie would get a portion of the sale price if he were ever sold to a major league club. This contract was also deemed illegal. For all those Phillies fans who loved Richie, they have contract lawyers to thank.

When Harry Met Richie

Although he had a very good playing career, the real love affair with Whitey and Phillies fans developed during his broadcasting days. He began his broadcasting career in 1963 working in the booth with longtime Phillies announcers By Saam and Bill Campbell.

A good or colorful baseball announcer really becomes part of a baseball fan's family. Great announcers like Red Barber, Ernie Harwell, Vince Scully, By Saam, Jack Brickhouse, Harry Kalas, and many others are really woven into the fabric of a fan's life. A fan will watch or listen to a game on TV or radio and the announcers will paint the picture of the game as if they are sitting right next to the listener. When you listened to Rich Ashburn, you were listening to a good friend. He could make even bad baseball fun to listen to.

Whitey was low key, was always relaxed, and possessed an amazing dry wit. But he could be emotional, as when Richie Allen hit a monstrous home run over the 447-foot sign in Connie Mack Stadium in his rookie year in 1964: "It's over the 447-foot sign! It's over the 447-foot sign!"

But the one thing that really set Richie apart was the chemistry between him and fellow broadcaster Harry Kalas, which was truly unique and delightful.

Kalas, whom I brought to Philadelphia in 1971 after working with him and listening to him in Houston for five years, called Whitey his best friend. Harry wrote an ode to "His Whiteness" and updated it the day after Richie's death. It went like this:

> His Cornhusker roots have served him well
> The dry wit, the humor, you could immediately tell
> But the enduring traits we readily see,
> His human compassion and love of family
> The greatest tribute to an athlete and man
> Is that in whatever pursuit, he did the best that he can.
> His charitable efforts in memory of Jan
> Remind us how fragile is one's life span
> Will we ever forget that August in '95
> When thousands took that wonderful drive
> To Cooperstown, the home of the Hall
> An emotional time for us all
> When His Whiteness got his just due
> We were not surprised because we knew
> At Cooperstown on this August day
> They honored a man who's a Hall of Famer in every way
> When Whitey turned 70, a pipe or hat, I did not send
> Rather my lifelong loyalty as a true friend

Now the man all Phillyland loved
Has gone to join Jan in the heavens above
And Don Richie Ashburn by any measure
Was a man whose memory we will forever treasure

The on- and off-air relationship between Harry and Richie was warm, caring, fun, and real. "When I first joined the Phillies in 1971, Richie took me under his wing and made me feel welcome in Philadelphia and with the Phillies," Kalas recalled. "He had such a great knowledge of the game and had the experience as a Hall of Fame player. He understood the nuances of the game. Whitey was a superb color analyst. As he told me, if he didn't have anything to say, he was going to keep quiet."

Richie created a number of signature lines, and every Phillies fan who watched and listened to games between 1963 and 1997 heard them many times. How many times did we hear Richie utter these memorable phrases?

"Hard to believe, Harry."

"He looks hitterish."

"He looks runnerish."

"Right down the middle for a ball."

"You can bet the house on it, Harry."

"It's a lead-pipe cinch, Harry."

His on-air humor would usually pop up unexpectedly. For example, in one of his first games working with Kalas, the two of them watched a player break his bat.

"Richie, the game bat must be very important to a player," Kalas said.

"It really is, Harry," Ashburn said with a straight face. "In fact, when I was playing and doing well with a certain bat, I would not trust leaving it around the dugout or in the clubhouse. I used to take it back to my room and go to bed with it. In fact, I've been in bed with a lot of old bats in my day."

In 1980 Richie was working with Tim McCarver in the booth, and McCarver related a story about Phillies pitcher Larry Christenson making a trip to Mount St. Helens and bringing home some ash from the volcano. McCarver explained that the ash from the side of the mountain where the explosion had taken place was finer than the ash from the other side.

Without batting an eye, Ashburn leaned into the mic and said, "I think if you've seen one piece of ash, you've seen them all."

The fans in Philadelphia loved Ashburn so much that when the Phillies beat the Astros to go to the World Series in 1980, many of our listeners spent the next day neither celebrating nor recovering from celebrating but instead calling up the commissioner's office to complain that they would not be able to hear Whitey and Harry call the games on the radio. As a result of this outcry, Major League Baseball changed their policy the next year and allowed local announcers to handle the radio calls for World Series games. Ashburn and his partner were both very touched by this display of loyalty from the Philadelphia fans, who are never shy about letting themselves be heard.

The Induction

Those same fans were heard on July 30, 1995, which was one of the highlights of my entire life. It was the day that both Richie Ashburn and Mike Schmidt were inducted into baseball's Hall of Fame in Cooperstown, New York. I adored both of them so much— Schmittie for his baseball talent and Richie, well, for being Richie. I wasn't alone in my adoration. It was the single largest crowd ever to attend an induction ceremony, and the 20,000-plus people were all wearing Phillies shirts and caps. It was a sea of red.

"There was complete joy and fulfillment," Richie's wife, Herbie, said. "It was a wonderful day for our family. I've never seen two more popular players enter the Hall than Mike Schmidt and Rich. It was a fantastic event."

I had never seen Richie as emotional as he was on that hot August day in Cooperstown. You could see the pride and gratitude in his face and eyes. I thought a lot about that day two years later when I got the news that my friend was gone.

Family Comes First

The greatest miracle in life is not winning the World Series or winning the lottery—the greatest miracle of life is family and friends. These are the final words that I use in almost every speech I have given over the last 20 years.

I am very fortunate to have great friends like John and Sara Mashek, Josh and Lissa Thompson, Frank and Trudy Rosato, Larry and Diane Zullinger, Dan and Margo Polett, Sheila and Lou Rice, Cathy Rice, Claire Rice, Dick and Jean Dicken, Dick and Jane Hogan, Mary and Jim Brockhoff, and a thousand apologies to anyone I may have missed. My family these days is my wife, Nancy; son Michael, his wife, Nanette, and their children, Will and Lowie; son Joe, his wife, Paula, and their children, Caroline, Dana, Molly, and Max; and my son Chris, his wife, Amy, and their children, Eliza and Warren.

Making a "Grate" First Impression

This family probably would not have happened had I not been playing the part of the Animal, a dimwitted Betty Grable–loving character in the play *Stalag 17* at Denison University. I had to dye my sandy hair black and wear long underwear and galoshes.

It was in the fall of 1954 when the Sigma Chi fraternity house, where I lived my sophomore and junior years in college, invited the Pi Beta Phi sorority for dinner.

Because I was practicing for the play, I arrived for dinner 10 minutes late, and the only seat remaining was next to a pretty, dark-haired girl by the name of Nancy Jane Kirwin.

The first words out of my mouth were: "You must be quite popular—the only seat open is next to you."

And it actually went downhill after that. I did not say one nice thing to her, and I did some cute little things like putting salt in her coffee. After dinner, she moved to the living room to play bridge, and I stood behind her and made fun of every play she made.

It was love at first sight. One way, of course. She was beautiful, sweet, and had a great smile. I still remember the white mock turtle cashmere sweater and brown skirt she wore that night. I was really in love, so I called her the next day for a date and she said she never wanted to go out with me.

But I kept asking. I even asked her to go to the Christmas prom and she told me she had a date with John Briggs—a guy she knew I despised. I found out later she did not have a date with John Briggs—she didn't even go to the prom. But I never gave up and she finally agreed to go to a movie with me in nearby Newark, Ohio. I picked her up at her dorm in my little black and white Chevy. She sat as far away from me as possible. Five minutes into the ride to Newark, we stopped at a red traffic light. I reached over and pulled her to me, kissed her on the lips, and exclaimed:

"You do not realize it, but you and I are going to get married and go to Hawaii on our honeymoon."

Honeymoon in Hawaii…and Vegas

Eighteen months later we were sunbathing on Waikiki Beach as Mr. and Mrs. Bill Giles. We had been married on June 17, 1956, in her hometown of San Diego. My father was my best man, and he announced to Father Nightingale and everyone at the rehearsal dinner, "I am truly the best man here."

My father had given me $1,500 for my honeymoon, and on our way back from Hawaii to Cincinnati, Nancy and I spent three days in San Francisco and two days in Las Vegas. I had $500 left when we got to Vegas, so after seeing a few floor shows I said to Nancy, "Why don't I take $200 of the remaining $500 and we go play a little blackjack to win back the money we spent on the honeymoon?"

She said she just wanted to sleep, so I gave her $300 and took the $200 to the tables. It took me only about an hour to lose the $200, so I went back to our room to go to sleep. Guess what? Nancy was sound asleep and her $300 was on the dresser. So I said to myself, "Nancy will be mad that I lost that $200, so I will just take the $300 and get us back to at least $500."

I'm sure you know what happened. It's amazing we've been married 50 years!

We lived in my father's log cabin for six weeks while waiting for my air force career to begin in September 1956. My wife wanted the first home-cooked meal as Mrs. Bill Giles to include my father and for the meal to be cooked in the little kitchen in his cabin. It was to be fried chicken. As the cooking began, a horrible odor permeated the entire cabin. It turned out that a squirrel was being fried in wires behind the stove. The three of us went out to dinner.

It's a Boy

Three years in the air force was both educational and fun, but nothing I wanted to do for a long time. During the three years, we lived in nine different apartments or houses in San Antonio then Harlingen, Texas, and Lincoln, Nebraska. It was in Lincoln that we bought our first house—for $11,500 with monthly payments of $66 per month. We sold it 18 months later for $12,600, so I figured we lived in the house for almost nothing.

It was in Lincoln that our first son arrived. Michael Warren Giles was born on June 2, 1959, but it was not routine. I was stationed in the Azores for 90 days on temporary duty during the time he was to be born. The air force gave you a 72-hour pass for maternity issues, so I took the trip from the Azores—an island chain in the Atlantic Ocean about a thousand miles off the coast of Portugal—to Lincoln two days prior to the due date hoping to see our first son born. But nothing happened my first 48 hours home, so the doctors decided to induce the baby so I could see him before I had to return to the Azores. Nancy was in labor for 28 hours before Michael was born. I always kid Mike that he has been a "pain" ever since.

A Lucky Quarter

It was back in the Azores that the Giles family almost ended up being just Nancy and Mike. I nearly killed 300 people, including myself. I was a navigator in the 98th Air Squadron, and we were ordered to spend 10 days at an air base near London. On our return from London to the Azores—which, if you look at a map, is in the middle of the ocean with no other land around for miles and miles—I was the lead navigator. Our plane had 18 other KC-97 planes following us with 300 people in all the planes. In those days, navigation was primarily done by using a sextant to view the stars and the sun and to time your ground speed by looking through a bomb site to pick up buildings on the ground or waves in the ocean and timing your speed with a stopwatch.

Unfortunately, on this historic day (for me, anyway) the entire squadron was flying in the "soup." You could not see above you or below you. I had to navigate entirely on the preflight plan, which was based on what the weather guys had told us about the winds prior to our takeoff. Now, when you get within 100 miles of an air base, you could pick up a radar signal and from there it was easy. We were flying merrily along until we got to a point where we should have been able to pick up the radar from the Azores base.

"Lieutenant Giles, this is Captain Flori," my pilot said. "We only have 15 minutes of fuel left, and we can't pick up the radar. What do you suggest?"

I calmly took a quarter out of my flight suit and said to myself that if it lands heads we'll turn right, and if it's tails we'll turn left. I flipped the coin and it came up heads.

"Captain Flori," I said with a faked confidence, "turn 90 degrees right."

Thank God, within four minutes we picked up the radar at the Azores AFB and everyone landed safely. That night at the officers club, I was being toasted as the greatest navigator in the history of the 98th Air Squadron. Little did they know! I often wonder what would have happened if that quarter had turned up tails.

My Three Sons

Thanks in part to that quarter, our second son, Joe, was born on May 11, 1962, in Houston, and our third son, Chris, was born in Houston on September 27, 1965. When Chris was born, I did a little takeoff on my scoreboard antics of "Kibler did it again" by giving out cigars with "the Giles did it again" on the wrappers of the cigars because we now had three handsome sons.

Of course, my wife always wanted a girl, but she is now delighted to have three beautiful daughters-in-law and four beautiful grand-daughters to buy clothes for and to knit for.

I thank God, my mom, and my dad for bringing me into the world, and I thank my wife, Nancy, for hanging in there with me and raising our family so well. When I look back on my 50 years of married life, I wonder how our sons turned out so well. In 1962, when I was both traveling secretary and publicity director of the Houston Colt .45s, I was home for dinner only two nights during a 12-month period. Then when I became CEO of the Phillies and endured the stress of being responsible for every loss and every win, plus every ticket sold, it couldn't have been easy for my wife. I very seldom threw things or got real mad about anything, but Nancy knew when I was not happy. I didn't say much, but I wanted to be alone—I worked in the yard or swam in the pool to ease my frustration.

As you go through 50 years of married life there are many cycles—romance and growing a family, making your career both enjoyable and successful, raising your children properly and enjoy-ing the spouses they choose. Now it is time to enjoy what may be the greatest reward of family—watching your grandchildren develop and grow into what you hope and believe will be special.

Family Traditions…and a Notorious Moment or Two

Traveling, camping, and sporting events occupied much of the growing-up time for Nancy, me, and the boys. Our last camping trip was at Hickory Run State Park in the Poconos in Pennsylvania in the late 1970s. All five of us were cuddled in a tent and a severe cold front came through the area. It got so cold the boys and I retired to our blue Pontiac station wagon, turned on the heater, and slept. Nancy was left in the tent and was not a happy camper when she woke up to find her four males staying warm in the car. That was our last camping trip as a family.

Watching my sons play sports and play them well was another special treat for me. And as the sons of a baseball executive, there were some perks—like using the major league batting cages in spring training, catching fly balls as I hit them with a fungo bat after many spring-training games, and, of course, having easy access to players' autographs.

Despite my encouragement to play baseball, they all switched from baseball to lacrosse when they were about 13. Each of them was very talented and became captain of the Episcopal Academy lacrosse team. Mike was a goalie, Joe an attack man, and Chris a crease attack man. One of my most enjoyable experiences was watching their lacrosse games, even if that sport does require the use of funny-looking baseball bats. I also enjoyed watching Mike and Chris play high school football and Joe do well in cross-country.

Nancy deserves most of the credit for raising our sons the right way, but the boys and I did have a special bond. One of the most significant "bonding" occasions was a fly-fishing trip to Alaska in 1996, camping out at the Bering Sea, and catching beautiful rainbow trout and king salmon. Another was the Giles Cup golf tournament. The Giles Cup is a golf tournament that I created in 1996 when we all had given up team sports for tennis, squash, and golf. The four of us all had handicaps around 18, so we were quite equal in ability. We would play as a foursome 15 to 25 times a year, often traveling to the Caribbean at Christmas with our entire family and squeezing in three or four rounds of the Giles Cup on the trip. The guy who won the most matches in a calendar year got his name engraved on a big silver cup we display in our cottage in the Poconos.

December 26 to January 3 has always been the real family vacation time because it is hard for a baseball guy to get everyone together in the summer. We got on a skiing kick for a number of years and went to Vail and Telluride in Colorado and Lech, Austria, for about eight years. When the grandkids started to arrive on the scene, we switched our Christmas family trip to warm weather sites so the grandkids could enjoy the beach and the guys could get a little golf in.

Another special bond for the Giles family was the Tomato Bowl. The Tomato Bowl was a football game played every Thanksgiving Day at 11:00 AM on our street in Gladwyne. All the kids and fathers (usually around 30 people in all) would play a fun football game. The reason it was called the Tomato Bowl was that my father always served Bloody Marys at halftime.

Inducting My Father

I had many opportunities to bond with my father throughout my life, but one of the most special occasions was a time we weren't together—at least not physically. It was August 5, 1979, one of my many visits to Cooperstown for Induction Day, but certainly my most memorable. My father had died six months earlier, and I was there to deliver the acceptance speech for his induction into the Baseball Hall of Fame. The following is a transcript of my speech:

> Having spent the last 24 to 48 hours here, I understand why my father felt that this was the greatest weekend in his life. It's an honor for me to be here in his place, but the greatest thing about this weekend is we have had 27 of my dad's

family here from all across the country. I'd like all of them, but particularly the people that my father was so proud of, his daughter-in-law and two of his grandsons, Nancy, Joe, Mike and the rest of you, stand up and take a bow.

On July 21, 1952, 27 years ago, my father was here at the Hall of Fame and related these words, "I wonder if we fully appreciate the single honor which has been bestowed upon these men. To do so one must realize that more than 8,000 major league players have become eligible as nominees for the Hall of Fame. Yet only 58 players, so far, have withstood the rigid, critical, conscientious screening necessary for election to this baseball pantheon."

In the same speech my dad went on to say, "There must be some very special qualifications or special characteristics that these players possessed that others did not. To my way of thinking the most important must have been their desire and determination to perform far beyond their rate of capacity." My father had that desire and determination to perform far beyond his rate of capacity, and on behalf of my dad, who I know is really with us here today, I want to sincerely thank the Hall of Fame Committee for recognizing his great accomplishments. My father did have great desire and determination, as his record proves, and he would have been particularly proud today to be inducted with two other National Leaguers, Hack Wilson and a fellow named Willie Mays.

He had many more great qualities, other than just desire and determination, and the reason I'm here pinch-hitting for him today is a good example of one of his most significant great qualities—he was unselfish. There are givers and there are takers on this good earth, and my father was a true giver. He gave his love and attention to his family, friends, and baseball, and he gave this same love and dedication to the Baseball Hall of Fame, and that's why he did not receive this great honor in person some time ago. For years, Joe Cronin and my dad's other good friends tried to get him to retire from the Hall of Fame Selection Committee so that he could receive this recognition himself, but he always felt that he wanted to give to this great game and not to take from it.

He gave in 1950 when he and Ford Frick were tied in the election for the Office of Commissioner. He withdrew from the election because he thought it was in the best interest of baseball. When he was asked to become president of the National League, he said he would accept the honor only if he could keep the office in Cincinnati because he felt it was in the best interest of his son, for me to finish my high school career among my friends. He really never took anything and he just gave and gave to everyone, but particularly baseball, except for one time.

When I was PR director of the Houston club, I ran the scoreboard in Houston and one of the great umpires, John Kibler, kicked one of our players out on four consecutive days, so I put in great big letters on the scoreboard, "Kibler did it again." Well, the fans started to throw a few things at him, and my father was head of the umpires at the time. So the next morning, I got a call and he said, "Bill, who was it that put the message on the board about the umpires?" and I said, "Gee Dad, I don't know who it was, but I'll tell him not to do it again." And he said, "Well when you find out tell him his allowance is cut off, will ya?" So you see, he did have a sense of humor. He always had a twinkle in his eye. He made people smile. He made them happy. He just plain made this world a better place.

He taught me to learn to make decisions. When I was 15 years old, I asked him what I should do for a career. He said, "That's your decision, but whatever you decide, be the best at what you do. Even if you decide to be a garbage collector, collect more garbage than anybody else." As my old boss, Bob Carpenter, says, "When Warren Giles made a decision, you knew it was the right one."

I want to take just a moment to thank many of you here today and people everywhere, particularly so many in the news media, who wrote and recognized my father in such a fine and loving manner. When he passed away last winter, so many of his fine qualities were recognized. So many nice things have been said by the commissioner today, but the one word that was most important in his whole life, particularly his baseball life, was the word *integrity*. How many times did he say we have got to maintain the integrity of this great game? When I spent those final days in that Cincinnati hospital with my dad last February, I cannot forget a few of his last words, "Bill, have you ever thought what a mess this world would be in if there were no sports, and particularly baseball?" May God give all of us the courage and determination to uphold the desires and feelings that were my father's. I thank you for being here today, and, Dad, we all love you.

And that's the story of my life under the baseball big top—so far. I gave you the last word, Dad. You deserve nothing less.

Sources

In addition to Bill Giles's personal treasure trove of priceless baseball memories, the authors benefited greatly from interviews with Dallas Green, Tal Smith, Pat Gillick, Harry Kalas, Dave Montgomery, and a number of long-time Phillies employees during the summer of 2006.

Bodley, Hal. *The Team That Wouldn't Die*. Woburn, MA: Serendipity Press, 1981.

Fitzpatrick, Frank. *You Can't Lose 'Em All*. Lanham, MD: Taylor Trade Publishing, 2004.

Gordon, Robert, and Tom Burgoyne. *More Than Beards, Bellies, and Biceps*. Champaign, IL: Sports Publishing, 2006.

http://www.baseball-reference.com

Lowry, Philip. *Green Cathedrals*. Boston: Addison-Wesley, 1992.

Moran, Barbara, "Artificial Turf and How It Grew," *Invention & Technology*. Spring 2005.

Orodenker, Richard. *The Phillies Reader*. Philadelphia: Temple University Press, 2005.

Reichler, Joe. *The Baseball Encyclopedia*. New York: Macmillan Publishing Company, 1987.

Solomon, Burt. *The Baseball Timeline*. New York: DK Press, 2001.

Westcott, Rich, and Frank Bilovsky. *The Phillies Encyclopedia*. Philadelphia: Temple University Press, 2004.

Zimniuch, Fran. *Richie Ashburn Remembered*. Champaign, IL: Sports Publishing, 2005.

Index